SCOTT
Serving collectors since 1863.

1985 POSTAGE STAMP CATALOGUE
& INVENTORY CHECKLIST

SCOTT PUBLISHING COMPANY

BARNES & NOBLE BOOKS
A DIVISION OF HARPER & ROW, PUBLISHERS
New York, Cambridge, Philadelphia, San Francisco
London, Mexico City, São Paulo, Sydney

The contents of this book, are owned exclusively by Scott Publishing Co. and all rights thereto are reserved under the Pan American and Universal Copyright Conventions.

COPYRIGHT NOTE

Permission is hereby given for the use of material in this book and covered by copyright if:

(a) The material is used in advertising matter, circulars or price lists for the purpose of offering stamps for sale or purchase at the prices listed therein; and

(b) Such use is incidental to the business of buying and selling stamps and is limited in scope and length, i.e., it does not cover a substantial portion of the total number of stamps issued by any country or of any special category of stamps of any country; and

(c) Such material is not used as part of any catalogue, stamp album or computerized or other system based upon the Scott catalogue numbers, or in any updated valuations of stamps not offered for sale or purchase; and

(d) Such use is not competitive with the business of the copyright owner.

Any use of the material in this book which does not satisfy all the foregoing conditions is forbidden in any form unless permission in each instance is given in writing by the copyright owner.

TRADEMARK NOTICE

The terms SCOTT, SCOTT'S, SCOTT CATALOGUE NUMBERING SYSTEM, SCOTT CATALOGUE NUMBER, SCOTT NUMBER and abbreviations thereof, are trademarks of Scott Publishing Co., used to identify its publications and its copyrighted system for identifying and classifying postage stamps for dealers and collectors. These trademarks are to be used only with the prior consent of Scott Publishing Co.

SCOTT 1985 POSTAGE STAMP CATALOGUE & INVENTORY CHECKLIST. Copyright © 1985 by Scott Publishing Company. All rights reserved. Printed in the United States of America. No part of ths book may be used or reproduced in any manner whatsoever without written permission except in the case of brief quotations embodied in critical articles and reviews. For information address Harper & Row, Publishers, Inc., 10 East 53rd Street, New York, N.Y. 10022. Published simultaneously in Canada by Fitzhenry & Whiteside Limited, Toronto.

ISBN: 0-06-465157-6

85 86 87 88 89 10 9 8 7 6 5 4 3 2 1

CONTENTS

HOW TO USE THIS BOOK 4
INTRODUCTION TO STAMP COLLECTING 5
UNITED STATES 13
   Air Post Stamps 175
   Air Post Special Delivery Stamps 187
   Special Delivery Stamp 187
   Registration Stamp 188
   Certified Mail Stamp 188
   Postage Due Stamps 188
   U.S. Offices in China 192
   Official Stamps 193
   Newspaper Stamps 197
   Parcel Post Stamps 203
   Special Handling Stamps 203
   Parcel Post Postage Due Stamps 203
   Carrier's Stamps 203
   Plate Number Block, Sheet and
      First Day Cover Prices 204

How To Use This Book

Scott Number®	Illustration; Design No.	Denomination	Color or Description	Color of the stamp paper	Prices Unused	Used
1811	A984	1c	dk blue,	*greenish*	.05	.05

The number (1811) in the first column is the stamp's identifying Scott® number. The letter-number combination (A984) indicates the design and refers to the illustration having this same (A984) designation. Following that is the denomination of the stamp and its color or description along with the color of the paper in italics if other than white. Finally, the price, unused and used is shown.

INTRODUCTION TO STAMP COLLECTING

A fascinating hobby, an engrossing avocation and a universal pastime, stamp collecting is pursued by millions. Young and old, rich and poor, cultured and uncultured, they are all involved in that king of indoor sport, "the paper chase."

It was 140 years ago that Rowland Hill's far-reaching postal reforms became a reality and the world's first adhesive postage stamp was put on sale throughout the post offices of Great Britain. The date was May 6, 1840. Not too long after, the world's first stamp collector came into being and a hobby was born that has continued to grow ever since.

Although for the next seven years there were only three stamps in England, the 1p black, 2p blue and 1p red, there were people who saved them. One apocryphal story has it that a stylish Victorian lady had a room papered with the ebon-hued "Penny Black." In 1850 there were reportedly collectors who were even more rabid. The Illustrated London News for May 8th of that year reports the dire tale of another Victorian damsel, this one in desperate need of help. Her collector father declared he would place her in a convent if she did not amass one million used postage stamps within a certain time. The story aroused concern and sympathy and the stamps poured in, "...many from persons of the highest rank, expressing the most kindly feeling." Shades of Rumpelstiltskin! Fortunately, few collectors have risen to the aberrative heights of those fabled fanatics. Stamp collecting, however, continued to spread, and as country after country began to issue stamps the fraternity flourished. Today, their numbers are legion, as are the number of stamp issuing countries.

Specialization can take many forms. There are those that collect the stamps of a single country. There are those that collect a single issue and those that collect a single stamp in all its nuances and variations. Some collect a particular type of postage stamp such as air mails, commemoratives, etc. Others specialize in cancellations and postmarks and collect their stamps on "cover" that is on the entire envelope. Most popular, however, is collecting by country-especially one's own country. The catalogue you now hold is designed to aid in forming just such a collection; it lists the stamps of the United States. A simplified edition of the 1985 Scott Standard Postage Stamp Catalogue, it has many uses. We will go into them later. First let us briefly discuss some of the ways of forming a collection.

Although the methods of collecting postage stamps are varied and many, anyone can enjoy them. One may begin by attempting to gather a single specimen of every stamp issued by a country. As one becomes more experienced, the collection may be enlarged to include the different types of each stamp such as perforation varieties, watermark varieties, different printings and color changes. The stamps may be collected on cover complete with all postal markings. Thus, the postal rates, cancellations and postmarks and any other postal information that helps speed a letter to its destination may be studied.

A very popular form of collecting practiced today is called "topical" collecting. Here, the subject depicted on the stamp is the paramount attraction. The topics or themes from which to choose are myriad. Animals, flowers, music and musicians, ships, birds and famous people on stamps make interesting collections as do transportation, exploration of space, artists and famous paintings. The list is endless.

Building such a collection is simple. Pick a topic that interests you, check it out on one of the many available lists of stamps dealing with that subject and begin. If your subject is broad enough, forming an interesting and meaningful collection should not be difficult.

Let us not forget another very popular form of collecting, the "First Day Cover." These are envelopes franked with a new stamp and cancelled on the first day of use, usually at a specially designated location. The envelope ordinarily contains a cachet commemorating the event or person for which the stamp was issued.

Collections may be limited to types of stamps. The postage stamps issued by most countries are divided into such categories as definitives, commemoratives, air mail stamps, special delivery stamps, postage due stamps, etc. Any of those groups provide the means for building a good collection.

Definitive stamps are those regular issues used on most of the mail sent out on a daily basis. Issued in a rising series of values that allows a mailer to meet any current postal rate, they range in the U.S. from one cent to five dollars. Printed in huge quantities, they are kept in service by the post office for long periods of time.

Commemoratives meet another need. They are stamps issued to celebrate an important event, honor a famous person or promote a special project. Such stamps are issued on a limited basis for a limited time. They are usually more colorful and of a larger size than the definitives, making them of special interest to the collector.

Although few air mail stamps are issued by the United States they remain highly popular among collectors. They, too, are **subject** to several ways of collecting. Besides amassing the actual stamps, enthusiasts eagerly pursue "First Flight Covers," "Airport Dedications" and even "Crash Covers."

Not as important, but often collected as a unit are the special delivery stamps which secure speedier delivery of a letter and postage due stamps which indicate that a letter did not carry enough postage to pay for its delivery, subjecting the recipient to a fee to make up the difference.

Let us move on to the tools of collecting. They are not many, but they are both useful and necessary. First a home for your collection is needed.

THE ALBUM

Stamps, to display them at their best, should be properly housed. A good album not only achieves this, but gives protection from dirt, loss and damage. When choosing one, however, make sure of three things. That the album is within your means, meets your special interests and is the best you can afford. There are many on the market and they are geared to fit every taste and pocketbook.

Loose-leaf albums are recommended. Not only will they allow for expansion of a collection, but the pages may be removed for mounting and for display. A special advantage of the loose-leaf album is that in a good many cases it may be kept up-to-date with supplements that are published annually on matching pages and are available at your stamp dealer.

MOUNTS AND HINGES

Along with the album one must have mounts and hinges. Let us consider the mount first. These days, when the never-hinged stamp has assumed some importance, the mount has become a necessary accessory. It is a must for mint stamps.

Most mounts consist of a pre-glued, clear plastic container that holds a stamp safely and can be affixed to an album page with minimum effort. They are available in sizes to fit any stamp, block or even whole envelopes.

Although the mount is important, the hinge is equally so. Many a stamp in the old days was ruined beyond redemption by being glued to an album page. Hinges are cheap and effective. The best ones are peelable and may be removed from a stamp or album page without leaving an unsightly mark or causing damage. They are perfect for less expensive stamps, used stamps and stamps that have previously been hinged. Using them is simple. Merely fold back about a quarter of the hinge, adhesive side out. Moisten the folded part and affix it to the back of the stamp. Then, holding the stamp with a pair of tongs, moisten the bottom part and place it and the stamp in its proper place on the album page.

STAMP TONGS

We mentioned tongs above. This simple, but important, accessory should always be used when handling a stamp. They cost little and will quickly pay for themselves. The ones with round ends are preferable, those with sharp ends may damage a stamp. Once you get used to using them you will find them easier to work with than your fingers. What's more, your stamps will be the better for it.

MAGNIFYING GLASS

A good magnifying glass for scrutinizing stamps in detail is another extremely useful philatelic tool. It lets you see flaws that are otherwise invisible to the naked eye. It makes minute parts of a design large enough to see. It saves wear and tear on the eyesight. It too pays for itself.

PERFORATION GAUGE and WATERMARK DETECTOR

As one becomes familiar with stamps he will discover that although many stamps appear to be exactly alike, they are not. The color and design may be identical, but there is a difference. The perforations around the edge of the stamp are not the same, nor is the watermark. To determine these differences a perforation gauge and a watermark detector are needed. Often, the perforations or the watermark found in the paper on which a stamp is printed are the only ways to classify it properly.

The perforation gauge, printed on plastic or cardboard, contains a graded scale that measures the size of the perforations used for most stamps. Placing the stamp on the gauge and moving it up or down until the dots on the gauge and the teeth of the perforation mesh gives one the size of the perforation. Most gauges also contain a small millimeter rule that allows one to accurately determine the dimensions of the stamps.

Watermarks are not quite so easy to detect. They are a design or device impressed into the paper on which the stamp is printed. Occasionally a watermark may be seen by holding a stamp up to the light, but normally a watermark detector is necessary to bring it out. Many types of detectors exist, but the simplest and most useful is that old standby, the small black tray. The stamp is placed face down in it, some lighter fluid is poured over the stamp causing the watermark to become visible.

CONDITION

As collectors and stamp collecting become more sophisticated, "condition" becomes more and more important. "Condition," speaking philatelically, means the state of a stamp - superb, mediocre or below average. Like anything else, a stamp in fine condition will always bring more than the same item in poor condition

A stamp when added to a collection should be the best obtainable. If it is unused, it should be well-centered and have a clean, fresh look. The gum should be intact. Stamps that have been hinged sell for less than those with pristine gum and stamps with part gum sell for much less.

Used stamps should be well-centered and lightly cancelled. They should not be faded or dirty. They should not have any thinning.

When buying a stamp labeled "superb," it should be of top quality, perfectly centered, brilliant in color and have perfect gum. Used copies should be fresh, lightly cancelled and sound in every respect.

When buying a stamp labeled "fine," it should be without flaws, but with average centering. The gum may have light hinge marks. Used copies are not quite as fresh as "superb," centering is average and the cancels are heavier.

A stamp listed as "good" or "average" is usually off-center, but attractive. It may have minor defects such as disturbed gum, tiny thins or heavy hinge marks. Used copies, except for the gum, fall into the same classification. Stamps that fall below these standards should be ignored.

THE CATALOGUE

The catalogue is one of the collector's most valued tools. Without it he is liable to be as lost as a sailor at sea without a compass. An illustrated and priced list of the postage stamps issued by every country of the world, it is a prime source of basic information pertaining to stamps and stamp collecting. Issued annually, it is the chief and handiest guide to what postage stamps exist. Its illustrations make it easy to identify one's stamps and are a guide to the fundamental elements of the hobby.

Scott's Standard Postage Stamp Catalogue is the leading general catalogue in the United States. It identifies every stamp and its major varieties by color, design and denomination. It gives the date of issue, the printing method, perforation size and watermark, if any, of each stamp where possible and the reason for its issuance. Every stamp is priced used and unused. In addition, every stamp has an identifying number. These are used by dealers and collectors as a quick method of identifying stamps they wish to buy or sell.

This pocket edition of the "Standard Catalogue" which you hold in your hand is a simplified version of the parent volume. Limited to the United States, it does not go into the massive detail that the larger one does. Nevertheless, it is a valuable and useful tool containing the basic information needed to identify and assign the stamps to your collection. Besides giving the current market value of each stamp it gives their philatelic details as well. As in the parent catalogue, the following style of listing is used.

The number in the first column is its Scott number or identifying number. The letter and number that come next (A41) indicate the design and refer to the illustration so designated. Following that is the denomination of the stamp and its color. Finally, the price, unused and used is shown.

Especially useful in this catalogue is the provision for making your own inventory and checklist. It allows one to keep a complete record of his holdings with a minimum of effort.

Above the columns of boxes are spaces in which a collector may indicate such designations as, "Mint," "Used," "Block," "Plate Block," "First Day Cover," or any other classification he desires. A mark in any of the boxes below makes a quickly visible checklist that instantly shows the status of his collection. A handy pocket inventory, it eliminates such chores as the compiling of buying lists.

The following is a list of color abbreviations used in this catalogue

amb	amber	ind	indigo
anil	aniline	int	intense
ap	apple	lav	lavender
aqua	aquamarine	lem	lemon
az	azure	lil	lilac
bis	bister	lt	light
bl	blue	mag	magenta
bld	blood	man	manila
blk	black	mar	maroon
bril	brilliant	mlky	milky
brn	brown	multi	multicolored
brnsh	brownish	mv	mauve
brnt	burnt	myr	myrtle
brnz	bronze	ol	olive
brt	bright	olvn	olivine
car	carmine	org	orange
cer	cerise	pck	peacock
cham	chamois	pnksh	pinkish
chlky	chalky	Prus	Prussian
chnt	chestnut	pur	purple
choc	chocolate	redsh	reddish
chr	chrome	res	reseda
cit	citron	ros	rosine
cl	claret	ryl	royal
cob	cobalt	sal	salmon
cop	copper	saph	sapphire
crim	crimson	scar	scarlet
cr	cream	sep	sepia
db	drab	sien	sienna
dk	dark	sil	silver
dl	dull	sl	slate
dp	deep	stl	steel
emer	emerald	turq	turquoise
gldn	golden	ultra	ultramarine
grn	green	ven	Venetian
grnsh	greenish	ver	vermillion
grysh	grayish	vio	violet
hel	heliotrope	yel	yellow
hn	henna	yelsh	yellowish

Benjamin Franklin
A1
A3

George Washington
A2
A4

Reproductions. The letters R. W. H. & E. at the bottom of each stamp are less distinct on the reproductions than on the originals.

5c. On the originals the left side of the white shirt frill touches the oval on a level with the top of the "F" of "Five." On the reproductions it touches the oval about on a level with the top of the figure "5."

10c. On the reproductions, line of coat at left points to right tip of "X" and line of coat at right points to center of "S" of CENTS. On the originals, line of coat points to "T" of TEN and between "T" and "S" of CENTS. On the reproductions the eyes have a sleepy look, the line of the mouth is straighter, and in the curl of hair near the left cheek is a strong black dot, while the originals have only a faint one.

Franklin
A5

A5

ONE CENT.

Type I. Has complete curved lines outside the labels with "U.S. Postage" and "One Cent." The scrolls below the lower label are turned under, forming little balls. The ornaments at top are substantially complete.

Type Ib. Same as I but balls below the bottom label are not so clear. The plume-like scrolls at bottom are not complete.

A6

Type Ia. Same as I at bottom but top ornaments and outer line at top are partly cut away.

A7

Type II. The little balls of the bottom scrolls and the bottoms of the lower plume ornaments are missing. The side ornaments are complete.

A8

Type III. The top and bottom curved lines outside the labels are broken in the middle. The side ornaments are complete.

Type IIIa. Similar to type III with the outer line broken at top or bottom but not both.

A9

Type IV. Similar to type II, but with the curved lines outside the labels recut at top or bottom or both.

Prices for types I and III are for stamps showing the marked characteristics plainly. Copies of type I showing the balls indistinctly and of type III with the lines only slightly broken, sell for much lower prices.

UNITED STATES

Scott® No.	Illus No.	Description	Unused Price	Used Price	/////
1847		All Issues from 1847 to 1894 are Unwatermarked.			
1	A1	5c red brown, *bluish*	5000.00	800.00	☐☐☐☐☐
2	A2	10c black, *bluish*	20000.00	2500.00	☐☐☐☐☐
1875		REPRODUCTIONS.	Bluish paper without gum.		
3	A3	5c red brown	1650.00		☐☐☐☐☐
4	A4	10c black	2000.00		☐☐☐☐☐
1851-56					
5	A5	1c blue, Type I	100000.00	20000.00	☐☐☐☐☐
5A	A5	1c blue, Type Ib	10500.00	3500.00	☐☐☐☐☐
6	A6	1c blue, Type Ia	13500.00	4250.00	☐☐☐☐☐
7	A7	1c blue, Type II	450.00	85.00	☐☐☐☐☐
8	A8	1c blue, Type III	4500.00	1250.00	☐☐☐☐☐
8A	A8	1c blue, Type IIIa	1550.00	525.00	☐☐☐☐☐
9	A9	1c blue, Type IV ('52)	300.00	75.00	☐☐☐☐☐
10	A10	3c orange brown, Type I	1250.00	65.00	☐☐☐☐☐
11	A10	3c dl red, Type I	120.00	7.00	☐☐☐☐☐
12	A11	5c red brown, Type I ('56)	9000.00	1300.00	☐☐☐☐☐
13	A12	10c green, Type I ('55)	7500.00	675.00	☐☐☐☐☐
14	A13	10c green, Type II ('55)	1500.00	275.00	☐☐☐☐☐
15	A14	10c green, Type III ('55)	1550.00	285.00	☐☐☐☐☐
16	A15	10c green, Type IV ('55)	9500.00	1350.00	☐☐☐☐☐
17	A16	12c black	1850.00	250.00	☐☐☐☐☐
1857-61		*Perf. 15*			
18	A5	1c blue, Type I ('61)	675.00	325.00	☐☐☐☐☐
19	A6	1c blue, Type Ia	8500.00	2000.00	☐☐☐☐☐
20	A7	1c blue, Type II	425.00	120.00	☐☐☐☐☐
21	A8	1c blue, Type III	3250.00	950.00	☐☐☐☐☐
22	A8	1c blue, Type IIIa	575.00	200.00	☐☐☐☐☐
23	A9	1c blue, Type IV	1500.00	265.00	☐☐☐☐☐
24	A20	1c blue, Type V	120.00	22.50	☐☐☐☐☐
25	A10	3c rose, Type I	650.00	27.50	☐☐☐☐☐
26	A21	3c dl red, Type II	50.00	2.75	☐☐☐☐☐
26a		3c dl red, Type IIa	110.00	20.00	☐☐☐☐☐
27	A11	5c brick red, Type I ('58)	6500.00	900.00	☐☐☐☐☐
28	A11	5c red brown, Type I	1350.00	275.00	☐☐☐☐☐
28A	A11	5c indian red, Type I ('58)	8000.00	1200.00	☐☐☐☐☐
29	A11	5c brown, Type I ('59)	675.00	200.00	☐☐☐☐☐
30	A22	5c orange brown, Type II ('61)	750.00	900.00	☐☐☐☐☐
30A	A22	5c brown, Type II ('60)	425.00	170.00	☐☐☐☐☐
31	A12	10c green, Type I	4500.00	500.00	☐☐☐☐☐
32	A13	10c green, Type II	1400.00	150.00	☐☐☐☐☐
33	A14	10c green, Type III	1450.00	160.00	☐☐☐☐☐
34	A15	10c green, Type IV	12000.00	1400.00	☐☐☐☐☐
35	A23	10c green, Type V ('59)	175.00	57.50	☐☐☐☐☐
36	A16	12c black, plate I	300.00	75.00	☐☐☐☐☐
36b		12c black, plate III ('59)	225.00	85.00	☐☐☐☐☐

Washington
A10

Thomas Jefferson
A11

A13

Type II. The design is complete at the top. The outer line at the bottom is broken in the middle. The shells are partly cut away.

A10

THREE CENTS.

Type I. There is an outer frame line at top and bottom.

A11

FIVE CENTS.

Type I. There are projections on all four sides.

A12

A14

Type III. The outer lines are broken above the top label and the "X" numerals. The outer line at the bottom and the shells are partly cut away, as in Type II.

A15

Type IV. The outer lines have been recut at top or bottom or both.

Types I, II, III and IV have complete ornaments at the sides of the stamps and three pearls at each outer edge of the bottom panel.

A12

TEN CENTS.

Type I. The "shells" at the lower corners are practically complete. The outer line below the label is very nearly complete. The outer lines are broken above the middle of the top label and the "X" in each upper corner.

A16

14

Same Designs as 1851-56 Issues.

Franklin
A20

ONE CENT.

Type V. Similar to type III of 1851-56 but with side ornaments partly cut away.

A21

THREE CENTS.

Type II. The outer frame line has been removed at top and bottom. The side frame lines were recut so as to be continuous from the top to the bottom of the plate.

Type IIa. The side frame lines extend only to the top and bottom of the stamp design.

A22

A22

FIVE CENTS.

Type II. The projections at top and bottom are partly cut away.

A23
(Two typical examples).

TEN CENTS.

Type V. The side ornaments are slightly cut away. Usually only one pearl remains at each end of the lower label but some copies show two or three pearls at the right side. At the bottom the outer line is complete and the shells nearly so. The outer lines at top are complete except over the right "X".

TWELVE CENTS.

Plate I. Outer frame lines complete.
Plate III. Outer frame lines noticeably uneven or broken, sometimes partly missing.

15

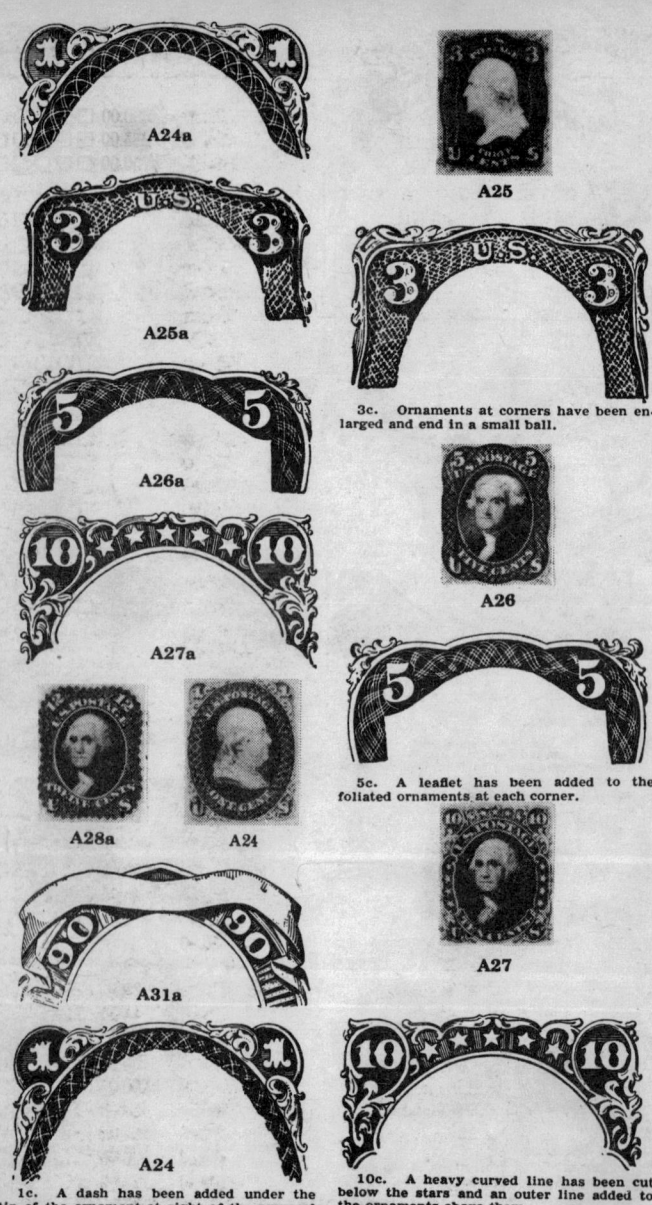

3c. Ornaments at corners have been enlarged and end in a small ball.

5c. A leaflet has been added to the foliated ornaments at each corner.

1c. A dash has been added under the tip of the ornament at right of the numeral in upper left corner.

10c. A heavy curved line has been cut below the stars and an outer line added to the ornaments above them.

Scott® No.	Illus No.	Description	Unused Price	Used Price	/ / / / / /
37	A17	24c gray lilac ('60)	650.00	200.00	☐☐☐☐☐
38	A18	30c orange ('60)	800.00	285.00	☐☐☐☐☐
39	A19	90c blue ('60)	1450.00	2750.00	☐☐☐☐☐
1875		**GOVERNMENT REPRINTS.**	**Without Gum.**		*Perf. 12.*
40	A5	1c bright blue	500.00		☐☐☐☐☐
41	A10	3c scarlet	2750.00		☐☐☐☐☐
42	A22	5c orange brown	900.00		☐☐☐☐☐
43	A12	10c blue green	2250.00		☐☐☐☐☐
44	A16	12c greenish black	2450.00		☐☐☐☐☐
45	A17	24c black violet	2750.00		☐☐☐☐☐
46	A18	30c yellow orange	2850.00		☐☐☐☐☐
47	A19	90c dp blue	4000.00		☐☐☐☐☐
1861					
55	A24a	1c indigo	16500.00		☐☐☐☐☐
56	A25a	3c brown rose	700.00		☐☐☐☐☐
57	A26a	5c brown	12000.00		☐☐☐☐☐
58	A27a	10c dk green	4750.00		☐☐☐☐☐
59	A28a	12c black	35000.00		☐☐☐☐☐
60	A29	24c dk violet	5000.00		☐☐☐☐☐
61	A30	30c red orange	15000.00		☐☐☐☐☐
62	A31a	90c dl blue	19000.00		☐☐☐☐☐

The paper of Nos. 55–62 is thin and semitransparent. That of the following issues is thicker and more opaque, except Nos. 62B, 70c, and 70d.
It is doubtful that Nos. 55–62 were regularly issued.

62B	A27a	10c dk green	4750.00	450.00	☐☐☐☐☐

No. 62B unused cannot be distinguished from No. 58 which does not exist used.

1861-62

Scott No.	Illus No.	Description	Unused Price	Used Price	
63	A24	1c blue	100.00	17.50	☐☐☐☐☐
64	A25	3c pink	3250.00	250.00	☐☐☐☐☐
64a		3c pigeon blood pink	—	1200.00	☐☐☐☐☐
64b		3c rose pink	250.00	45.00	☐☐☐☐☐
65	A25	3c rose	45.00	1.10	☐☐☐☐☐
66	A25	3c lake	1350.00		☐☐☐☐☐
67	A26	5c buff	3850.00	350.00	☐☐☐☐☐
68	A27	10c yellow green	235.00	32.50	☐☐☐☐☐
69	A28	12c black	425.00	45.00	☐☐☐☐☐
70	A29	24c red lilac ('62)	475.00	60.00	☐☐☐☐☐
70a		24c brown lilac	425.00	55.00	☐☐☐☐☐
70b		24c steel blue	3000.00	250.00	☐☐☐☐☐
70c		24c violet	2500.00	450.00	☐☐☐☐☐
70d		24c grayish lilac	900.00	250.00	☐☐☐☐☐
71	A30	30c orange	450.00	60.00	☐☐☐☐☐
72	A31	90c blue	1100.00	225.00	☐☐☐☐☐

Nos. 70c and 70d are on a thinner, harder and more transparent paper than Nos. 70, 70a, 70b, or the later No. 78.

A28

A34

A35

12c. Ovals and scrolls have been added to the corners.

A36

A37

A29   A30

A31   Grill

A38

A39

A40

A41

A42

A43

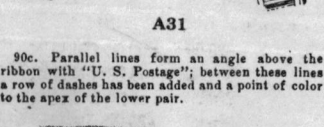

A31

90c. Parallel lines form an angle above the ribbon with "U. S. Postage"; between these lines a row of dashes has been added and a point of color to the apex of the lower pair.

A40

FIFTEEN CENTS. Type I. Picture unframed.

A32

A33

A40a

Type II. Picture framed.
Type III. Same as type I but without fringe of brown shading lines around central vignette.

18

Scott® No.	Illus No.	Description	Unused Price	Used Price	/////
1861-66					
73	A32	2c black ('63)	110.00	20.00	☐☐☐☐☐
74	A25	3c scarlet	3750.00		☐☐☐☐☐
75	A26	5c red brown ('62)	1200.00	185.00	☐☐☐☐☐
76	A26	5c brown ('63)	275.00	47.50	☐☐☐☐☐
77	A33	15c black ('66)	450.00	60.00	☐☐☐☐☐
78	A29	24c lilac ('63)	250.00	45.00	☐☐☐☐☐

Same as 1861-66 Issues.
Embossed with grills of various sizes.
Grill with Points Up

1867   A. Grill covering the entire stamp. *Perf. 12.*

79	A25	3c rose	1650.00	425.00	☐☐☐☐☐
80	A26	5c brown	40000.00	—	☐☐☐☐☐
80a		5c dk brown		37500.00	☐☐☐☐☐
81	A30	30c orange		32500.00	☐☐☐☐☐

B. Grill about 18x15 mm.
(22 by 18 points.)

82	A25	3c rose		35000.00	☐☐☐☐☐

C. Grill about 13x16 mm.
(16 to 17 by 18 to 21 points.)

83	A25	3c rose	1450.00	300.00	☐☐☐☐☐

Grill with Points Down.
D. Grill about 12x14 mm.
(15 by 17 to 18 points.)

84	A32	2c black	2400.00	725.00	☐☐☐☐☐
85	A25	3c rose	1100.00	325.00	☐☐☐☐☐

Z. Grill about 11x14 mm.
(13 to 14 by 17 to 18 points.)

85A	A24	1c blue	—	110000.00	☐☐☐☐☐
85B	A32	2c black	900.00	275.00	☐☐☐☐☐
85C	A25	3c rose	2500.00	750.00	☐☐☐☐☐
85D	A27	10c green	—	23500.00	☐☐☐☐☐
85E	A28	12c black	1450.00	500.00	☐☐☐☐☐
85F	A33	15c black		35000.00	☐☐☐☐☐

E. Grill about 11x13 mm.
(14 by 15 to 17 points.)

86	A24	1c blue	625.00	200.00	☐☐☐☐☐
87	A32	2c black	300.00	65.00	☐☐☐☐☐
88	A25	3c rose	200.00	9.50	☐☐☐☐☐
89	A27	10c green	1000.00	150.00	☐☐☐☐☐
90	A28	12c black	1200.00	170.00	☐☐☐☐☐
91	A33	15c black	2400.00	400.00	☐☐☐☐☐

F. Grill about 9x13 mm.
(11 to 12 by 15 to 17 points.)

92	A24	1c blue	225.00	75.00	☐☐☐☐☐
93	A32	2c black	110.00	22.50	☐☐☐☐☐
94	A25	3c red	75.00	2.50	☐☐☐☐☐
95	A26	5c brown	750.00	185.00	☐☐☐☐☐

A44

A45

A48

A49

A44

A48

A45

A49

A46

A50

A46

A47

A50

A47

A51

Scott® No.	Illus No.	Description	Unused Price	Used Price	//////
96	A27	10c yellow green	550.00	85.00	☐☐☐☐☐
97	A28	12c black	600.00	90.00	☐☐☐☐☐
98	A33	15c black	600.00	100.00	☐☐☐☐☐
99	A29	24c gray lilac	1100.00	425.00	☐☐☐☐☐
100	A30	30c orange	1250.00	325.00	☐☐☐☐☐
101	A31	90c blue	3500.00	850.00	☐☐☐☐☐
1875		Re-issue. Without Grill.			*Perf. 12.*
102	A24	1c blue	475.00	650.00	☐☐☐☐☐
103	A32	2c black	2500.00	3250.00	☐☐☐☐☐
104	A25	3c brown red	3000.00	4000.00	☐☐☐☐☐
105	A26	5c brown	1600.00	1850.00	☐☐☐☐☐
106	A27	10c green	2100.00	2500.00	☐☐☐☐☐
107	A28	12c black	2850.00	3350.00	☐☐☐☐☐
108	A33	15c black	2850.00	3500.00	☐☐☐☐☐
109	A29	24c dp violet	3500.00	5500.00	☐☐☐☐☐
110	A30	30c brownish orange	4250.00	6500.00	☐☐☐☐☐
111	A31	90c blue	5500.00	9500.00	☐☐☐☐☐

These stamps can be distinguished from the 1861–66 issues by the shades and the paper which is hard and very white instead of yellowish. The gum is white and crackly.

G. Grill measuring 9½x9 mm.

		(12 by 11 to 11½ points)			*Perf. 12*
1869					
112	A34	1c buff	225.00	60.00	☐☐☐☐☐
113	A35	2c brown	160.00	25.00	☐☐☐☐☐
114	A36	3c ultra	135.00	5.50	☐☐☐☐☐
115	A37	6c ultra	775.00	85.00	☐☐☐☐☐
116	A38	10c yellow	850.00	95.00	☐☐☐☐☐
117	A39	12c green	750.00	85.00	☐☐☐☐☐
118	A40	15c brown & blue, Type I	1750.00	235.00	☐☐☐☐☐
119	A40a	15c brown & blue, Type II	850.00	115.00	☐☐☐☐☐
119b		Center inverted	130000.00	17000.00	☐☐☐☐☐
120	A41	24c green & violet	2500.00	500.00	☐☐☐☐☐
120b		Center invtd.	100000.00	16500.00	☐☐☐☐☐
121	A42	30c blue & carmine	2250.00	250.00	☐☐☐☐☐
121b		Flags invtd.	115000.00	45000.00	☐☐☐☐☐
122	A43	90c carmine & black	8000.00	1250.00	☐☐☐☐☐
1875		Re-issues. Without Grill. Hard White Paper.			*Perf. 12*
123	A34	1c buff	325.00	225.00	☐☐☐☐☐
124	A35	2c brown	375.00	325.00	☐☐☐☐☐
125	A36	3c blue	3000.00	1400.00	☐☐☐☐☐
126	A37	6c blue	850.00	500.00	☐☐☐☐☐
127	A38	10c yellow	1400.00	1000.00	☐☐☐☐☐
128	A39	12c green	1500.00	1000.00	☐☐☐☐☐
129	A40	15c brown & blue, Type III	1300.00	500.00	☐☐☐☐☐
130	A41	24c green & violet	1250.00	500.00	☐☐☐☐☐

A52

A46a

3c. The under part of the upper tail of the left ribbon is heavily shaded.

A53

A54

A47a

6c. The first four vertical lines of the shading in the lower part of the left ribbon have been strengthened.

A44a

1c. In pearl at left of numeral "1" is a small crescent.

A48a

7c. Two small semi-circles are drawn around the ends of the lines which outline the ball in the lower right hand corner.

A45a

2c. Under the scroll at the left of "U. S." there is a small diagonal line. This mark seldom shows clearly. The stamp, No. 157, can be distinguished by its color.

A49a

10c. There is a small semi-circle in the scroll at the right end of the upper label.

Scott® No.	Illus No.	Description	Unused Price	Used Price	/ / / / / /
131	A42	30c blue & carmine	1750.00	1000.00	☐☐☐☐☐
132	A43	90c carmine & black	5500.00	8000.00	☐☐☐☐☐

1880 — Soft Porous Paper.

133	A34	1c buff	200.00	135.00	☐☐☐☐☐
133a		1c brown orange	175.00	120.00	☐☐☐☐☐

H. Grill about 10x12 mm. (11 to 13 by 14 to 16 points.) On all values, 1c to 90c.
I. Grill about 8½x10 mm. (10 to 11 by 10 to 13 points.) On 1, 2, 3, 6, 7c.

Two varieties of grill are known on this issue.

On the 1870-71 stamps the grill impressions are usually faint or incomplete. This is especially true of the H grill, which often shows only a few points.

Prices are for stamps showing well defined grills.

1870-71 — White Wove Paper. *Perf. 12.*

134	A44	1c ultra	425.00	50.00	☐☐☐☐☐
135	A45	2c red brown	300.00	30.00	☐☐☐☐☐
136	A46	3c green	225.00	8.50	☐☐☐☐☐
137	A47	6c carmine	1400.00	250.00	☐☐☐☐☐
138	A48	7c vermilion ('71)	1000.00	225.00	☐☐☐☐☐
139	A49	10c brown	1350.00	375.00	☐☐☐☐☐
140	A50	12c dl violet	11500.00	1500.00	☐☐☐☐☐
141	A51	15c orange	1600.00	675.00	☐☐☐☐☐
142	A52	24c purple	—	10500.00	☐☐☐☐☐
143	A53	30c black	3750.00	800.00	☐☐☐☐☐
144	A54	90c carmine	5000.00	700.00	☐☐☐☐☐

1870-71 — Without Grill. White Wove Paper. *Perf. 12.*

145	A44	1c ultra	135.00	6.50	☐☐☐☐☐
146	A45	2c red brown	40.00	4.50	☐☐☐☐☐
147	A46	3c green	90.00	.40	☐☐☐☐☐
148	A47	6c carmine	185.00	11.00	☐☐☐☐☐
149	A48	7c vermilion ('71)	300.00	50.00	☐☐☐☐☐
150	A49	10c brown	185.00	12.00	☐☐☐☐☐
151	A50	12c dl violet	475.00	45.00	☐☐☐☐☐
152	A51	15c bright orange	450.00	50.00	☐☐☐☐☐
153	A52	24c purple	525.00	65.00	☐☐☐☐☐
154	A53	30c black	900.00	80.00	☐☐☐☐☐
155	A54	90c carmine	1100.00	150.00	☐☐☐☐☐

1873 — White Wove Paper, thin to thick Without Grill* *Perf. 12.*

156	A44a	1c ultra	45.00	1.75	☐☐☐☐☐
157	A45a	2c brown	130.00	7.00	☐☐☐☐☐
158	A46a	3c green	35.00	.15	☐☐☐☐☐
159	A47a	6c dl pink	160.00	8.00	☐☐☐☐☐
160	A48a	7c orange vermilion	375.00	50.00	☐☐☐☐☐
161	A49a	10c brown	165.00	8.25	☐☐☐☐☐
162	A50a	12c black violet	550.00	55.00	☐☐☐☐☐

A50a

12c. The balls of the figure "2" are crescent shaped.

A51a

15c. In the lower part of the triangle in the upper left corner two lines have been made heavier forming a "V". This mark can be found on some of the Continental and American (1879) printings, but not all stamps show it.

Secret marks were added to the dies of the 24c, 30c and 90c but new plates were not made from them. The various printings of these stamps can be distinguished only by the shades and paper.

A55　　　　A56

A44b

1c. The vertical lines in the upper part of the stamp have been so deepened that the background often appears to be solid. Lines of shading have been added to the upper arabesques.

A46b

3c. The shading at the sides of the central oval appears only about one-half the previous width. A short horizontal dash has been cut about 1mm. below the "TS" of "CKNTS."

A47b

6c. On the original stamps four vertical lines can be counted from the edge of the panel to the outside of the stamp. On the re-engraved stamps there are but three lines in the same place.

A49b

10c. On the original stamps there are five vertical lines between the left side of the oval and the edge of the shield. There are only four lines on the re-engraved stamps. In the lower part of the latter, also, the horizontal lines of the background have been strengthened.

HOW TO USE THIS BOOK

The number in the first column is its Scott number or identifying number. The letter and number that come next (A41) indicate the design and refer to the illustration so designated. Following that is the denomination of the stamp and its color. Finally, the price, unused and used is shown.

Scott® No.	Illus No.	Description	Unused Price	Used Price	/ / / / /
1873					
163	A51a	15c yellow orange	475.00	45.00	☐☐☐☐☐
165	A53	30c gray black	475.00	45.00	☐☐☐☐☐
166	A54	90c rose carmine	1150.00	160.00	☐☐☐☐☐

* All values except 90c exist with experimental (J) grill, about 7x9½ mm.

Special Printing. Without Gum.

1875 Hard, White Wove Paper. *Perf. 12*

167	A44a	1c ultra	5500.00		☐☐☐☐☐
168	A45a	2c dk brown	3000.00		☐☐☐☐☐
169	A46a	3c blue green	8500.00	—	☐☐☐☐☐
170	A47a	6c dl rose	7000.00		☐☐☐☐☐
171	A48a	7c reddish vermilion	1850.00		☐☐☐☐☐
172	A49a	10c pale brown	6000.00		☐☐☐☐☐
173	A50a	12c dk violet	2350.00		☐☐☐☐☐
174	A51a	15c bright orange	6500.00		☐☐☐☐☐
175	A52	24c dl purple	1650.00	—	☐☐☐☐☐
176	A53	30c greenish black	6000.00		☐☐☐☐☐
177	A54	90c violet carmine	6000.00		☐☐☐☐☐

1875 Yellowish Wove Paper. *Perf. 12.*

178	A45a	2c vermilion	125.00	4.00	☐☐☐☐☐
179	A55	5c blue	135.00	7.50	☐☐☐☐☐

Special Printing. Without Gum.

1875 Hard, White Wove Paper.

180	A45a	2c carmine vermilion	17000.00		☐☐☐☐☐
181	A55	5c bright blue	31500.00		☐☐☐☐☐

Same as 1870-75 Issues. Varying from Thin to Thick.

1879 Soft Porous Paper. *Perf. 12*

182	A44a	1c dk ultra	90.00	1.20	☐☐☐☐☐
183	A45a	2c vermilion	50.00	1.20	☐☐☐☐☐
184	A46a	3c green	37.50	.10	☐☐☐☐☐
185	A55	5c blue	175.00	7.50	☐☐☐☐☐
186	A47a	6c pink	400.00	10.00	☐☐☐☐☐
187	A49	10c brown (without secret mark)	600.00	12.00	☐☐☐☐☐
188	A49a	10c brown (with secret mark)	400.00	13.00	☐☐☐☐☐
189	A51a	15c red orange	150.00	13.50	☐☐☐☐☐
190	A53	30c full black	425.00	21.00	☐☐☐☐☐
191	A54	90c carmine	1000.00	140.00	☐☐☐☐☐

Special Printing. Without Gum.

1880 Soft Porous Paper. *Perf. 12.*

192	A44a	1c dk ultra	8000.00		☐☐☐☐☐
193	A45a	2c black brown	4500.00		☐☐☐☐☐
194	A46a	3c blue green	11500.00		☐☐☐☐☐
195	A47a	6c dl rose	8500.00		☐☐☐☐☐
196	A48a	7c scarlet vermilion	2250.00		☐☐☐☐☐
197	A49a	10c dp brown	7500.00		☐☐☐☐☐
198	A50a	12c black purple	4250.00		☐☐☐☐☐

HOW TO USE THIS BOOK

The number in the first column is its Scott number or identifying number. The letter and number that come next (A41) indicate the design and refer to the illustration so designated. Following that is the denomination of the stamp and its color. Finally, the price, unused and used is shown.

Scott® No.	Illus No.	Description	Unused Price	Used Price	/////
1880					
199	A51a	15c orange	7000.00		☐☐☐☐☐
200	A52	24c dk violet	2350.00		☐☐☐☐☐
201	A53	30c greenish black	6250.00		☐☐☐☐☐
202	A54	90c dl carmine	6250.00		☐☐☐☐☐
203	A45a	2c scarlet vermilion	16000.00		☐☐☐☐☐
204	A55	5c dp blue	27500.00		☐☐☐☐☐
1882		*Perf. 12.*			
205	A56	5c yellow brown	90.00	4.00	☐☐☐☐☐
1882		Special Printing. Soft Porous Paper.	Without Gum.		
205C	A56	5c gray brown	16500.00		☐☐☐☐☐
1881-82					
206	A44b	1c gray blue	30.00	.40	☐☐☐☐☐
207	A46b	3c blue green	35.00	.12	☐☐☐☐☐
208	A47b	6c rose ('82)	235.00	40.00	☐☐☐☐☐
208a		6c brown red	210.00	55.00	☐☐☐☐☐
209	A49b	10c brown ('82)	67.50	2.25	☐☐☐☐☐
1883					
210	A57	2c red brown	28.50	.08	☐☐☐☐☐
211	A58	4c blue green	140.00	7.00	☐☐☐☐☐
		Special Printing. Soft Porous Paper.			
211B	A57	2c pale red brown	675.00		☐☐☐☐☐
211D	A58	4c dp blue green	13000.00		☐☐☐☐☐
1887-88					
212	A59	1c ultra	50.00	.65	☐☐☐☐☐
213	A57	2c green	20.00	.08	☐☐☐☐☐
214	A46b	3c vermilion	42.50	32.50	☐☐☐☐☐
215	A58	4c carmine	140.00	10.00	☐☐☐☐☐
216	A56	5c indigo	120.00	6.00	☐☐☐☐☐
217	A53	30c orange brown	350.00	70.00	☐☐☐☐☐
218	A54	90c purple	725.00	130.00	☐☐☐☐☐
1890-93					
219	A60	1c dl blue	20.00	.10	☐☐☐☐☐
219D	A61	2c lake	150.00	.45	☐☐☐☐☐
220	A61	2c carmine	16.50	.05	☐☐☐☐☐
220a		Cap on left "2"	35.00	1.00	☐☐☐☐☐
220c		Cap on both "2's"	110.00	7.00	☐☐☐☐☐
221	A62	3c purple	55.00	4.50	☐☐☐☐☐
222	A63	4c dk brown	52.50	1.50	☐☐☐☐☐
223	A64	5c chocolate	52.50	1.50	☐☐☐☐☐
224	A65	6c brown red	52.50	13.00	☐☐☐☐☐
225	A66	8c lilac ('93)	40.00	8.50	☐☐☐☐☐
226	A67	10c green	100.00	1.50	☐☐☐☐☐
227	A68	15c indigo	150.00	15.00	☐☐☐☐☐
228	A69	30c black	225.00	18.50	☐☐☐☐☐
229	A70	90c orange	375.00	85.00	☐☐☐☐☐

TWO CENTS.

Type I. The horizontal lines of the ground work run across the triangle and are of the same thickness within it as without.

Type II. The horizontal lines cross the triangle but are thinner within it than without.

Type III. The horizontal lines do not cross the double frame lines of the triangle. The lines within the triangle are thin, as in type II.

Scott® No.	Illus No.	Description	Unused Price	Used Price	/ / / / / /
1893					
230	A71	1c dp blue	25.00	.30	☐☐☐☐☐
231	A72	2c brown violet	22.50	.06	☐☐☐☐☐
232	A73	3c green	50.00	15.00	☐☐☐☐☐
233	A74	4c ultra	75.00	6.00	☐☐☐☐☐
233a		4c blue (error)	6500.00	2500.00	☐☐☐☐☐
234	A75	5c chocolate	85.00	7.00	☐☐☐☐☐
235	A76	6c purple	75.00	20.00	☐☐☐☐☐
236	A77	8c magenta	50.00	8.00	☐☐☐☐☐
237	A78	10c black brown	130.00	6.50	☐☐☐☐☐
238	A79	15c dk green	225.00	65.00	☐☐☐☐☐
239	A80	30c orange brown	325.00	90.00	☐☐☐☐☐
240	A81	50c slate blue	400.00	140.00	☐☐☐☐☐
241	A82	$1 salmon	1100.00	575.00	☐☐☐☐☐
242	A83	$2 brown red	1250.00	500.00	☐☐☐☐☐
243	A84	$3 yellow green	2600.00	900.00	☐☐☐☐☐
244	A85	$4 crimson lake	3500.00	1300.00	☐☐☐☐☐
245	A86	$5 black	3850.00	1500.00	☐☐☐☐☐
1894		*Perf. 12.* Unwmkd.			
246	A87	1c ultra	21.00	3.00	☐☐☐☐☐
247	A87	1c blue	52.50	1.25	☐☐☐☐☐
248	A88	2c pink, Type I	17.50	2.00	☐☐☐☐☐
249	A88	2c carmine lake, Type I	125.00	1.35	☐☐☐☐☐
250	A88	2c carmine, Type I	21.00	.25	☐☐☐☐☐
251	A88	2c carmine, Type II	165.00	2.50	☐☐☐☐☐
252	A88	2c carmine, Type III	85.00	3.25	☐☐☐☐☐
253	A89	3c purple	80.00	6.25	☐☐☐☐☐
254	A90	4c dk brown	90.00	2.50	☐☐☐☐☐
255	A91	5c chocolate	70.00	3.50	☐☐☐☐☐
256	A92	6c dl brown	135.00	14.00	☐☐☐☐☐
257	A93	8c violet brown ('95)	100.00	10.00	☐☐☐☐☐
258	A94	10c dk green	185.00	6.50	☐☐☐☐☐
259	A95	15c dk blue	275.00	45.00	☐☐☐☐☐
260	A96	50c orange	375.00	75.00	☐☐☐☐☐
261	A97	$1 black, Type I	950.00	225.00	☐☐☐☐☐
261A	A97	$1 black, Type II	2000.00	450.00	☐☐☐☐☐
262	A98	$2 bright blue	2400.00	550.00	☐☐☐☐☐
263	A99	$5 dk green	3750.00	1000.00	☐☐☐☐☐
1895	Wmkd.	USPS in Doublelined Capitals. (191)			
264	A87	1c blue	6.00	.10	☐☐☐☐☐
265	A88	2c carmine, Type I	25.00	.65	☐☐☐☐☐
266	A88	2c carmine, Type II	22.50	2.50	☐☐☐☐☐
267	A88	2c carmine, Type III	4.50	.05	☐☐☐☐☐
268	A89	3c purple	32.50	1.00	☐☐☐☐☐
269	A90	4c dk brown	35.00	1.10	☐☐☐☐☐
270	A91	5c chocolate	32.50	1.75	☐☐☐☐☐
271	A92	6c dl brown	75.00	3.50	☐☐☐☐☐

ONE DOLLAR.

Type I. The circles enclosing "$1" are broken where they meet the curved line below "One Dollar." The fifteen left vertical rows of impressions from plate 76 are Type I, the balance being Type II.

Type II. The circles are complete.

TEN CENTS

Type I. Tips of foliate ornaments do not impinge on white curved line below "TEN CENTS".

Type II. Tips of ornaments break curved line below "E" of "TEN" and "T" of "CENTS".

Scott® No.	Illus No.	Description	Unused Price	Used Price	//////
1895					
271a		Wmkd. USIR	1850.00	350.00	☐☐☐☐☐
272	A93	8c violet brown	35.00	1.00	☐☐☐☐☐
272a		Wmkd. USIR	700.00	110.00	☐☐☐☐☐
273	A94	10c dk green	60.00	1.20	☐☐☐☐☐
274	A95	15c dk blue	185.00	8.25	☐☐☐☐☐
275	A96	50c orange	265.00	20.00	☐☐☐☐☐
276	A97	$1 black, Type I	625.00	65.00	☐☐☐☐☐
276A	A97	$1 black, Type II	1350.00	120.00	☐☐☐☐☐
277	A98	$2 bright blue	975.00	250.00	☐☐☐☐☐
278	A99	$5 dk green	2100.00	375.00	☐☐☐☐☐
1898					
279	A87	1c dp green	10.00	.06	☐☐☐☐☐
279B	A88	2c red, Type III	9.00	.05	☐☐☐☐☐
279e		Booklet pane of 6	375.00	200.00	☐☐☐☐☐
280	A90	4c rose brown	30.00	.70	☐☐☐☐☐
281	A91	5c dk blue	37.50	.65	☐☐☐☐☐
282	A92	6c lake	45.00	2.00	☐☐☐☐☐
282C	A94	10c brown, Type I	160.00	2.00	☐☐☐☐☐
283	A94	10c orange brown, Type II	100.00	1.75	☐☐☐☐☐
284	A95	15c olive green	120.00	6.75	☐☐☐☐☐
1898					
285	A100	1c dk yellow green	30.00	5.50	☐☐☐☐☐
286	A101	2c copper red	27.50	1.50	☐☐☐☐☐
287	A102	4c orange	150.00	22.50	☐☐☐☐☐
288	A103	5c dl blue	125.00	20.00	☐☐☐☐☐
289	A104	8c violet brown	180.00	40.00	☐☐☐☐☐
290	A105	10c gray violet	200.00	20.00	☐☐☐☐☐
291	A106	50c sage green	800.00	165.00	☐☐☐☐☐
292	A107	$1 black	2000.00	600.00	☐☐☐☐☐
293	A108	$2 orange brown	3000.00	825.00	☐☐☐☐☐
1901					
294	A109	1c green & black	22.50	4.00	☐☐☐☐☐
294a		Center invtd.	11000.00	3000.00	☐☐☐☐☐
295	A110	2c carmine & black	22.50	1.10	☐☐☐☐☐
295a		Center invtd.	50000.00	12000.00	☐☐☐☐☐
296	A111	4c dp red brown & black	105.00	19.00	☐☐☐☐☐
296a		Center invtd.	14000.00		☐☐☐☐☐
297	A112	5c ultra & black	120.00	20.00	☐☐☐☐☐
298	A113	8c brown violet & black	150.00	75.00	☐☐☐☐☐
299	A114	10c yellow brown & black	225.00	35.00	☐☐☐☐☐
1902-03		*Perf. 12*			
300	A115	1c blue green ('03)	10.00	.05	☐☐☐☐☐
300b		Bklt. pane of 6	550.00	250.00	☐☐☐☐☐
301	A116	2c carmine ('03)	12.50	.05	☐☐☐☐☐
301c		Booklet pane of 6	475.00	250.00	☐☐☐☐☐

A109   A110   A111   A112

A113   A114

A115   A116   A117   A118

A119   A120   A121   A122

A123   A124   A125   A126

A127   A128   A129

Scott® No.	Illus No.	Description	Unused Price	Used Price	/ / / / / /
1902-03					
302	A117	3c bright violet ('03)	55.00	3.00 ☐☐☐☐☐
303	A118	4c brown ('03)	55.00	1.00 ☐☐☐☐☐
304	A119	5c blue ('03)	65.00	1.00 ☐☐☐☐☐
305	A120	6c claret ('03)	70.00	2.25 ☐☐☐☐☐
306	A121	8c violet black	40.00	2.00 ☐☐☐☐☐
307	A122	10c pale red brown ('03)	70.00	1.50 ☐☐☐☐☐
308	A123	13c purple black	40.00	8.50 ☐☐☐☐☐
309	A124	15c olive green ('03)	160.00	6.00 ☐☐☐☐☐
310	A125	50c orange ('03)	525.00	25.00 ☐☐☐☐☐
311	A126	$1 black ('03)	900.00	55.00 ☐☐☐☐☐
312	A127	$2 dk blue ('03)	1200.00	175.00 ☐☐☐☐☐
313	A128	$5 dk green ('03)	3000.00	625.00 ☐☐☐☐☐
1906-08		*Imperf.*			
314	A115	1c blue green	35.00	21.00 ☐☐☐☐☐
314A	A118	4c brown ('08)	17500.00	9000.00 ☐☐☐☐☐
315	A119	5c blue ('08)	650.00	300.00 ☐☐☐☐☐
		Coil Stamps.			
1908		*Perf. 12 Horizontally.*			
316	A115	1c blue green, pair	22500.00	— ☐☐☐☐☐
317	A119	5c blue, pair	4500.00	— ☐☐☐☐☐
		Perf. 12 Vertically.			
318	A115	1c blue green, pair	3500.00	— ☐☐☐☐☐
1903		*Perf. 12.*			
319	A129	2c carmine	7.00	.05 ☐☐☐☐☐
319g		Booklet pane of 6	120.00	20.00 ☐☐☐☐☐
1906		*Imperf.*			
320	A129	2c carmine	32.50	20.00 ☐☐☐☐☐
		Coil Stamps.			
1908		*Perf. 12 Horizontally.*			
321	A129	2c carmine, pair	35000.00	— ☐☐☐☐☐
		Perf. 12 Vertically.			
322	A129	2c carmine, pair	4750.00	— ☐☐☐☐☐
1904					
323	A130	1c green	30.00	5.00 ☐☐☐☐☐
324	A131	2c carmine	27.50	1.50 ☐☐☐☐☐
325	A132	3c violet	90.00	35.00 ☐☐☐☐☐
326	A133	5c dk blue	120.00	22.50 ☐☐☐☐☐
327	A134	10c red brown	225.00	35.00 ☐☐☐☐☐
1907					
328	A135	1c green	22.50	4.00 ☐☐☐☐☐
329	A136	2c carmine	30.00	2.50 ☐☐☐☐☐
330	A137	5c blue	130.00	27.50 ☐☐☐☐☐
1908-09		Wmkd. USPS (191) *Perf. 12.*			
331	A138	1c green	8.00	.05 ☐☐☐☐☐
331a		Booklet pane of 6	150.00	35.00 ☐☐☐☐☐

A130

A131

A132

A133

A134

A135

A136

A137

Franklin
A138

Washington
A139

Washington
A140

Franklin
A148

A141

HOW TO USE THIS BOOK

The number in the first column is its Scott number or identifying number. The letter and number that come next (A41) indicate the design and refer to the illustration so designated. Following that is the denomination of the stamp and its color. Finally, the price, unused and used is shown.

Scott® No.	Illus No.	Description	Unused Price	Used Price	/ / / / / /
1908-09					
332	A139	2c carmine	7.50	.05	☐☐☐☐☐
332a		Bklt. pane of 6	120.00	35.00	☐☐☐☐☐
333	A140	3c dp violet, Type I	27.50	3.00	☐☐☐☐☐
334	A140	4c orange brown	30.00	1.00	☐☐☐☐☐
335	A140	5c blue	40.00	2.00	☐☐☐☐☐
336	A140	6c red orange	50.00	4.50	☐☐☐☐☐
337	A140	8c olive green	32.50	2.50	☐☐☐☐☐
338	A140	10c yellow ('09)	65.00	1.50	☐☐☐☐☐
339	A140	13c blue green ('09)	35.00	22.50	☐☐☐☐☐
340	A140	15c pale ultra ('09)	60.00	5.75	☐☐☐☐☐
341	A140	50c violet ('09)	325.00	15.00	☐☐☐☐☐
342	A140	$1 violet brown ('09)	500.00	85.00	☐☐☐☐☐
		Imperf.			
343	A138	1c green	8.00	3.50	☐☐☐☐☐
344	A139	2c carmine	11.00	3.00	☐☐☐☐☐
345	A140	3c dp violet, Type I ('09)	22.50	13.50	☐☐☐☐☐
346	A140	4c orange brown ('09)	40.00	20.00	☐☐☐☐☐
347	A140	5c blue ('09)	60.00	35.00	☐☐☐☐☐
1908-10		Coil Stamps. *Perf. 12 Horizontally*			
348	A138	1c green	22.50	12.00	☐☐☐☐☐
349	A139	2c carmine ('09)	45.00	5.50	☐☐☐☐☐
350	A140	4c orange brown ('10)	110.00	57.50	☐☐☐☐☐
351	A140	5c blue ('09)	130.00	75.00	☐☐☐☐☐
1909		*Perf. 12 Vertically.*			
352	A138	1c green	55.00	17.50	☐☐☐☐☐
353	A139	2c carmine	45.00	5.50	☐☐☐☐☐
354	A140	4c orange brown	120.00	45.00	☐☐☐☐☐
355	A140	5c blue	130.00	65.00	☐☐☐☐☐
356	A140	10c yellow	1200.00	350.00	☐☐☐☐☐
1909		Bluish Paper *Perf. 12.*			
357	A138	1c green	110.00	100.00	☐☐☐☐☐
358	A139	2c carmine	100.00	75.00	☐☐☐☐☐
359	A140	3c dp violet, Type I	1450.00	1000.00	☐☐☐☐☐
360	A140	4c orange brown	14000.00		☐☐☐☐☐
361	A140	5c blue	3500.00	4000.00	☐☐☐☐☐
362	A140	6c red orange	950.00	600.00	☐☐☐☐☐
363	A140	8c olive green	14000.00		☐☐☐☐☐
364	A140	10c yellow	975.00	650.00	☐☐☐☐☐
365	A140	13c blue green	2000.00	1000.00	☐☐☐☐☐
366	A140	15c pale ultra	950.00	650.00	☐☐☐☐☐
1909		*Perf. 12.*			
367	A141	2c carmine	8.50	2.75	☐☐☐☐☐
		Imperf.			
368	A141	2c carmine	40.00	30.00	☐☐☐☐☐
		Bluish Paper. *Perf. 12.*			
369	A141	2c carmine	300.00	175.00	☐☐☐☐☐

A142

A143

A144

A145

A146

A147

TYPE I

THREE CENTS.

Type I. The top line of the toga rope is weak and the rope shading lines are thin. The fifth line from the left is missing.

The line between the lips is thin.

Used on both flat plate and rotary press printings.

Scott® No.	Illus No.	Description	Unused Price	Used Price	/ / / / / /

1909 *Perf. 12*

370	A142	2c carmine	13.00	2.25	☐☐☐☐☐

Imperf.

371	A142	2c carmine	55.00	35.00	☐☐☐☐☐

1909 *Perf. 12.*

372	A143	2c carmine	16.00	4.75	☐☐☐☐☐

Imperf.

373	A143	2c carmine	60.00	35.00	☐☐☐☐☐

Wmkd. USPS in Single lined Capitals. (190)

1910-11 *Perf. 12*

374	A138	1c green	7.50	.06	☐☐☐☐☐
374a		Bklt. pane of 6	135.00	30.00	☐☐☐☐☐
375	A139	2c carmine	7.00	.05	☐☐☐☐☐
375a		Booklet pane of 6	110.00	25.00	☐☐☐☐☐
376	A140	3c dp violet, Type I ('11)	17.50	1.50	☐☐☐☐☐
377	A140	4c brown ('11)	25.00	.50	☐☐☐☐☐
378	A140	5c blue ('11)	25.00	.50	☐☐☐☐☐
379	A140	6c red orange ('11)	35.00	.75	☐☐☐☐☐
380	A140	8c olive green ('11)	115.00	12.50	☐☐☐☐☐
381	A140	10c yellow ('11)	105.00	4.00	☐☐☐☐☐
382	A140	15c pale ultra ('11)	250.00	15.00	☐☐☐☐☐

1911 *Imperf.*

383	A138	1c green	4.00	3.00	☐☐☐☐☐
384	A139	2c carmine	6.00	1.50	☐☐☐☐☐

Coil Stamps.

1910 *Perf. 12 Horizontally*

385	A138	1c green	25.00	12.00	☐☐☐☐☐
386	A139	2c carmine	37.50	10.00	☐☐☐☐☐

1910-11 *Perf. 12 Vertically.*

387	A138	1c green	75.00	20.00	☐☐☐☐☐
388	A139	2c carmine	550.00	70.00	☐☐☐☐☐
389	A140	3c dp violet, Type I ('11)	12000.00	4250.00	☐☐☐☐☐

1910 *Perf. 8½ Horizontally.*

390	A138	1c green	4.50	2.75	☐☐☐☐☐
391	A139	2c carmine	32.50	7.50	☐☐☐☐☐

1910-13 *Perf. 8½ Vertically.*

392	A138	1c green	20.00	14.00	☐☐☐☐☐
393	A139	2c carmine	40.00	5.00	☐☐☐☐☐
394	A140	3c dp violet, Type I ('11)	50.00	25.00	☐☐☐☐☐
395	A140	4c brown ('12)	50.00	25.00	☐☐☐☐☐
396	A140	5c blue ('13)	50.00	25.00	☐☐☐☐☐

1913 *Perf. 12.*

397	A144	1c green	20.00	1.75	☐☐☐☐☐
398	A145	2c carmine	22.50	.50	☐☐☐☐☐
399	A146	5c blue	90.00	11.00	☐☐☐☐☐
400	A147	10c orange yellow	165.00	25.00	☐☐☐☐☐
400A	A147	10c orange	275.00	18.50	☐☐☐☐☐

1914-15 *Perf. 10.*

401	A144	1c green	30.00	6.50	☐☐☐☐☐

TYPE I

TWO CENTS.

Type I. There is one shading line in the first curve of the ribbon above the left "2" and one in the second curve of the ribbon above the right "2."

The button of the toga has a faint outline.

The top line of the toga rope, from the button to the front of the throat, is also very faint.

The shading lines at the face terminate in front of the ear with little or no joining, to form a lock of hair.

Used on both flat and rotary press printings.

TYPE II

TWO CENTS.

Type II. Shading lines in ribbons as on type I.

The toga button, rope, and shading lines are heavy.

The shading lines of the face at the lock of hair end in a strong vertical curved line.

Used on rotary press printings only.

TYPE III

TWO CENTS.

Type III. Two lines of shading in the curves of the ribbons.

Other characteristics similar to type II.

Used on rotary press printings only.

HOW TO USE THIS BOOK

The number in the first column is its Scott number or identifying number. The letter and number that come next (A41) indicate the design and refer to the illustration so designated. Following that is the denomination of the stamp and its color. Finally, the price, unused and used is shown.

Scott® No.	Illus No.	Description	Unused Price	Used Price	/ / / / / /
1914-15					
402	A145	2c carmine ('15)	95.00	1.50	☐☐☐☐☐
403	A146	5c blue ('15)	210.00	17.50	☐☐☐☐☐
404	A147	10c orange ('15)	1550.00	72.50	☐☐☐☐☐
1912-14		Wmkd. USPS (190) Perf. 12.			
405	A140	1c green	7.00	.06	☐☐☐☐☐
405b		Bklt. pane of 6	65.00	7.50	☐☐☐☐☐
406	A140	2c carmine, Type I	6.00	.05	☐☐☐☐☐
406a		Bklt. pane of 6	70.00	17.50	☐☐☐☐☐
407	A140	7c black ('14)	100.00	7.00	☐☐☐☐☐
1912		*Imperf.*			
408	A140	1c green	1.50	.60	☐☐☐☐☐
409	A140	2c carmine, Type I	1.65	.60	☐☐☐☐☐
1912		Coil Stamps. *Perf. 8½ Horizontally.*			
410	A140	1c green	6.25	3.00	☐☐☐☐☐
411	A140	2c carmine, Type I	7.75	3.25	☐☐☐☐☐
		Perf. 8½ Vertically.			
412	A140	1c green	21.00	5.00	☐☐☐☐☐
413	A140	2c carmine, Type I	35.00	.50	☐☐☐☐☐
1912-14		Perf. 12			
414	A148	8c pale olive green	35.00	1.25	☐☐☐☐☐
415	A148	9c salmon red ('14)	47.50	13.50	☐☐☐☐☐
416	A148	10c orange yellow	35.00	.30	☐☐☐☐☐
417	A148	12c claret brown ('14)	37.50	4.00	☐☐☐☐☐
418	A148	15c gray	75.00	3.00	☐☐☐☐☐
419	A148	20c ultra ('14)	175.00	15.00	☐☐☐☐☐
420	A148	30c orange red ('14)	120.00	15.00	☐☐☐☐☐
421	A148	50c violet ('14)	525.00	15.00	☐☐☐☐☐
1912		Wmkd. USPS (191) Perf. 12.			
422	A148	50c violet	275.00	15.00	☐☐☐☐☐
423	A148	$1 violet brown	625.00	70.00	☐☐☐☐☐
1914-15		Wmkd. USPS (190) Perf. 10			
424	A140	1c green	3.00	.06	☐☐☐☐☐
424a		Perf. 12x10	300.00	250.00	☐☐☐☐☐
424b		Perf. 10x12	.	125.00	☐☐☐☐☐
424d		Booklet pane of 6	4.00	.75	☐☐☐☐☐
425	A140	2c rose red, Type I	2.75	.05	☐☐☐☐☐
425d		Perf. 12 x 10		250.00	☐☐☐☐☐
425e		Booklet pane of 6	15.00	3.00	☐☐☐☐☐
426	A140	3c dp violet, Type I	12.50	1.25	☐☐☐☐☐
427	A140	4c brown	32.50	.40	☐☐☐☐☐
428	A140	5c blue	27.50	.40	☐☐☐☐☐
428a		Perf. 12x10		400.00	☐☐☐☐☐
429	A140	6c red orange	37.50	1.20	☐☐☐☐☐
430	A140	7c black	90.00	4.25	☐☐☐☐☐

TYPE Ia

TWO CENTS.

Type Ia. Design characteristics similar to type I except that all lines of design are stronger.

The toga button, toga rope and rope shading lines are heavy. The latter characteristics are those of type II, which, however, occur only on impressions from rotary plates.

Used only on flat plates 10208 and 10209.

TYPE II

THREE CENTS.

Type II. The top line of the toga rope is strong and the rope shading lines are heavy and complete. The line between the lips is heavy.

Used on both flat plate and rotary press printings.

TYPE IV

TWO CENTS.

Type IV. Top line of toga rope is broken. Shading lines in toga button are so arranged that the curving of the first and last form "QID".

Line of color in left "2" is very thin and usually broken.

Used on offset printings only.

Scott® No.	Illus No.	Description	Unused Price	Used Price	/ / / / / /
1914-15					
431	A148	8c pale olive green	35.00	1.50	☐☐☐☐☐
432	A148	9c salmon red	47.50	7.50	☐☐☐☐☐
433	A148	10c orange yellow	45.00	.25	☐☐☐☐☐
434	A148	11c dk green ('15)	20.00	5.50	☐☐☐☐☐
435	A148	12c claret brown	22.50	3.75	☐☐☐☐☐
437	A148	15c gray	125.00	6.25	☐☐☐☐☐
438	A148	20c ultra	250.00	3.50	☐☐☐☐☐
439	A148	30c orange red	300.00	12.00	☐☐☐☐☐
440	A148	50c violet ('15)	850.00	15.00	☐☐☐☐☐

1914 — Coil Stamps. *Perf. 10 Horizontally*

441	A140	1c green	1.00	.75	☐☐☐☐☐
442	A140	2c carmine, Type I	10.00	6.50	☐☐☐☐☐

Perf. 10 Vertically.

443	A140	1c green	22.50	5.00	☐☐☐☐☐
444	A140	2c carmine, Type I	35.00	1.00	☐☐☐☐☐
445	A140	3c violet, Type I	225.00	100.00	☐☐☐☐☐
446	A140	4c brown	140.00	32.50	☐☐☐☐☐
447	A140	5c blue	47.50	20.00	☐☐☐☐☐

1915-16 — Coil Stamps Rotary Press Printing *Perf. 10 Horizontally*

448	A140	1c green	6.50	2.75	☐☐☐☐☐
449	A140	2c red, Type I	1500.00	130.00	☐☐☐☐☐
450	A140	2c carmine, Type III ('16)	12.00	2.75	☐☐☐☐☐

1914-16 *Perf. 10 Vertically.*

452	A140	1c green	10.00	1.50	☐☐☐☐☐
453	A140	2c carmine rose, Type I	120.00	3.75	☐☐☐☐☐
454	A140	2c red, Type II	125.00	13.50	☐☐☐☐☐
455	A140	2c carmine, Type III	11.00	.85	☐☐☐☐☐
456	A140	3c violet, Type I ('16)	300.00	85.00	☐☐☐☐☐
457	A140	4c brown ('16)	32.50	15.00	☐☐☐☐☐
458	A140	5c blue ('16)	32.50	15.00	☐☐☐☐☐

1914 *Imperf.*

459	A140	2c carmine, Type I	475.00	600.00	☐☐☐☐☐

1915 *Wmk. 191 Perf. 10*

460	A148	$1 violet black	950.00	85.00	☐☐☐☐☐

1915 *Wmk. 190 Perf. 11*

461	A140	2c pale carmine red, Type I	90.00	80.00	☐☐☐☐☐

1916-17 *Perf. 10. Unwmkd.*

462	A140	1c green	7.50	.20	☐☐☐☐☐
462a		Booklet pane of 6	12.00	1.00	☐☐☐☐☐
463	A140	2c carmine, Type I	4.25	.10	☐☐☐☐☐
463a		Booklet pane of 6	75.00	15.00	☐☐☐☐☐
464	A140	3c violet, Type I	90.00	11.00	☐☐☐☐☐
465	A140	4c orange brown	45.00	1.50	☐☐☐☐☐

TYPE V

TWO CENTS.

Type V. Top line of toga is complete.
Five vertical shading lines in toga button.
Line of color in left "2" is very thin and usually broken.
Shading dots on the nose and lip are as indicated on the diagram.
Used on offset printings only.

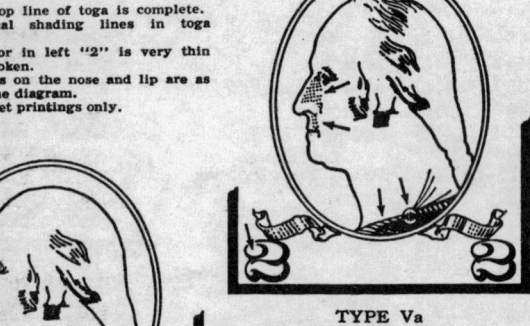

TYPE Va

TWO CENTS.

Type Va. Characteristics same as type V, except in shading dots of nose. Third row from bottom has 4 dots instead of 6. Overall height of type Va is 1/3 mm. less than type V.

Used on offset printings only.

TYPE VI

TWO CENTS.

Type VI. General characteristics same as type V, except that line of color in left "2" is very heavy.

Used on offset printings only.

HOW TO USE THIS BOOK

The number in the first column is its Scott number or identifying number. The letter and number that come next (A41) indicate the design and refer to the illustration so designated. Following that is the denomination of the stamp and its color. Finally, the price, unused and used is shown.

Scott® No.	Illus No.	Description	Unused Price	Used Price	/ / / / / /
1916-17					
466	A140	5c blue	80.00	1.40	☐☐☐☐☐
467	A140	5c carmine (error in plate of 2c, '17)	800.00	525.00	☐☐☐☐☐
468	A140	6c red orange	95.00	7.50	☐☐☐☐☐
469	A140	7c black	125.00	12.00	☐☐☐☐☐
470	A148	8c olive green	50.00	5.00	☐☐☐☐☐
471	A148	9c salmon red	57.50	15.00	☐☐☐☐☐
472	A148	10c orange yellow	110.00	1.00	☐☐☐☐☐
473	A148	11c dk green	27.50	15.00	☐☐☐☐☐
474	A148	12c claret brown	47.50	4.25	☐☐☐☐☐
475	A148	15c gray	175.00	10.00	☐☐☐☐☐
476	A148	20c lt ultra	275.00	11.00	☐☐☐☐☐
476A	A148	30c orange red	—	—	☐☐☐☐☐
477	A148	50c lt violet ('17)	1500.00	67.50	☐☐☐☐☐
478	A148	$1 violet black	950.00	15.00	☐☐☐☐☐
479	A127	$2 dk blue	550.00	40.00	☐☐☐☐☐
480	A128	$5 lt green	450.00	42.50	☐☐☐☐☐
1916-17		*Imperf.*			
481	A140	1c green	1.10	.75	☐☐☐☐☐
482	A140	2c carmine, Type I	1.50	1.50	☐☐☐☐☐
482A	A140	2c carmine, Type Ia		5500.00	☐☐☐☐☐
483	A140	3c violet, Type I ('17)	18.00	8.50	☐☐☐☐☐
484	A140	3c violet, Type II	12.00	4.00	☐☐☐☐☐
485	A140	5c carmine (error in plate of 2c) ('17)	13500.00		☐☐☐☐☐
1916-19		Coil Stamps Rotary Press Printing	*Perf. 10 Horizontally.*		
486	A140	1c green ('18)	1.00	.15	☐☐☐☐☐
487	A140	2c carmine, Type II	20.00	2.50	☐☐☐☐☐
488	A140	2c carmine, Type III ('19)	3.50	1.50	☐☐☐☐☐
489	A140	3c violet, Type I ('17)	5.50	1.00	☐☐☐☐☐
1916-22		*Perf. 10 Vertically.*			
490	A140	1c green	.75	.15	☐☐☐☐☐
491	A140	2c carmine, Type II	1450.00	185.00	☐☐☐☐☐
492	A140	2c carmine, Type III	10.00	.15	☐☐☐☐☐
493	A140	3c violet, Type I ('17)	22.50	3.00	☐☐☐☐☐
494	A140	3c violet, Type II ('18)	12.50	.60	☐☐☐☐☐
495	A140	4c orange brown ('17)	12.50	3.50	☐☐☐☐☐
496	A140	5c blue ('19)	4.50	.60	☐☐☐☐☐
497	A148	10c orange yellow ('22)	26.50	8.50	☐☐☐☐☐
1917-19		*Perf. 11*			
498	A140	1c green	.25	.05	☐☐☐☐☐
498e		Booklet pane of 6	1.75	.35	☐☐☐☐☐
498f		Booklet pane of 30	575.00		☐☐☐☐☐
499	A140	2c rose, Type I	.25	.05	☐☐☐☐☐
499e		Booklet pane of 6	2.00	.50	☐☐☐☐☐
499f		Bklt. pane of 30	8500.00		☐☐☐☐☐

TYPE VII

TWO CENTS.

Type VII. Line of color in left "2" is invariably continuous, clearly defined, and heavier than in type V or Va, but not as heavy as in type VI.

Additional vertical row of dots has been added to the upper lip.

Numerous additional dots have been added to hair on top of head.

Used on offset printings only.

TYPE III

THREE CENTS.

Type III. The top line of the toga rope is strong but the fifth shading line is missing as in type I.

Center shading line of the toga button consists of two dashes with a central dot.

The "P" and "O" of "POSTAGE" are separated by a line of color.

The frame line at the bottom of the vignette is complete.

Used on offset printings only.

TYPE IV

THREE CENTS.

Type IV. Shading lines of toga rope are complete.

Second and fourth shading lines in toga button are broken in the middle and the third line is continuous with a dot in the center.

"P" and "O" of "POSTAGE" are joined.

Frame line at bottom of vignette is broken.

Used on offset printings only.

Scott® No.	Illus No.	Description	Unused Price	Used Price	//////
1917-19					
500	A140	2c dp rose, Type Ia	275.00	120.00	☐☐☐☐☐
501	A140	3c lt violet, Type I	15.00	.10	☐☐☐☐☐
501b		Booklet pane of 6	75.00	15.00	☐☐☐☐☐
502	A140	3c dk violet, Type II	18.50	.25	☐☐☐☐☐
502b		Booklet pane of 6	50.00	10.00	☐☐☐☐☐
503	A140	4c brown	13.00	.20	☐☐☐☐☐
504	A140	5c blue	9.00	.08	☐☐☐☐☐
505	A140	5c rose (error in plate of 2c)	550.00	400.00	☐☐☐☐☐
506	A140	6c red orange	15.00	.30	☐☐☐☐☐
507	A140	7c black	32.50	1.20	☐☐☐☐☐
508	A148	8c olive bister	13.50	.70	☐☐☐☐☐
509	A148	9c salmon red	17.50	2.25	☐☐☐☐☐
510	A148	10c orange yellow	20.00	.10	☐☐☐☐☐
511	A148	11c lt green	10.00	3.25	☐☐☐☐☐
512	A148	12c claret brown	10.50	.45	☐☐☐☐☐
513	A148	13c apple green ('19)	13.00	7.00	☐☐☐☐☐
514	A148	15c gray	47.50	1.00	☐☐☐☐☐
515	A148	20c lt ultra	60.00	.30	☐☐☐☐☐
516	A148	30c orange red	50.00	.95	☐☐☐☐☐
517	A148	50c red violet	100.00	.65	☐☐☐☐☐
518	A148	$1 violet brown	85.00	1.75	☐☐☐☐☐
1917		Wmkd. USPS (191)		Perf. 11.	
519	A139	2c carmine	250.00	225.00	☐☐☐☐☐
1918					
523	A149	$2 orange red & black	1300.00	175.00	☐☐☐☐☐
524	A149	$5 dp green & black	500.00	25.00	☐☐☐☐☐
1918-20		Offset Printing.		Perf. 11	
525	A140	1c gray green	2.25	.60	☐☐☐☐☐
526	A140	2c carmine, Type IV ('20)	30.00	4.00	☐☐☐☐☐
527	A140	2c carmine, Type V	17.50	1.00	☐☐☐☐☐
528	A140	2c carmine, Type Va	9.00	.15	☐☐☐☐☐
528A	A140	2c carmine, Type VI	45.00	1.00	☐☐☐☐☐
528B	A140	2c carmine, Type VII	20.00	.12	☐☐☐☐☐
529	A140	3c violet, Type III	2.25	.10	☐☐☐☐☐
530	A140	3c purple, Type IV	.70	.06	☐☐☐☐☐
		Imperf.			
531	A140	1c green ('19)	10.00	8.00	☐☐☐☐☐
532	A140	2c carmine rose, Type IV ('20)	40.00	25.00	☐☐☐☐☐
533	A140	2c carmine, Type V	275.00	65.00	☐☐☐☐☐
534	A140	2c carmine, Type Va	13.50	9.00	☐☐☐☐☐
534A	A140	2c carmine, Type VI	40.00	25.00	☐☐☐☐☐
534B	A140	2c carmine, Type VII	1750.00	425.00	☐☐☐☐☐
535	A140	3c violet, Type IV	10.00	6.50	☐☐☐☐☐
		Perf. 12½.			
536	A140	1c gray green	15.00	12.50	☐☐☐☐☐

A149

A150

A151

A152

A153

A154

A155

A156

A157

A158

A159

A160

A161

A162

A163

A164

A165

A166

A167

A168

A169

Scott® No.	Illus No.	Description	Unused Price	Used Price	//////
1919		*Perf. 11.*			
537	A150	3c violet	12.50	4.25	☐☐☐☐☐
1919		*Perf. 11x10.*			
538	A140	1c green	10.00	9.00	☐☐☐☐☐
539	A140	2c carmine rose, Type II	2150.00	675.00	☐☐☐☐☐
540	A140	2c carmine rose, Type III	11.00	9.00	☐☐☐☐☐
541	A140	3c violet, Type II	37.50	35.00	☐☐☐☐☐
1920	Size: 19 mm. by 22½–22¾ mm.		*Perf. 10x11.*		
542	A140	1c green	6.50	1.00	☐☐☐☐☐
1921	Size: 19x22½mm.		*Perf. 10.*		
543	A140	1c green	.50	.06	☐☐☐☐☐
1923	Size: 19x22½mm.		*Perf. 11*		
544	A140	1c green	6500.00	1500.00	☐☐☐☐☐
1921	Size: 19½–20 mm. by 22 mm.		*Perf. 11*		
545	A140	1c green	150.00	90.00	☐☐☐☐☐
546	A140	2c carmine rose, Type III	100.00	70.00	☐☐☐☐☐
1920		*Perf. 11.*			
547	A149	$2 carmine & black	450.00	35.00	☐☐☐☐☐
548	A151	1c green	6.50	3.00	☐☐☐☐☐
549	A152	2c carmine rose	10.00	2.25	☐☐☐☐☐
550	A153	5c dp blue	60.00	18.50	☐☐☐☐☐
1922-25		*Perf. 11*			
551	A154	½c olive brown ('25)	.15	.05	☐☐☐☐☐
552	A155	1c dp green ('23)	2.50	.07	☐☐☐☐☐
553	A156	1½c yellow brown ('25)	4.00	.20	☐☐☐☐☐
554	A157	2c carmine ('23)	2.00	.05	☐☐☐☐☐
554c		Booklet pane of 6	7.00	1.00	☐☐☐☐☐
555	A158	3c violet ('23)	22.50	1.25	☐☐☐☐☐
556	A159	4c yellow brown ('23)	22.50	.20	☐☐☐☐☐
557	A160	5c dk blue	22.50	.06	☐☐☐☐☐
558	A161	6c red orange	42.50	.85	☐☐☐☐☐
559	A162	7c black ('23)	10.00	.75	☐☐☐☐☐
560	A163	8c olive green ('23)	55.00	.85	☐☐☐☐☐
561	A164	9c rose ('23)	17.00	1.25	☐☐☐☐☐
562	A165	10c orange ('23)	23.50	.10	☐☐☐☐☐
563	A166	11c lt blue	2.25	.25	☐☐☐☐☐
564	A167	12c brown violet ('23)	9.00	.08	☐☐☐☐☐
565	A168	14c blue ('23)	6.00	.85	☐☐☐☐☐
566	A169	15c gray	24.00	.06	☐☐☐☐☐
567	A170	20c carmine rose ('23)	27.50	.06	☐☐☐☐☐
568	A171	25c yellow green	27.50	.50	☐☐☐☐☐
569	A172	30c olive brown ('23)	45.00	.35	☐☐☐☐☐
570	A173	50c lilac	80.00	.12	☐☐☐☐☐
571	A174	$1 violet black ('23)	60.00	.45	☐☐☐☐☐
572	A175	$2 dp blue ('23)	175.00	9.50	☐☐☐☐☐
573	A176	$5 carmine & blue ('23)	425.00	15.00	☐☐☐☐☐

A170

A171

A172

A173

A174

A175

A176

A177

Type I—No heavy hair lines at top center of head. Outline of left acanthus scroll generally faint at top and toward base at left side.

Type II—The heavy hair lines at top center of head; two being outstanding in the white area. Outline of left acanthus scroll very strong and clearly defined at top (under left edge of lettered panel) and at lower curve (above and to left of numeral oval). Type II is found only on Nos. 599A and 634A.

A178

A179

A180

Scott® No.	Illus No.	Description	Unused Price	Used Price	/////
1923-26		*Imperf.*			
575	A155	1c green	11.00	3.50	☐☐☐☐☐
576	A156	1½c yellow brown ('25)	2.50	1.75	☐☐☐☐☐
577	A157	2c carmine	3.00	2.00	☐☐☐☐☐
		Perf. 11x10.			
578	A155	1c green	80.00	65.00	☐☐☐☐☐
579	A157	2c carmine	57.50	50.00	☐☐☐☐☐
1923-26		*Perf. 10.*			
581	A155	1c green	7.00	.65	☐☐☐☐☐
582	A156	1½c brown ('25)	5.00	.60	☐☐☐☐☐
583	A157	2c carmine ('24)	2.50	.05	☐☐☐☐☐
583a		Bklt. pane of 6	75.00	25.00	☐☐☐☐☐
584	A158	3c violet ('25)	30.00	1.75	☐☐☐☐☐
585	A159	4c yellow brown ('25)	17.00	.40	☐☐☐☐☐
586	A160	5c blue ('25)	16.00	.18	☐☐☐☐☐
587	A161	6c red orange ('25)	9.00	.40	☐☐☐☐☐
588	A162	7c black ('26)	11.50	5.00	☐☐☐☐☐
589	A163	8c olive green ('26)	30.00	3.00	☐☐☐☐☐
590	A164	9c rose ('26)	5.50	2.25	☐☐☐☐☐
591	A165	10c orange ('25)	65.00	.06	☐☐☐☐☐
		Perf. 11.			
594	A155	1c green	7000.00	1850.00	☐☐☐☐☐
595	A157	2c carmine	200.00	150.00	☐☐☐☐☐

Nos. 594–595 were made from coil waste of Nos. 597 and 599, and measure approximately 19¾x22¼mm.

Perf. 11

596	A155	1c green		13500.00	☐☐☐☐☐

No. 596 measures approximately 19¼x22¾mm. Most copies carry the Bureau precancel "Kansas City, Mo."

1923-29		Coil Stamps	*Perf. 10 Vertically*		
597	A155	1c green	.35	.06	☐☐☐☐☐
598	A156	1½c brown ('25)	.75	.10	☐☐☐☐☐
599	A157	2c carmine, Type I ('23)	.30	.05	☐☐☐☐☐
599A	A157	2c carmine, Type II ('29)	140.00	10.00	☐☐☐☐☐
600	A158	3c violet ('24)	8.00	.08	☐☐☐☐☐
601	A159	4c yellow brown	4.00	.40	☐☐☐☐☐
602	A160	5c dk blue ('24)	1.50	.18	☐☐☐☐☐
603	A165	10c orange ('24)	4.00	.08	☐☐☐☐☐
		Perf. 10 Horizontally			
604	A155	1c yellow green	.25	.08	☐☐☐☐☐
605	A156	1½c yellow brown ('25)	.30	.15	☐☐☐☐☐
606	A157	2c carmine	.30	.12	☐☐☐☐☐
1923		Flat Plate Printing (19¼x22¼mm.)	*Perf. 11*		
610	A177	2c black	.85	.10	☐☐☐☐☐
		Imperf.			
611	A177	2c black	15.00	6.00	☐☐☐☐☐

A181

A182

A183

A184

A185

A186

A187

A188

A190

A189

A191

A192

A193

Scott® No.	Illus No.	Description	Unused Price	Used Price	//////
1923		*Perf. 10*			
612	A177	2c black	25.00	2.50	☐☐☐☐☐
		Perf. 11 (19¼x22¾mm.)			
613	A177	2c black		13500.00	☐☐☐☐☐
1924					
614	A178	1c dk green	5.50	5.00	☐☐☐☐☐
615	A179	2c carmine rose	9.50	3.50	☐☐☐☐☐
616	A180	5c dk blue	55.00	22.50	☐☐☐☐☐
1925					
617	A181	1c dp green	5.50	5.50	☐☐☐☐☐
618	A182	2c carmine rose	10.00	7.50	☐☐☐☐☐
619	A183	5c dk blue	50.00	20.00	☐☐☐☐☐
620	A184	2c carmine & black	9.00	5.00	☐☐☐☐☐
621	A185	5c dk blue & black	30.00	22.50	☐☐☐☐☐
1925-26		*Perf. 11*			
622	A186	13c green ('26)	20.00	.65	☐☐☐☐☐
623	A187	17c black	27.50	.35	☐☐☐☐☐
1926					
627	A188	2c carmine rose	4.25	.60	☐☐☐☐☐
628	A189	5c gray lilac	11.00	5.00	☐☐☐☐☐
629	A190	2c carmine rose	2.75	2.25	☐☐☐☐☐
630	A190a	2c carmine rose, sheet of 25	525.00	425.00	☐☐☐☐☐
		Imperf.			
631	A156	1½c yellow brown	2.50	2.10	☐☐☐☐☐
1926-34		*Perf. 11x10½.*			
632	A155	1c green ('27)	.15	.05	☐☐☐☐☐
632a		Booklet pane of 6	2.50	.25	☐☐☐☐☐
633	A156	1½c yellow brown ('27)	2.75	.08	☐☐☐☐☐
634	A157	2c carmine, Type I	.15	.05	☐☐☐☐☐
634d		Bklt. pane of 6	1.00	.15	☐☐☐☐☐
634A	A157	2c carmine, Type II ('28)	375.00	22.50	☐☐☐☐☐
635	A158	3c violet ('27)	.55	.05	☐☐☐☐☐
635a		3c bright violet ('34)	.35	.05	☐☐☐☐☐
636	A159	4c yellow brown ('27)	4.25	.08	☐☐☐☐☐
637	A160	5c dk blue ('27)	3.50	.05	☐☐☐☐☐
638	A161	6c red orange ('27)	3.50	.05	☐☐☐☐☐
639	A162	7c black ('27)	3.50	.08	☐☐☐☐☐
640	A163	8c olive green ('27)	3.50	.05	☐☐☐☐☐
641	A164	9c orange red ('31)	3.50	.05	☐☐☐☐☐
642	A165	10c orange ('27)	5.75	.05	☐☐☐☐☐
1927					
643	A191	2c carmine rose	1.65	1.65	☐☐☐☐☐
644	A192	2c carmine rose	5.50	3.75	☐☐☐☐☐
1928					
645	A193	2c carmine rose	1.25	.65	☐☐☐☐☐

No. 634 Overprinted	**MOLLY PITCHER**	Nos. 634 and 637 Overprinted	**HAWAII 1778 - 1928**
SCOTT 646		SCOTT 647-648	

A194

A195

A196

A197

A198

A199

A200

A201

A202

A203

A204

A205

HOW TO USE THIS BOOK

The number in the first column is its Scott number or identifying number. The letter and number that come next (A41) indicate the design and refer to the illustration so designated. Following that is the denomination of the stamp and its color. Finally, the price, unused and used is shown.

Scott® No.	Illus No.	Description	Unused Price	Used Price	/ / / / / /
1928-29					
646	A157	2c Molly Pitcher ovpt.	1.50	1.50	☐☐☐☐☐
647	A157	2c Hawaii ovpt.	7.00	6.00	☐☐☐☐☐
648	A160	5c Hawaii ovpt.	21.00	20.00	☐☐☐☐☐
649	A194	2c carmine rose	1.50	1.40	☐☐☐☐☐
650	A195	5c blue	8.50	5.00	☐☐☐☐☐
651	A196	2c carmine & black	.85	.80	☐☐☐☐☐
653	A154	½c olive brown	.05	.05	☐☐☐☐☐
654	A197	2c carmine rose, perf. 11	1.00	1.00	☐☐☐☐☐
655	A197	2c carmine rose, perf. 11 x 10½	.90	.25	☐☐☐☐☐
		Coil Stamp (Rotary Press) *Perf. 10 Vertically.*			
656	A197	2c carmine rose	20.00	2.00	☐☐☐☐☐
1929					
657	A198	2c carmine rose	1.00	.90	☐☐☐☐☐
		Overprinted **Kans.**			
658	A155	1c green	2.50	1.65	☐☐☐☐☐
659	A156	1½c brown	3.50	3.00	☐☐☐☐☐
660	A157	2c carmine	3.50	.65	☐☐☐☐☐
661	A158	3c violet	18.50	12.00	☐☐☐☐☐
662	A159	4c yellow brown	18.50	7.50	☐☐☐☐☐
663	A160	5c dp blue	14.00	9.00	☐☐☐☐☐
664	A161	6c red orange	28.50	17.50	☐☐☐☐☐
665	A162	7c black	30.00	22.50	☐☐☐☐☐
666	A163	8c olive green	85.00	72.50	☐☐☐☐☐
667	A164	9c lt rose	14.00	11.00	☐☐☐☐☐
668	A165	10c orange yellow	23.50	11.00	☐☐☐☐☐
		Overprinted **Nebr.**			
669	A155	1c green	2.50	2.00	☐☐☐☐☐
670	A156	1½c brown	3.25	2.25	☐☐☐☐☐
671	A157	2c carmine	2.25	.85	☐☐☐☐☐
672	A158	3c violet	12.50	8.75	☐☐☐☐☐
673	A159	4c yellow brown	18.50	11.00	☐☐☐☐☐
674	A160	5c dp blue	18.00	13.50	☐☐☐☐☐
675	A161	6c red orange	40.00	19.00	☐☐☐☐☐
676	A162	7c black	22.50	15.00	☐☐☐☐☐
677	A163	8c olive green	30.00	22.00	☐☐☐☐☐
678	A164	9c lt rose	35.00	25.00	☐☐☐☐☐
679	A165	10c orange yellow	110.00	17.50	☐☐☐☐☐
680	A199	2c carmine rose	1.00	1.00	☐☐☐☐☐
681	A200	2c carmine rose	.80	.80	☐☐☐☐☐
1930					
682	A201	2c carmine rose	.80	.60	☐☐☐☐☐
683	A202	2c carmine rose	1.75	1.60	☐☐☐☐☐
		Perf. 11x10½.			
684	A203	1½c brown	.25	.05	☐☐☐☐☐
685	A204	4c brown	.50	.06	☐☐☐☐☐
		Coil Stamps *Perf. 10 Vertically*			
686	A203	1½c brown	1.60	.07	☐☐☐☐☐

A206   A207   A208   A209

A210   A211   A212   A213

A214   A215   A216   A217

A218   A219   A220   A221

A222   A223   A224   A225

A226   A227   A228

Scott® No.	Illus No.	Description	Unused Price	Used Price	/ / / / / /
1930					
687	A204	4c brown	2.75	.50	☐☐☐☐☐
1930					
688	A205	2c carmine rose	1.40	1.40	☐☐☐☐☐
689	A206	2c carmine rose	.80	.75	☐☐☐☐☐
1931					
690	A207	2c carmine rose	.25	.18	☐☐☐☐☐
1931		*Perf. 11x10½.*			
692	A166	11c lt blue	3.00	.10	☐☐☐☐☐
693	A167	12c brown violet	6.50	.06	☐☐☐☐☐
694	A186	13c yellow green	2.75	.10	☐☐☐☐☐
695	A168	14c dk blue	4.00	.30	☐☐☐☐☐
696	A169	15c gray	10.00	.06	☐☐☐☐☐
		Perf. 10½x11.			
697	A187	17c black	5.25	.20	☐☐☐☐☐
698	A170	20c carmine rose	13.00	.05	☐☐☐☐☐
699	A171	25c blue green	11.00	.08	☐☐☐☐☐
700	A172	30c brown	18.50	.07	☐☐☐☐☐
701	A173	50c lilac	60.00	.07	☐☐☐☐☐
1931					
702	A208	2c black & red	.15	.12	☐☐☐☐☐
703	A209	2c carmine rose & black	.40	.35	☐☐☐☐☐
1932					
704	A210	½c olive brown	.08	.05	☐☐☐☐☐
705	A211	1c green	.13	.05	☐☐☐☐☐
706	A212	1½c brown	.55	.08	☐☐☐☐☐
707	A213	2c carmine rose	.10	.05	☐☐☐☐☐
708	A214	3c dp violet	.60	.06	☐☐☐☐☐
709	A215	4c lt brown	.30	.06	☐☐☐☐☐
710	A216	5c blue	2.25	.10	☐☐☐☐☐
711	A217	6c red orange	5.00	.06	☐☐☐☐☐
712	A218	7c black	.35	.20	☐☐☐☐☐
713	A219	8c olive bister	5.00	.90	☐☐☐☐☐
714	A220	9c pale red	4.25	.25	☐☐☐☐☐
715	A221	10c orange yellow	16.50	.10	☐☐☐☐☐
716	A222	2c carmine rose	.50	.25	☐☐☐☐☐
717	A223	2c carmine rose	.18	.08	☐☐☐☐☐
718	A224	3c violet	2.00	.06	☐☐☐☐☐
719	A225	5c blue	3.25	.30	☐☐☐☐☐
1932		*Perf. 11x10½.*			
720	A226	3c dp violet	.15	.05	☐☐☐☐☐
720b		Booklet pane of 6	22.50	5.00	☐☐☐☐☐
		Coil Stamps *Perf. 10 Vertically*			
721	A226	3c dp violet	3.00	.08	☐☐☐☐☐
		Perf. 10 Horizontally.			
722	A226	3c dp violet	1.85	.45	☐☐☐☐☐
		Perf. 10 Vertically.			
723	A161	6c dp orange	12.50	.25	☐☐☐☐☐

A229

A230

A231

A232

A233

A234

A235

A236

A237

A238

HOW TO USE THIS BOOK

The number in the first column is its Scott number or identifying number. The letter and number that come next (A41) indicate the design and refer to the illustration so designated. Following that is the denomination of the stamp and its color. Finally, the price, unused and used is shown.

Scott® No.	Illus No.	Description	Unused Price	Used Price	/ / / / / /
1932					
724	A227	3c violet	.35	.25 ☐☐☐☐☐
725	A228	3c violet	.50	.40 ☐☐☐☐☐
1933					
726	A229	3c violet	.35	.25 ☐☐☐☐☐
727	A230	3c violet	.15	.10 ☐☐☐☐☐
728	A231	1c yellow green	.12	.06 ☐☐☐☐☐
729	A232	3c violet	.18	.05 ☐☐☐☐☐
730	A231a	1c dp yellow green, sheet of 25	45.00	40.00 ☐☐☐☐☐
730a		Single stamp, imperf.	1.00	.50 ☐☐☐☐☐
731	A232a	3c dp violet, sheet of 25	40.00	37.50 ☐☐☐☐☐
731a		Single stamp, imperf.	.85	.50 ☐☐☐☐☐
732	A233	3c violet	.14	.05 ☐☐☐☐☐
733	A234	3c dk blue	.85	.85 ☐☐☐☐☐
734	A235	5c blue	.85	.40 ☐☐☐☐☐
1934					
735	A235a	3c dk blue, sheet of six	28.50	26.00 ☐☐☐☐☐
735a		Single stamp, imperf.	3.00	2.50 ☐☐☐☐☐
736	A236	3c carmine rose	.20	.20 ☐☐☐☐☐
1934		*Perf. 11x10½.*			
737	A237	3c dp violet	.15	.06 ☐☐☐☐☐
		Perf. 11.			
738	A237	3c dp violet	.20	.20 ☐☐☐☐☐
739	A238	3c dp violet	.20	.12 ☐☐☐☐☐
740	A239	1c green	.10	.06 ☐☐☐☐☐
741	A240	2c red	.15	.06 ☐☐☐☐☐
742	A241	3c dp violet	.20	.06 ☐☐☐☐☐
743	A242	4c brown	.55	.50 ☐☐☐☐☐
744	A243	5c blue	1.10	.90 ☐☐☐☐☐
745	A244	6c dk blue	2.00	1.25 ☐☐☐☐☐
746	A245	7c black	1.00	1.00 ☐☐☐☐☐
747	A246	8c sage green	2.85	2.50 ☐☐☐☐☐
748	A247	9c red orange	3.00	.90 ☐☐☐☐☐
749	A248	10c gray black	5.00	1.35 ☐☐☐☐☐
750	A248a	3c dp violet, sheet of six	45.00	35.00 ☐☐☐☐☐
750a		Single stamp, imperf.	5.00	4.50 ☐☐☐☐☐
751	A248b	1c green, sheet of six	18.50	15.00 ☐☐☐☐☐
751a		Single stamp, imperf.	2.00	1.75 ☐☐☐☐☐

Without Gum.

Note. In 1940 the P.O. Department offered to and did gum full sheets of Nos. 754 to 771 sent in by owners.

1935					
752	A230	3c violet	.20	.15 ☐☐☐☐☐
753	A234	3c dk blue	.60	.60 ☐☐☐☐☐
		Imperf.			
754	A237	3c dp violet	1.00	.60 ☐☐☐☐☐
755	A238	3c dp violet	1.00	.60 ☐☐☐☐☐

A240

A239

A241

A242

A243

A244

A245

A246

A247

A249

A248

A250

A252

A253

Scott® No.	Illus No.	Description	Unused Price	Used Price	/ / / / / /
1935		*Imperf.*			
756	A239	1c green	.30	.20 ☐☐☐☐☐
757	A240	2c red	.40	.35 ☐☐☐☐☐
758	A241	3c dp violet	.75	.70 ☐☐☐☐☐
759	A242	4c brown	2.00	2.00 ☐☐☐☐☐
760	A243	5c blue	3.00	2.25 ☐☐☐☐☐
761	A244	6c dk blue	4.00	2.75 ☐☐☐☐☐
762	A245	7c black	3.00	2.50 ☐☐☐☐☐
763	A246	8c sage green	3.50	2.75 ☐☐☐☐☐
764	A247	9c red orange	3.75	2.75 ☐☐☐☐☐
765	A248	10c gray black	6.25	5.50 ☐☐☐☐☐
766	A231a	1c yellow green, pane of 25	50.00	50.00 ☐☐☐☐☐
766a		Single stamp	1.00	.50 ☐☐☐☐☐
767	A232a	3c violet, pane of 25	45.00	40.00 ☐☐☐☐☐
767a		Single stamp	.85	.50 ☐☐☐☐☐
768	A235a	3c dk blue, pane of six	32.50	25.00 ☐☐☐☐☐
768a		Single stamp	3.25	2.75 ☐☐☐☐☐
769	A248b	1c green, pane of six	15.00	12.00 ☐☐☐☐☐
769a		Single stamp	1.75	1.75 ☐☐☐☐☐
770	A248a	3c dp violet, pane of six	35.00	25.00 ☐☐☐☐☐
770a		Single stamp	3.75	3.75 ☐☐☐☐☐
771	APSD1	16c dk blue	4.00	3.50 ☐☐☐☐☐
1935		*Perf. 11x10½, 11*			
772	A249	3c violet	.15	.06 ☐☐☐☐☐
773	A250	3c purple	.12	.06 ☐☐☐☐☐
774	A251	3c purple	.12	.06 ☐☐☐☐☐
775	A252	3c purple	.12	.06 ☐☐☐☐☐
1936					
776	A253	3c purple	.12	.06 ☐☐☐☐☐
777	A254	3c purple	.15	.06 ☐☐☐☐☐
778	A254a	Sheet of 4	3.50	3.50 ☐☐☐☐☐
778a		A249 3c violet	.70	.60 ☐☐☐☐☐
778b		A250 3c violet	.70	.60 ☐☐☐☐☐
778c		A252 3c violet	.70	.60 ☐☐☐☐☐
778d		A253 3c violet	.70	.60 ☐☐☐☐☐
782	A255	3c purple	.12	.06 ☐☐☐☐☐
783	A256	3c purple	.12	.06 ☐☐☐☐☐
784	A257	3c dk violet	.10	.05 ☐☐☐☐☐
1936-37					
785	A258	1c green	.10	.06 ☐☐☐☐☐
786	A259	2c carmine ('37)	.15	.06 ☐☐☐☐☐
787	A260	3c purple ('37)	.20	.08 ☐☐☐☐☐
788	A261	4c gray ('37)	.65	.15 ☐☐☐☐☐
789	A262	5c ultra ('37)	1.00	.15 ☐☐☐☐☐
790	A263	1c green	.10	.06 ☐☐☐☐☐
791	A264	2c carmine ('37)	.15	.06 ☐☐☐☐☐
792	A265	3c purple ('37)	.20	.08 ☐☐☐☐☐

A251

A255

A254

A256

A257

A258

A259

A260

A261

A262

A263

A264

A265

A266

A267

A268

A269

A269a

A270

A272

A273

A274

A275

A276

A271

A277

A278

61

 Thomas Jefferson A279	 James Madison A280	 White House A281	 James Monroe A282
 John Q. Adams A283	 Andrew Jackson A284	 Martin Van Buren A285	 William H. Harrison A286
 John Tyler A287	 James K. Polk A288	 Zachary Taylor A289	 Millard Fillmore A290
 Franklin Pierce A291	 James Buchanan A292	 Abraham Lincoln A293	 Andrew Johnson A294
 Ulysses S. Grant A295	 Rutherford B. Hayes A296	 James A. Garfield A297	 Chester A. Arthur A298
 Grover Cleveland A299	 Benjamin Harrison A300	 William McKinley A301	 Theodore Roosevelt A302

Scott® No.	Illus No.	Description	Unused Price	Used Price	/ / / / /
1936-37					
793	A266	4c gray ('37)	.65	.15	☐☐☐☐☐
794	A267	5c ultra ('37)	1.00	.15	☐☐☐☐☐
1937					
795	A268	3c red violet	.12	.06	☐☐☐☐☐
796	A269	5c gray blue	.35	.25	☐☐☐☐☐
797	A269a	10c blue green	1.25	.85	☐☐☐☐☐
798	A270	3c bright red violet	.15	.07	☐☐☐☐☐
799	A271	3c violet	.15	.07	☐☐☐☐☐
800	A272	3c violet	.15	.07	☐☐☐☐☐
801	A273	3c bright violet	.15	.07	☐☐☐☐☐
802	A274	3c lt violet	.15	.07	☐☐☐☐☐
1938-54		*Perf. 11x10½, 11.*			
803	A275	½c dp orange	.05	.05	☐☐☐☐☐
804	A276	1c green	.06	.05	☐☐☐☐☐
804b		Bklt. pane of 6	1.75	.20	☐☐☐☐☐
805	A277	1½c bister brown	.06	.05	☐☐☐☐☐
806	A278	2c rose carmine	.06	.05	☐☐☐☐☐
806b		Bklt. pane of 6	4.25	.50	☐☐☐☐☐
807	A279	3c dp violet	.10	.05	☐☐☐☐☐
807a		Bklt. pane of 6	8.50	.50	☐☐☐☐☐
808	A280	4c red violet	.45	.05	☐☐☐☐☐
809	A281	4½c dk gray	.20	.06	☐☐☐☐☐
810	A282	5c bright blue	.40	.05	☐☐☐☐☐
811	A283	6c red orange	.45	.05	☐☐☐☐☐
812	A284	7c sepia	.50	.05	☐☐☐☐☐
813	A285	8c olive green	.65	.05	☐☐☐☐☐
814	A286	9c rose pink	.70	.05	☐☐☐☐☐
815	A287	10c brown red	.50	.05	☐☐☐☐☐
816	A288	11c ultra	1.00	.08	☐☐☐☐☐
817	A289	12c bright violet	1.65	.06	☐☐☐☐☐
818	A290	13c blue green	1.75	.08	☐☐☐☐☐
819	A291	14c blue	1.75	.10	☐☐☐☐☐
820	A292	15c blue gray	.75	.05	☐☐☐☐☐
821	A293	16c black	1.75	.35	☐☐☐☐☐
822	A294	17c rose red	1.50	.12	☐☐☐☐☐
823	A295	18c brown carmine	3.00	.08	☐☐☐☐☐
824	A296	19c bright violet	1.85	.50	☐☐☐☐☐
825	A297	20c bright blue green	1.20	.05	☐☐☐☐☐
826	A298	21c dl blue	2.25	.10	☐☐☐☐☐
827	A299	22c vermilion	2.25	.50	☐☐☐☐☐
828	A300	24c gray black	7.00	.25	☐☐☐☐☐
829	A301	25c dp red lilac	1.40	.05	☐☐☐☐☐
830	A302	30c dp ultra	9.00	.05	☐☐☐☐☐
831	A303	50c lt red violet	13.50	.06	☐☐☐☐☐
832	A304	$1 purple & black	15.00	.10	☐☐☐☐☐
832b		Wmkd. USIR ('51)	350.00	90.00	☐☐☐☐☐
832c		$1 red violet & black ('54)	10.00	.15	☐☐☐☐☐

William Howard Taft
A303

Woodrow Wilson
A304

Warren G. Harding
A305

Calvin Coolidge
A306

A308

A307

A309

A311

A310

A312

A314

A313

A315

A316

A317

Scott® No.	Illus No.	Description	Unused Price	Used Price	/ / / / / /
1938-54					
833	A305	$2 yellow green & black	37.50	6.00 ☐☐☐☐☐
834	A306	$5 carmine & black	140.00	5.50 ☐☐☐☐☐
1938					
835	A307	3c dp violet	.25	.08 ☐☐☐☐☐
836	A308	3c red violet	.25	.10 ☐☐☐☐☐
837	A309	3c bright violet	.25	.08 ☐☐☐☐☐
838	A310	3c violet	.25	.08 ☐☐☐☐☐
1939		Coil Stamps	*Perf. 10 Vertically.*		
839	A276	1c green	.25	.06 ☐☐☐☐☐
840	A277	1½c bister brown	.30	.06 ☐☐☐☐☐
841	A278	2c rose carmine	.30	.05 ☐☐☐☐☐
842	A279	3c dp violet	.75	.04 ☐☐☐☐☐
843	A280	4c red violet	9.00	.35 ☐☐☐☐☐
844	A281	4½c dk gray	.60	.45 ☐☐☐☐☐
845	A282	5c bright blue	6.00	.35 ☐☐☐☐☐
846	A283	6c red orange	1.10	.20 ☐☐☐☐☐
847	A287	10c brown red	12.50	.40 ☐☐☐☐☐
		Perf. 10 Horizontally			
848	A276	1c green	.75	.12 ☐☐☐☐☐
849	A277	1½c bister brown	1.10	.40 ☐☐☐☐☐
850	A278	2c rose carmine	2.50	.50 ☐☐☐☐☐
851	A279	3c dp violet	2.25	.45 ☐☐☐☐☐
1939					
852	A311	3c bright purple	.12	.06 ☐☐☐☐☐
853	A312	3c dp purple	.15	.06 ☐☐☐☐☐
854	A313	3c bright red violet	.25	.10 ☐☐☐☐☐
855	A314	3c violet	.22	.08 ☐☐☐☐☐
856	A315	3c dp red violet	.22	.08 ☐☐☐☐☐
857	A316	3c violet	.12	.08 ☐☐☐☐☐
858	A317	3c rose violet	.12	.08 ☐☐☐☐☐
1940					
859	A318	1c bright blue green	.08	.06 ☐☐☐☐☐
860	A319	2c rose carmine	.10	.08 ☐☐☐☐☐
861	A320	3c bright red violet	.12	.06 ☐☐☐☐☐
862	A321	5c ultra	.35	.30 ☐☐☐☐☐
863	A322	10c dk brown	2.50	2.35 ☐☐☐☐☐
864	A323	1c bright blue green	.12	.08 ☐☐☐☐☐
865	A324	2c rose carmine	.10	.08 ☐☐☐☐☐
866	A325	3c bright red violet	.18	.06 ☐☐☐☐☐
867	A326	5c ultra	.35	.25 ☐☐☐☐☐
868	A327	10c dk brown	3.50	3.00 ☐☐☐☐☐
869	A328	1c bright blue green	.09	.08 ☐☐☐☐☐
870	A329	2c rose carmine	.10	.06 ☐☐☐☐☐
871	A330	3c bright red violet	.30	.06 ☐☐☐☐☐
872	A331	5c ultra	.50	.35 ☐☐☐☐☐

Washington Irving
A318

James Fenimore Cooper
A319

Ralph Waldo Emerson
A320

Louisa May Alcott
A321

Samuel L. Clemens (Mark Twain)
A322

Henry W. Longfellow
A323

John Greenleaf Whittier
A324

James Russell Lowell
A325

Walt Whitman
A326

James Whitcomb Riley
A327

Horace Mann
A328

Mark Hopkins
A329

Charles W. Eliot
A330

Frances E. Willard
A331

Booker T. Washington
A332

John James
Audubon
A333

Dr. Crawford
W. Long
A334

Luther Burbank
A335

Dr. Walter Reed
A336

Jane Addams
A337

Stephen Collins
Foster
A338

John Philip
Sousa
A339

Victor
Herbert
A340

Edward
MacDowell
A341

Ethelbert Nevin
A342

Gilbert Charles
Stuart
A343

James A. McNeill
Whistler
A344

Augustus
Saint-Gaudens
A345

Daniel Chester
French
A346

Frederic Remington— A347

Eli Whitney
A348

Samuel F. B. Morse
A349

Cyrus Hall McCormick
A350

Elias Howe
A351

A353

A352

A355

A356

A354

A361

A357

A359

A360

A362

A363

A364

A366

A367

Scott® No.	Illus No.	Description	Unused Price	Used Price / / / / / /
1940				
873	A332	10c dk brown	2.50	2.25 ☐☐☐☐☐
874	A333	1c bright blue green	.08	.06 ☐☐☐☐☐
875	A334	2c rose carmine	.10	.06 ☐☐☐☐☐
876	A335	3c bright red violet	.10	.06 ☐☐☐☐☐
877	A336	5c ultra	.30	.25 ☐☐☐☐☐
878	A337	10c dk brown	2.00	2.00 ☐☐☐☐☐
879	A338	1c bright blue green	.08	.06 ☐☐☐☐☐
880	A339	2c rose carmine	.10	.06 ☐☐☐☐☐
881	A340	3c bright red violet	.15	.06 ☐☐☐☐☐
882	A341	5c ultra	.60	.30 ☐☐☐☐☐
883	A342	10c dk brown	5.50	2.25 ☐☐☐☐☐
884	A343	1c bright blue green	.08	.06 ☐☐☐☐☐
885	A344	2c rose carmine	.10	.06 ☐☐☐☐☐
886	A345	3c bright red violet	.10	.06 ☐☐☐☐☐
887	A346	5c ultra	.40	.22 ☐☐☐☐☐
888	A347	10c dk brown	2.75	2.25 ☐☐☐☐☐
889	A348	1c bright blue green	.12	.08 ☐☐☐☐☐
890	A349	2c rose carmine	.10	.06 ☐☐☐☐☐
891	A350	3c bright red violet	.20	.06 ☐☐☐☐☐
892	A351	5c ultra	1.50	.40 ☐☐☐☐☐
893	A352	10c dk brown	15.50	3.25 ☐☐☐☐☐
894	A353	3c henna brown	.50	.15 ☐☐☐☐☐
895	A354	3c lt violet	.40	.12 ☐☐☐☐☐
896	A355	3c bright violet	.20	.08 ☐☐☐☐☐
897	A356	3c brown violet	.20	.08 ☐☐☐☐☐
898	A357	3c violet	.20	.08 ☐☐☐☐☐
899	A358	1c bright blue green	.05	.05 ☐☐☐☐☐
900	A359	2c rose carmine	.06	.05 ☐☐☐☐☐
901	A360	3c bright violet	.12	.05 ☐☐☐☐☐
902	A361	3c dp violet	.25	.15 ☐☐☐☐☐
1941				
903	A362	3c lt violet	.22	.10 ☐☐☐☐☐
1942				
904	A363	3c violet	.15	.12 ☐☐☐☐☐
905	A364	3c violet	.10	.05 ☐☐☐☐☐
906	A365	5c bright blue	.40	.30 ☐☐☐☐☐
1943				
907	A366	2c rose carmine	.08	.05 ☐☐☐☐☐
908	A367	1c bright blue green	.06	.05 ☐☐☐☐☐
1943-44				
909	A368	5c Poland Multicolored	.35	.20 ☐☐☐☐☐
910	A368	5c Czechoslovakia Multicolored	.30	.15 ☐☐☐☐☐
911	A368	5c Norway Multicolored	.25	.12 ☐☐☐☐☐

 A365
 A368
 A369
 A370
 A371
 A372
 A373
 A374
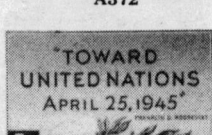 A375
 A377
 A376
 A378
 A379
 A380
 A381
 A382
 A383

Scott® No.	Illus No.	Description	Unused Price	Used Price	/ / / / / /
1943-44					
912	A368	5c Luxembourg Multicolored	.25	.12	☐☐☐☐☐
913	A368	5c Netherlands Multicolored	.25	.12	☐☐☐☐☐
914	A368	5c Belgium Multicolored	.25	.12	☐☐☐☐☐
915	A368	5c France Multicolored	.25	.10	☐☐☐☐☐
916	A368	5c Greece Multicolored	.85	.60	☐☐☐☐☐
917	A368	5c Yugoslavia Multicolored	.50	.40	☐☐☐☐☐
918	A368	5c Albania Multicolored	.50	.40	☐☐☐☐☐
919	A368	5c Austria Multicolored	.30	.25	☐☐☐☐☐
920	A368	5c Denmark Multicolored	.50	.50	☐☐☐☐☐
921	A368	5c Korea Multicolored	.28	.25	☐☐☐☐☐
1944					
922	A369	3c violet	.25	.15	☐☐☐☐☐
923	A370	3c violet	.15	.15	☐☐☐☐☐
924	A371	3c bright red violet	.12	.10	☐☐☐☐☐
925	A372	3c dp violet	.12	.12	☐☐☐☐☐
926	A373	3c dp violet	.12	.10	☐☐☐☐☐
1945					
927	A374	3c bright red violet	.10	.08	☐☐☐☐☐
928	A375	5c ultra	.12	.08	☐☐☐☐☐
929	A376	3c yellow green	.10	.05	☐☐☐☐☐
1945-46					
930	A377	1c blue green	.05	.05	☐☐☐☐☐
931	A378	2c carmine rose	.08	.08	☐☐☐☐☐
932	A379	3c purple	.10	.08	☐☐☐☐☐
933	A380	5c bright blue ('46)	.12	.08	☐☐☐☐☐
1945					
934	A381	3c olive	.10	.05	☐☐☐☐☐
935	A382	3c blue	.10	.05	☐☐☐☐☐
936	A383	3c bright blue green	.10	.05	☐☐☐☐☐
937	A384	3c purple	.10	.05	☐☐☐☐☐
938	A385	3c dk blue	.10	.05	☐☐☐☐☐
1946					
939	A386	3c blue green	.10	.05	☐☐☐☐☐
940	A387	3c dk violet	.10	.05	☐☐☐☐☐
941	A388	3c dk violet	.10	.05	☐☐☐☐☐
942	A389	3c dp blue	.10	.05	☐☐☐☐☐
943	A390	3c violet brown	.10	.05	☐☐☐☐☐
944	A391	3c brown violet	.10	.05	☐☐☐☐☐

 A384
 A385
 A386
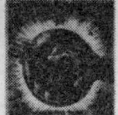 A387
 A388
 A389
 A390
 A391
 A392
 A393
 A394
 A399
 A395

 A396
 A397

 A401
 A400
 A402

A403

A404

A405

A406

A407

A408

A409

A410

A411

A412

A413

A414

A416

A415

A417

A418

A419

A420

A421

73

A422　　　A423　　　A424

A425　　　A426　　　A427

A428　　　A429

A430　　　A432

A433　　　A431

A434　　　A435　　　A436

Scott® No.	Illus No.	Description	Unused Price	Used Price	/ / / / / /
1947					
945	A392	3c bright red violet	.10	.05 ☐☐☐☐☐
946	A393	3c purple	.10	.05 ☐☐☐☐☐
947	A394	3c dp blue	.10	.05 ☐☐☐☐☐
948	A395	Sheet of two	1.75	1.00 ☐☐☐☐☐
948a		A1 5c blue	.35	.30 ☐☐☐☐☐
948b		A2 10c brown orange	.50	.30 ☐☐☐☐☐
949	A396	3c brown violet	.10	.05 ☐☐☐☐☐
950	A397	3c dk violet	.10	.05 ☐☐☐☐☐
951	A398	3c blue green	.10	.05 ☐☐☐☐☐
952	A399	3c bright green	.10	.05 ☐☐☐☐☐
1948					
953	A400	3c bright red violet	.10	.05 ☐☐☐☐☐
954	A401	3c dk violet	.10	.05 ☐☐☐☐☐
955	A402	3c brown violet	.10	.05 ☐☐☐☐☐
956	A403	3c gray black	.10	.05 ☐☐☐☐☐
957	A404	3c dk violet	.10	.05 ☐☐☐☐☐
958	A405	5c dp blue	.15	.10 ☐☐☐☐☐
959	A406	3c dk violet	.10	.05 ☐☐☐☐☐
960	A407	3c bright red violet	.10	.06 ☐☐☐☐☐
961	A408	3c blue	.10	.05 ☐☐☐☐☐
962	A409	3c rose pink	.10	.05 ☐☐☐☐☐
963	A410	3c dp blue	.10	.06 ☐☐☐☐☐
964	A411	3c brown red	.10	.10 ☐☐☐☐☐
965	A412	3c bright red violet	.10	.08 ☐☐☐☐☐
966	A413	3c blue	.12	.10 ☐☐☐☐☐
967	A414	3c rose pink	.10	.08 ☐☐☐☐☐
968	A415	3c sepia	.12	.08 ☐☐☐☐☐
969	A416	3c orange yellow	.12	.08 ☐☐☐☐☐
970	A417	3c violet	.12	.08 ☐☐☐☐☐
971	A418	3c bright rose carmine	.12	.08 ☐☐☐☐☐
972	A419	3c dk brown	.12	.08 ☐☐☐☐☐
973	A420	3c violet brown	.12	.10 ☐☐☐☐☐
974	A421	3c blue green	.12	.08 ☐☐☐☐☐
975	A422	3c bright red violet	.12	.08 ☐☐☐☐☐
976	A423	3c henna brown	.15	.08 ☐☐☐☐☐
977	A424	3c rose pink	.12	.08 ☐☐☐☐☐
978	A425	3c bright blue	.12	.08 ☐☐☐☐☐
979	A426	3c carmine	.12	.08 ☐☐☐☐☐
980	A427	3c bright red violet	.12	.08 ☐☐☐☐☐
1949					
981	A428	3c blue green	.10	.05 ☐☐☐☐☐
982	A429	3c ultra	.10	.05 ☐☐☐☐☐
983	A430	3c green	.10	.05 ☐☐☐☐☐
984	A431	3c aqua	.10	.05 ☐☐☐☐☐
985	A432	3c bright rose carmine	.10	.05 ☐☐☐☐☐
986	A433	3c bright red violet	.10	.05 ☐☐☐☐☐

A437

A438

A439

A440

A441

A442

A443

A444

A445

A446

A447

A448

A449

A450

A451

A452

A453

Scott® No.	Illus No.	Description	Unused Price	Used Price	/ / / / / /
1950					
987	A434	3c yellow green	.10	.05	☐☐☐☐☐
988	A435	3c bright red violet	.10	.05	☐☐☐☐☐
989	A436	3c bright blue	.10	.05	☐☐☐☐☐
990	A437	3c dp green	.10	.05	☐☐☐☐☐
991	A438	3c lt violet	.10	.05	☐☐☐☐☐
992	A439	3c bright red violet	.10	.05	☐☐☐☐☐
993	A440	3c violet brown	.10	.05	☐☐☐☐☐
994	A441	3c violet	.10	.05	☐☐☐☐☐
995	A442	3c sepia	.10	.06	☐☐☐☐☐
996	A443	3c bright blue	.10	.05	☐☐☐☐☐
997	A444	3c yellow orange	.10	.05	☐☐☐☐☐
1951					
998	A445	3c gray	.10	.05	☐☐☐☐☐
999	A446	3c lt olive green	.10	.05	☐☐☐☐☐
1000	A447	3c blue	.10	.05	☐☐☐☐☐
1001	A448	3c blue violet	.10	.05	☐☐☐☐☐
1002	A449	3c violet brown	.10	.05	☐☐☐☐☐
1003	A450	3c violet	.10	.05	☐☐☐☐☐
1952					
1004	A451	3c carmine rose	.10	.05	☐☐☐☐☐
1005	A452	3c blue green	.10	.05	☐☐☐☐☐
1006	A453	3c bright blue	.10	.05	☐☐☐☐☐
1007	A454	3c dp blue	.10	.05	☐☐☐☐☐
1008	A455	3c dp violet	.10	.05	☐☐☐☐☐
1009	A456	3c blue green	.10	.05	☐☐☐☐☐
1010	A457	3c bright blue	.10	.05	☐☐☐☐☐
1011	A458	3c blue green	.10	.05	☐☐☐☐☐
1012	A459	3c violet blue	.10	.05	☐☐☐☐☐
1013	A460	3c dp blue	.10	.05	☐☐☐☐☐
1014	A461	3c violet	.10	.05	☐☐☐☐☐
1015	A462	3c violet	.10	.05	☐☐☐☐☐
1016	A463	3c dp blue & carmine	.10	.05	☐☐☐☐☐
1953					
1017	A464	3c bright blue	.10	.05	☐☐☐☐☐
1018	A465	3c chocolate	.10	.05	☐☐☐☐☐
1019	A466	3c green	.10	.05	☐☐☐☐☐
1020	A467	3c violet brown	.10	.05	☐☐☐☐☐
1021	A468	5c green	.15	.10	☐☐☐☐☐
1022	A469	3c rose violet	.10	.05	☐☐☐☐☐
1023	A470	3c yellow green	.10	.05	☐☐☐☐☐
1024	A471	3c dp blue	.10	.05	☐☐☐☐☐
1025	A472	3c violet	.10	.05	☐☐☐☐☐
1026	A473	3c blue violet	.10	.05	☐☐☐☐☐
1027	A474	3c bright red violet	.10	.05	☐☐☐☐☐

A454   A455   A456

A457   A458   A459

A460   A461   A462

A463   A464   A465

A466   A467   A468

A469   A470   A471

Scott® No.	Illus No.	Description	Unused Price	Used Price
1953				
1028	A475	3c copper brown	.10	.05
1954				
1029	A476	3c blue	.10	.05
1954-68		*Perf. 11x10½, 10½x11, 11.*		
1030	A477	½c red orange ('55)	.05	.05
1031	A478	1c dk green	.05	.05
1031A	A478a	1¼c turquoise ('60)	.05	.05
1032	A479	1½c brown carmine ('56)	.08	.05
1033	A480	2c carmine rose	.05	.05
1034	A481	2½c gray blue ('59)	.08	.05
1035	A482	3c dp violet	.08	.05
1035a		Booklet pane of 6	3.00	.50
1035b		Tagged ('66)	.25	.20
1036	A483	4c red violet	.10	.05
1036a		Booklet pane of 6 ('58)	2.00	.50
1036b		Tagged ('63)	.75	.16
1037	A484	4½c blue green ('59)	.15	.08
1038	A485	5c dp blue	.17	.05
1039	A486	6c carmine ('55)	.40	.05
1040	A487	7c rose carmine ('56)	.25	.05
1041	A488	8c dk violet blue & carmine	.30	.06
1042	A489	8c dk violet blue & carmine rose ('58)	.30	.05
1042A	A489a	8c brown ('61)	.25	.05
1043	A490	9c rose lilac ('56)	.30	.05
1044	A491	10c rose lake ('56)	.35	.05
1044b		Tagged ('66)	1.50	1.25
1044A	A491a	11c carmine & dk violet blue ('61)	.30	.06
1044c		Tagged ('67)	2.00	1.60
1045	A492	12c red ('59)	.55	.05
1045a		Tagged ('68)	.55	.15
1046	A493	15c rose lake ('58)	.85	.03
1046a		Tagged ('66)	.90	.22
1047	A494	20c ultra ('56)	.90	.05
1048	A495	25c green ('58)	3.00	.05
1049	A496	30c black ('55)	2.00	.08
1050	A497	40c brown red ('55)	4.25	.10
1051	A498	50c bright purple ('55)	4.00	.04
1052	A499	$1 purple ('55)	15.00	.06
1053	A500	$5 black ('56)	120.00	8.00
1954-73		**Coil Stamps** *Perf. 10 Vertically Perf. 10 Horizontally*		
1054	A478	1c dk green	.35	.12
1054A	A478a	1¼c turquoise ('60)	.25	.20
1055	A480	2c rose carmine	.10	.05
1055a		Tagged ('68)	.10	.05
1056	A481	2½c gray blue ('59)	.55	.35

A472

A473

A474

A475

A476

A477

A478

A478a

A479

A480

A481

A482

A483

A484

A485

A486

A487

A488

A489

A489a

A490

A491

Scott® No.	Illus No.	Description	Unused Price	Used Price	/ / / / / /
1057	A482	3c dp violet	.15	.05 ☐☐☐☐☐
1057b		Tagged ('66)	.75	.25 ☐☐☐☐☐
1058	A483	4c red violet ('58)	.15	.05 ☐☐☐☐☐
1059	A484	4½c blue green ('59)	2.75	1.20 ☐☐☐☐☐
1059A	A495	25c green ('65)	.70	.30 ☐☐☐☐☐
1059b		Tagged ('73)	.70	.30 ☐☐☐☐☐

1954

1060	A507	3c violet	.10	.05 ☐☐☐☐☐
1061	A508	3c brown orange	.10	.05 ☐☐☐☐☐
1062	A509	3c violet brown	.10	.05 ☐☐☐☐☐
1063	A510	3c violet brown	.10	.05 ☐☐☐☐☐

1955

1064	A511	3c violet brown	.10	.05 ☐☐☐☐☐
1065	A512	3c green	.10	.05 ☐☐☐☐☐
1066	A513	8c dp blue	.20	.12 ☐☐☐☐☐
1067	A514	3c purple	.10	.05 ☐☐☐☐☐
1068	A515	3c green	.10	.05 ☐☐☐☐☐
1069	A516	3c blue	.10	.05 ☐☐☐☐☐
1070	A517	3c dp blue	.12	.05 ☐☐☐☐☐
1071	A518	3c lt brown	.10	.05 ☐☐☐☐☐
1072	A519	3c rose carmine	.10	.05 ☐☐☐☐☐

1956

1073	A520	3c bright carmine	.10	.05 ☐☐☐☐☐
1074	A521	3c dp blue	.10	.05 ☐☐☐☐☐
1075	A522	Sheet of two	5.25	4.50 ☐☐☐☐☐
1075a		A482 3c dp violet	1.35	1.10 ☐☐☐☐☐
1075b		A488 8c dk violet blue & carmine	1.75	1.50 ☐☐☐☐☐
1076	A523	3c dp violet	.10	.05 ☐☐☐☐☐
1077	A524	3c rose lake	.12	.05 ☐☐☐☐☐
1078	A525	3c brown	.12	.05 ☐☐☐☐☐
1079	A526	3c blue green	.12	.05 ☐☐☐☐☐
1080	A527	3c dk blue green	.10	.05 ☐☐☐☐☐
1081	A528	3c black brown	.10	.05 ☐☐☐☐☐
1082	A529	3c dp blue	.10	.05 ☐☐☐☐☐
1083	A530	3c *orange*	.10	.05 ☐☐☐☐☐
1084	A531	3c violet	.10	.05 ☐☐☐☐☐
1085	A532	3c dk blue	.10	.05 ☐☐☐☐☐

1957

1086	A533	3c rose red	.10	.05 ☐☐☐☐☐
1087	A534	3c red lilac	.10	.05 ☐☐☐☐☐
1088	A535	3c dk blue	.10	.05 ☐☐☐☐☐
1089	A536	3c red lilac	.10	.05 ☐☐☐☐☐
1090	A537	3c bright ultra	.10	.05 ☐☐☐☐☐
1091	A538	3c blue green	.10	.05 ☐☐☐☐☐
1092	A539	3c dk blue	.10	.05 ☐☐☐☐☐
1093	A540	3c rose lake	.10	.05 ☐☐☐☐☐

HOW TO USE THIS BOOK

The number in the first column is its Scott number or identifying number. The letter and number that come next (A41) indicate the design and refer to the illustration so designated. Following that is the denomination of the stamp and its color. Finally, the price, unused and used is shown.

Scott® No.	Illus No.	Description	Unused Price	Used Price	/ / / / / /
1957					
1094	A541	4c dk blue & dp carmine	.10	.05	☐☐☐☐☐
1095	A542	3c dp violet	.10	.05	☐☐☐☐☐
1096	A543	8c carmine, ultra & ocher	.22	.15	☐☐☐☐☐
1097	A544	3c rose lake	.10	.05	☐☐☐☐☐
1098	A545	3c blue, ocher & green	.10	.05	☐☐☐☐☐
1099	A546	3c black	.10	.05	☐☐☐☐☐
1958					
1100	A547	3c green	.10	.05	☐☐☐☐☐
1104	A551	3c dp claret	.10	.05	☐☐☐☐☐
1105	A552	3c purple	.10	.05	☐☐☐☐☐
1106	A553	3c green	.10	.05	☐☐☐☐☐
1107	A554	3c black & red orange	.10	.05	☐☐☐☐☐
1108	A555	3c lt green	.10	.05	☐☐☐☐☐
1109	A556	3c bright greenish blue	.10	.05	☐☐☐☐☐
1110	A557	4c olive bister	.10	.05	☐☐☐☐☐
1111	A557	8c carmine, ultra & ocher	.25	.15	☐☐☐☐☐
1112	A558	4c reddish purple	.10	.05	☐☐☐☐☐
1958-59					
1113	A559	1c green ('59)	.05	.05	■☐☐☐☐
1114	A560	3c purple ('59)	.10	.06	☐☐☐☐☐
1115	A561	4c sepia	.10	.05	☐☐☐☐☐
1116	A562	4c dk blue ('59)	.10	.05	☐☐☐☐☐
1958					
1117	A563	4c green	.10	.05	■☐☐☐☐
1118	A563	8c carmine, ultra & ocher	.22	.12	☐☐☐☐☐
1119	A564	4c black	.10	.05	☐☐☐☐☐
1120	A565	4c crimson rose	.10	.05	☐☐☐☐☐
1121	A566	4c dk carmine rose	.10	.05	☐☐☐☐☐
1122	A567	4c green, yellow & brown	.10	.05	■☐☐☐☐
1123	A568	4c blue	.10	.05	☐☐☐☐☐
1959					
1124	A569	4c blue green	.10	.05	☐☐☐☐☐
1125	A570	4c blue	.10	.05	☐☐☐☐☐
1126	A570	8c carmine, ultra & ocher	.20	.12	☐☐☐☐☐
1127	A571	4c blue	.10	.05	☐☐☐☐☐
1128	A572	4c bright greenish blue	.13	.05	☐☐☐☐☐
1129	A573	8c rose lake	.20	.12	☐☐☐☐☐
1130	A574	4c black	.10	.05	☐☐☐☐☐
1131	A575	4c red & dk blue	.10	.05	☐☐☐☐☐
1132	A576	4c ocher, dk blue & dp carmine	.10	.05	☐☐☐☐☐
1133	A577	4c blue, green & ocher	.10	.05	☐☐☐☐☐

A516

A515

A517

A520

A518   A519

A521   A523

Souvenir Sheet.

A522

A524   A525   A526

A527   A528

Scott® No.	Illus No.	Description	Unused Price	Used Price	/ / / / / /

1959
1134	A578	4c brown	.10	.05	☐☐☐☐☐
1135	A579	4c green	.10	.05	☐☐☐☐☐
1136	A580	4c gray	.10	.05	☐☐☐☐☐
1137	A580	8c carmine, ultra & ocher	.20	.12	☐☐☐☐☐
1138	A581	4c rose lake	.10	.05	☐☐☐☐☐

1960-61
1139	A582	4c dk violet blue & carmine	.18	.05	☐☐☐☐☐
1140	A583	4c olive bister & green	.18	.05	☐☐☐☐☐
1141	A584	4c gray & vermilion	.18	.05	☐☐☐☐☐
1142	A585	4c carmine & dk blue	.18	.05	☐☐☐☐☐
1143	A586	4c magenta & green	.18	.05	☐☐☐☐☐
1144	A587	4c green & brown ('61)	.18	.05	☐☐☐☐☐

1960
1145	A588	4c red, dk blue & dk bister	.10	.05	☐☐☐☐☐
1146	A589	4c dl blue	.10	.05	☐☐☐☐☐
1147	A590	4c blue	.10	.05	☐☐☐☐☐
1148	A590	8c carmine, ultra & ocher	.20	.12	☐☐☐☐☐
1149	A591	4c gray black	.10	.05	☐☐☐☐☐
1150	A592	4c dk blue, brown orange & green	.10	.05	☐☐☐☐☐
1151	A593	4c blue	.10	.05	☐☐☐☐☐
1152	A594	4c dp violet	.10	.05	☐☐☐☐☐
1153	A595	4c dk blue & red	.10	.05	☐☐☐☐☐
1154	A596	4c sepia	.10	.05	☐☐☐☐☐
1155	A597	4c dk blue	.10	.05	☐☐☐☐☐
1156	A598	4c green	.10	.05	☐☐☐☐☐
1157	A599	4c green & rose red	.10	.05	☐☐☐☐☐
1158	A600	4c blue & pink	.10	.05	☐☐☐☐☐
1159	A601	4c blue	.10	.05	☐☐☐☐☐
1160	A601	8c carmine, ultra & ocher	.20	.12	☐☐☐☐☐
1161	A602	4c dl violet	.10	.05	☐☐☐☐☐
1162	A603	4c dk blue	.10	.05	☐☐☐☐☐
1163	A604	4c indigo, slate & rose red	.10	.05	☐☐☐☐☐
1164	A605	4c dk blue & carmine	.10	.05	☐☐☐☐☐
1165	A606	4c blue	.10	.05	☐☐☐☐☐
1166	A606	8c carmine, ultra & ocher	.20	.12	☐☐☐☐☐
1167	A607	4c dk blue & bright red	.10	.05	☐☐☐☐☐
1168	A608	4c green	.10	.05	☐☐☐☐☐
1169	A608	8c carmine, ultra & ocher	.20	.12	☐☐☐☐☐
1170	A609	4c dl violet	.10	.05	☐☐☐☐☐
1171	A610	4c dp claret	.10	.05	☐☐☐☐☐
1172	A611	4c dl violet	.10	.05	☐☐☐☐☐

A529

A530

A531

A532

A534

A533

A535

A537

A536

A538

A539

A540

A541

A542

A543

A544

 A545
 A546
 A547

 A551
 A552
 A553

 A554
 A555
 A556

 A557
 A558
 A559

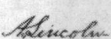
 A560
 A561 A562
 A564
 A563

A565

A566

A568

A567

A569

A570

A572

A571

A573

A574

A578

A575

A577

A576

A580

A579

A581

A582

A583

A584

A589

A585

A586

A587

A588

A590

A591

A592

A593

A594

A595

A596

A597

A598

A599

A600

A604

A608

A603

A601

A613

A605

A606

A602

A609

A610

A611

A612

A607

A614

Scott® No.	Illus No.	Description	Unused Price	Used Price	/ / / / /
1960					
1173	A612	4c dp violet	.35	.12 ☐☐☐☐☐
1961					
1174	A613	4c red orange	.10	.05 ☐☐☐☐☐
1175	A613	8c carmine, ultra & ocher	.20	.12 ☐☐☐☐☐
1176	A614	4c blue, slate & brown orange	.10	.05 ☐☐☐☐☐
1177	A615	4c dl violet	.10	.05 ☐☐☐☐☐
1178	A616	4c lt green	.18	.05 ☐☐☐☐☐
1179	A617	4c *peach blossom* ('62)	.15	.05 ☐☐☐☐☐
1180	A618	5c gray & blue ('63)	.15	.05 ☐☐☐☐☐
1181	A619	5c dk red & black ('64)	.15	.05 ☐☐☐☐☐
1182	A620	5c Prussian blue & black ('65)	.15	.05 ☐☐☐☐☐
1961					
1183	A621	4c brown, dk red & green, *yellow*	.10	.05 ☐☐☐☐☐
1184	A622	4c blue green	.10	.05 ☐☐☐☐☐
1185	A623	4c blue	.10	.05 ☐☐☐☐☐
1186	A624	4c ultra, *grayish*	.10	.05 ☐☐☐☐☐
1187	A625	4c multi	.12	.05 ☐☐☐☐☐
1188	A626	4c blue	.10	.05 ☐☐☐☐☐
1189	A627	4c brown	.10	.05 ☐☐☐☐☐
1190	A628	4c blue, green, orange & black	.10	.05 ☐☐☐☐☐
1962					
1191	A629	4c lt blue, maroon & bister	.10	.05 ☐☐☐☐☐
1192	A630	4c carmine, violet blue & green	.10	.05 ☐☐☐☐☐
1193	A631	4c dk blue & yellow	.10	.10 ☐☐☐☐☐
1194	A632	4c blue & bister	.10	.05 ☐☐☐☐☐
1195	A633	4c *buff*	.10	.05 ☐☐☐☐☐
1196	A634	4c red & dk blue	.10	.05 ☐☐☐☐☐
1197	A635	4c blue, dk slate green & red	.10	.05 ☐☐☐☐☐
1198	A636	4c slate	.10	.05 ☐☐☐☐☐
1199	A637	4c rose red	.10	.05 ☐☐☐☐☐
1200	A638	4c violet	.10	.05 ☐☐☐☐☐
1201	A639	4c *yellow bister*	.10	.05 ☐☐☐☐☐
1202	A640	4c dk blue & red brown	.10	.05 ☐☐☐☐☐
1203	A641	4c black, brown & yellow	.10	.05 ☐☐☐☐☐
1204	A641	4c black, brown & yellow (yel. inverted)	.12	.08 ☐☐☐☐☐
1205	A642	4c green & red	.10	.05 ☐☐☐☐☐
1206	A643	4c blue green & black	.10	.05 ☐☐☐☐☐
1207	A644	4c multi	.15	.05 ☐☐☐☐☐
1963-66					
1208	A645	5c blue & red	.12	.05 ☐☐☐☐☐
1208a		Tagged ('66)	.25	.05 ☐☐☐☐☐
1962-66		*Perf. 11x10½*			
1209	A646	1c green ('63)	.05	.05 ☐☐☐☐☐

 A616
 A615
 A617
 A618
 A619
 A621
 A622
 A620
 A623
 A624
 A625
 A626
 A627
 A628
 A629
 A631
 A630

A633

A632

A634

A637

A636

A640

A638

A635

A639

A642

A646

A650

A645

A663

A644

A643

A641

A662

A664

A665

93

A666

A667

A668

A669

A670

A671

A675

A676

A680

A672

A678

A679

A673

A677

A674

A681

A682

Scott® No.	Illus No.	Description	Unused Price	Used Price	/ / / / / /
1962-66					
1209a		Tagged ('66)	.06	.05 ☐☐☐☐☐
1213	A650	5c dk blue gray	.12	.05 ☐☐☐☐☐
1213a		Bklt. pane 5 + label	2.00	.75 ☐☐☐☐☐
1213b		Tagged ('63)	.65	.30 ☐☐☐☐☐
1213c		As "a," tagged ('63)	1.25	.50 ☐☐☐☐☐
		Coil Stamps *Perf. 10 Vertically*		
1225	A646	1c green ('63)	.20	.03 ☐☐☐☐☐
1225a		Tagged ('66)	.12	.05 ☐☐☐☐☐
1229	A650	5c dk blue gray	1.75	.03 ☐☐☐☐☐
1229a		Tagged ('63)	1.25	.06 ☐☐☐☐☐
1963					
1230	A662	5c dk carmine & brown	.12	.05 ☐☐☐☐☐
1231	A663	5c green, buff & red	.12	.05 ☐☐☐☐☐
1232	A664	5c green, red & black	.12	.05 ☐☐☐☐☐
1233	A665	5c dk blue, black & red	.12	.05 ☐☐☐☐☐
1234	A666	5c ultra & green	.12	.05 ☐☐☐☐☐
1235	A667	5c blue green	.12	.05 ☐☐☐☐☐
1236	A668	5c bright purple	.12	.05 ☐☐☐☐☐
1237	A669	5c Prussian blue & black	.12	.05 ☐☐☐☐☐
1238	A670	5c gray, dk blue & red	.12	.05 ☐☐☐☐☐
1239	A671	5c bluish black & red	.12	.05 ☐☐☐☐☐
1240	A672	5c dk blue, bluish black & red	.12	.05 ☐☐☐☐☐
1240a		Tagged	1.00	.40 ☐☐☐☐☐
1241	A673	5c dk blue & multi	.12	.05 ☐☐☐☐☐
1964					
1242	A674	5c black	.12	.05 ☐☐☐☐☐
1243	A675	5c indigo, red brown & olive	.15	.05 ☐☐☐☐☐
1244	A676	5c blue green	.12	.05 ☐☐☐☐☐
1245	A677	5c brown, green, yellow green & olive	.12	.05 ☐☐☐☐☐
1246	A678	5c blue gray	.12	.05 ☐☐☐☐☐
1247	A679	5c bright ultra	.12	.05 ☐☐☐☐☐
1248	A680	5c red, yellow & blue	.12	.05 ☐☐☐☐☐
1249	A681	5c dk blue & red	.12	.05 ☐☐☐☐☐
1250	A682	5c black brown, *tan*	.12	.05 ☐☐☐☐☐
1251	A683	5c green	.12	.05 ☐☐☐☐☐
1252	A684	5c red, black & blue	.12	.05 ☐☐☐☐☐
1253	A685	5c multi	.12	.05 ☐☐☐☐☐
1254	A686	5c green, carmine & black	.75	.05 ☐☐☐☐☐
1254a		Tagged	1.50	.50 ☐☐☐☐☐
1255	A687	5c carmine, green & black	.75	.05 ☐☐☐☐☐
1255a		Tagged	1.50	.50 ☐☐☐☐☐
1256	A688	5c carmine, green & black	.75	.05 ☐☐☐☐☐
1256a		Tagged	1.50	.50 ☐☐☐☐☐
1257	A689	5c black, green & carmine	.75	.05 ☐☐☐☐☐
1257a		Tagged	1.50	.50 ☐☐☐☐☐

A684

A683

A685

A686

A687

A688

A689

A690

A691

A692

A696

A694

A695

A697

A693

A698

Scott® No.	Illus No.	Description	Unused Price	Used Price	//////
1964					
1257b		Block of 4, # 1254-1257	3.50	1.25	☐☐☐☐☐
1257c		Block of 4, tagged	6.50	3.00	☐☐☐☐☐
1258	A690	5c blue green	.12	.05	☐☐☐☐☐
1259	A691	5c ultra, black & dl red	.12	.05	☐☐☐☐☐
1260	A692	5c red lilac	.12	.05	☐☐☐☐☐
1965					
1261	A693	5c dp carmine, violet blue & gray	.12	.05	☐☐☐☐☐
1262	A694	5c maroon & black	.12	.05	☐☐☐☐☐
1263	A695	5c black, purple & red orange	.12	.05	☐☐☐☐☐
1264	A696	5c black	.12	.05	☐☐☐☐☐
1265	A697	5c black, yellow ocher & red lilac	.12	.05	☐☐☐☐☐
1266	A698	5c dl blue & black	.12	.05	☐☐☐☐☐
1267	A699	5c red, black & dk blue	.12	.05	☐☐☐☐☐
1268	A700	5c maroon, *tan*	.12	.05	☐☐☐☐☐
1269	A701	5c rose red	.12	.05	☐☐☐☐☐
1270	A702	5c black & blue	.12	.05	☐☐☐☐☐
1271	A703	5c red, yellow & black	.12	.05	☐☐☐☐☐
1272	A704	5c emerald, black & red	.12	.05	☐☐☐☐☐
1273	A705	5c black, brown & olive	.15	.05	☐☐☐☐☐
1274	A706	11c black, carmine & bister	.50	.25	☐☐☐☐☐
1275	A707	5c pale blue, black, carmine & violet blue	.12	.05	☐☐☐☐☐
1276	A708	5c carmine, dk olive green & bister	.12	.05	☐☐☐☐☐
1276a		Tagged	.50	.15	☐☐☐☐☐
1965-78		*Perf. 11x10½, 10½x11*			
1278	A710	1c green, tagged ('68)	.05	.05	■☐☐☐☐
1278a		Booklet pane of 8 ('68)	1.00	.25	☐☐☐☐☐
1278b		Bklt. pane of 4 + 2 labels ('71)	.75	.20	☐☐☐☐☐
1278c		Untagged (Bureau precanceled)		.07	☐☐☐☐☐
1279	A711	1¼c lt green ('67)	.10	.05	☐☐☐☐☐
1280	A712	2c dk blue gray, tagged ('66)	.05	.05	■☐☐☐☐
1280a		Booklet pane of 5 + label ('68)	1.20	.40	☐☐☐☐☐
1280b		Untagged (Bureau precanceled)		.10	☐☐☐☐☐
1280c		Booklet pane of 6 ('71)	1.00	.35	☐☐☐☐☐
1281	A713	3c violet, tagged ('67)	.06	.05	☐☐☐☐☐
1281a		Untagged (Bureau precanceled)		.12	☐☐☐☐☐
1282	A714	4c black	.12	.05	☐☐☐☐☐
1282a		Tagged	.08	.05	☐☐☐☐☐
1283	A715	5c blue ('66)	.18	.05	■☐☐☐☐
1283a		Tagged ('66)	.10	.05	☐☐☐☐☐

A700

A706

A701

A703

A702

A705

A704

A708

A707

A699

A710

A711

A712

A713

A714

A715

A715a Redrawn

A716

A717

Scott® No.	Illus No.	Description	Unused Price	Used Price	/ / / / / /
1965-78					
1283B	A715a	5c blue, tagged ('67)	.12	.05	
1283d		Untagged (Bureau precanceled)		.15	
1284	A716	6c gray brown ('66)	.18	.05	
1284a		Tagged ('66)	.12	.05	
1284b		Booklet pane of 8 ('67)	1.50	.50	
1284c		Booklet pane of 5 + label ('68)	1.25	.50	
1285	A717	8c violet ('66)	.25	.05	
1285a		Tagged ('66)	.16	.05	
1286	A718	10c lilac, tagged ('67)	.25	.05	
1286b		Untagged (Bureau precanceled)		.20	
1286A	A718a	12c black, tagged ('68)	.30	.05	
1286c		Untagged (Bureau precanceled)		.25	
1287	A719	13c brown, tagged ('67)	.30	.05	
1287a		Untagged (Bureau precanceled)		.25	
1288	A720	15c rose claret, tagged ('68)	.30	.06	
1288a		Untagged (Bureau precanceled)		.30	
1288d		Type II	.30	.06	
		Perf. 10			
1288B	A720	15c dk rose claret (from bklt. pane) ('78)	.30	.05	
1288c		Booklet pane of 8	2.40	1.25	
		Perf. 11x10½, 10½x11			
1289	A721	20c dp olive ('67)	.55	.06	
1289a		Tagged ('73)	.40	.06	
1290	A722	25c rose lake ('67)	.60	.05	
1290a		Tagged ('73)	.50	.05	
1291	A723	30c red lilac ('68)	.75	.08	
1291a		Tagged ('73)	.60	.06	
1292	A724	40c blue black ('68)	.95	.10	
1292a		Tagged ('73)	.80	.08	
1293	A725	50c rose magenta ('68)	1.10	.05	
1293a		Tagged ('73)	1.00	.05	
1294	A726	$1 dl purple ('67)	2.40	.08	
1294a		Tagged ('73)	2.00	.08	
1295	A727	$5 gray black ('66)	12.50	2.00	
1295a		Tagged ('73)	10.00	2.00	
1966-81		Coil Stamps Tagged	*Perf. 10 Horiz.*		
1297	A713	3c violet ('75)	.12	.05	
1297b		Untagged (Bureau precanceled)		.12	
1298	A716	6c gray brown ('67)	.30	.05	

A718

A718a

A719

A720

A721

A723

A722

A724

A725

A726

A727

A727a

A730

A732

A731

A728

A729

A734

A733

A735

Scott® No.	Illus No.	Description	Unused Price	Used Price	/////
1966-81		*Perf. 10 Vertically*			
1299	A710	1c green ('68)	.06	.05 □□□□□	
1299a		Untagged (Bureau precanceled)		.07 □□□□□	
1303	A714	4c black	.15	.05 □□□□□	
1303a		Untagged (Bureau precanceled)		.15 □□□□□	
1304	A715	5c blue	.15	.05 □□□□□	
1304a		Untagged (Bureau precanceled)		.15 □□□□□	
1304C	A715a	5c blue ('81)	.15	.05 □□□□□	
1305	A727a	6c gray brown ('68)	.20	.05 □□□□□	
1305b		Untagged (Bureau precanceled)		.20 □□□□□	
1305C	A726	$1 dl purple ('73)	2.25	.20 □□□□□	
1305E	A720	15c rose claret ('78)	.30	.05 □□□□□	
1305f		Untagged (Bureau precanceled)		.30 □□□□□	
1306	A728	5c black, crimson & dk blue	.12	.05 □□□□□	
1307	A729	5c orange brown & black	.12	.05 □□□□□	
1308	A730	5c yellow, ocher & violet blue	.12	.05 □□□□□	
1309	A731	5c multi	.12	.05 □□□□□	
1310	A732	5c multi	.12	.05 □□□□□	
1311	A733	5c multi	.30	.15 □□□□□	
1312	A734	5c carmine, dk & lt blue	.12	.05 □□□□□	
1313	A735	5c red	.12	.05 □□□□□	
1314	A736	5c yellow, black & green	.12	.05 □□□□□	
1314a		Tagged	.30	.15 □□□□□	
1315	A737	5c black, bister, red & ultra	.12	.05 □□□□□	
1315a		Tagged	.30	.15 □□□□□	
1316	A738	5c black, pink & blue	.12	.05 □□□□□	
1316a		Tagged	.30	.15 □□□□□	
1317	A739	5c green, red & black	.12	.05 □□□□□	
1317a		Tagged	.30	.15 □□□□□	
1318	A740	5c emerald, pink & black	.12	.05 □□□□□	
1318a		Tagged	.30	.15 □□□□□	
1319	A741	5c vermilion, yellow, blue & green	.12	.05 □□□□□	
1319a		Tagged	.30	.15 □□□□□	
1320	A742	5c red, dk blue, lt blue & black	.12	.05 □□□□□	
1320a		Tagged	.30	.15 □□□□□	
1321	A743	5c multi	.12	.05 □□□□□	
1321a		Tagged	.25	.10 □□□□□	
1322	A744	5c multi	.20	.05 □□□□□	
1322a		Tagged	.45	.15 □□□□□	
1967					
1323	A745	5c multi	.12	.05 □□□□□	
1324	A746	5c multi	.12	.05 □□□□□	
1325	A747	5c multi	.12	.05 □□□□□	
1326	A748	5c blue, red & black	.12	.05 □□□□□	

A737

A736

A739

A738

A741

A743

A745

A740

A747

A744

A742

A746

A749

A748

A751

A750

A752

102

Scott® No.	Illus No.	Denom	Description	Unused Price	Used Price	/ / / / / /
1967						
1327	A749	5c	red, black & green	.12	.05 ☐☐☐☐☐
1328	A750	5c	dk red brown, lemon & yellow	.12	.05 ☐☐☐☐☐
1329	A751	5c	red, blue, black & carmine	.12	.05 ☐☐☐☐☐
1330	A752	5c	green, black & yellow	.12	.05 ☐☐☐☐☐
1331	A753	5c	multi	.90	.25 ☐☐☐☐☐
1331a			Pair, # 1331-1332	3.50	1.50 ☐☐☐☐☐
1332	A754	5c	multi	.90	.25 ☐☐☐☐☐
1333	A755	5c	dk blue, lt blue & black	.15	.05 ☐☐☐☐☐
1334	A756	5c	blue	.15	.05 ☐☐☐☐☐
1335	A757	5c	gold & multi	.18	.05 ☐☐☐☐☐
1336	A758	5c	multi	.12	.05 ☐☐☐☐☐
1337	A759	5c	bright greenish blue, green & red brown	.15	.05 ☐☐☐☐☐
1968-71			*Perf. 11*			
1338	A760	6c	dk blue, red & green	.15	.05 ☐☐☐☐☐
			Perf. 11x10½			
1338D	A760	6c	dk blue, red & green ('70)	.15	.05 ☐☐☐☐☐
1338F	A760	8c	multi ('71)	.16	.05 ☐☐☐☐☐
1969-71			*Coil Stamps Perf. 10 Vert.*			
1338A	A760	6c	dk blue, red & green	.20	.05 ☐☐☐☐☐
1338G	A760	8c	multi ('71)	.20	.05 ☐☐☐☐☐
1968						
1339	A761	6c	multi	.18	.05 ☐☐☐☐☐
1340	A762	6c	blue, rose red & white	.18	.05 ☐☐☐☐☐
1341	A763	$1	sepia, dk blue, ocher & brown red	6.00	3.00 ☐☐☐☐☐
1342	A764	6c	ultra & orange red	.18	.05 ☐☐☐☐☐
1343	A765	6c	chalky blue, black & red	.18	.05 ☐☐☐☐☐
1344	A766	6c	black, yellow & orange	.18	.05 ☐☐☐☐☐
1345	A767	6c	dk blue	1.00	.50 ☐☐☐☐☐
1346	A768	6c	dk blue & red	1.00	.50 ☐☐☐☐☐
1347	A769	6c	dk blue & olive green	.60	.50 ☐☐☐☐☐
1348	A770	6c	dk blue & red	.60	.40 ☐☐☐☐☐
1349	A771	6c	dk blue, yellow & red	.60	.45 ☐☐☐☐☐
1350	A772	6c	dk blue & red	.60	.35 ☐☐☐☐☐
1351	A773	6c	dk blue, olive green & red	.60	.35 ☐☐☐☐☐
1352	A774	6c	dk blue & red	.60	.35 ☐☐☐☐☐
1353	A775	6c	dk blue, yellow & red	.80	.35 ☐☐☐☐☐
1354	A776	6c	dk blue, red & yellow	.80	.40 ☐☐☐☐☐
1354a			Strip of 10, Nos. 1345-1354	8.25	7.50 ☐☐☐☐☐
1355	A777	6c	multi	.20	.05 ☐☐☐☐☐
1356	A778	6c	black, apple green & orange brown	.20	.05 ☐☐☐☐☐
1357	A779	6c	yellow, dp yellow, maroon & black	.20	.05 ☐☐☐☐☐

A753　　A754

A755

A757

A756

A758

A759

A760

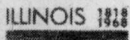

A761

A764

A762

A765

A763

A769

A766

A787

A788

A789

A790

A795

A791

A792

A793

A796

A794

A797

A798

A799

A800

A801

Scott® No.	Illus No.	Description	Unused Price	Used Price	/ / / / / /
1968					
1358	A780	6c bright blue, dk blue & black	.20	.05 ☐☐☐☐☐
1359	A781	6c lt gray brown & black brown	.20	.05 ☐☐☐☐☐
1360	A782	6c brown	.20	.05 ☐☐☐☐☐
1361	A783	6c multi	.25	.05 ☐☐☐☐☐
1362	A784	6c black & multi	.30	.05 ☐☐☐☐☐
1363	A785	6c multi	.20	.05 ☐☐☐☐☐
1363a		Untagged	.20	.05 ☐☐☐☐☐
1364	A786	6c black & multi	.40	.05 ☐☐☐☐☐
1969					
1365	A787	6c multi	1.10	.15 ☐☐☐☐☐
1366	A788	6c multi	1.10	.15 ☐☐☐☐☐
1367	A789	6c multi	1.10	.15 ☐☐☐☐☐
1368	A790	6c multi	1.10	.15 ☐☐☐☐☐
1368a		Block of 4, #1365-1368	5.50	3.50 ☐☐☐☐☐
1369	A791	6c red, blue & black	.20	.05 ☐☐☐☐☐
1370	A792	6c multi	.25	.05 ☐☐☐☐☐
1371	A793	6c black, blue & ocher	.30	.06 ☐☐☐☐☐
1372	A794	6c multi	.20	.05 ☐☐☐☐☐
1373	A795	6c multi	.20	.05 ☐☐☐☐☐
1374	A796	6c multi	.20	.05 ☐☐☐☐☐
1375	A797	6c multi	.20	.05 ☐☐☐☐☐
1376	A798	6c multi	1.50	.15 ☐☐☐☐☐
1377	A799	6c multi	1.50	.15 ☐☐☐☐☐
1378	A800	6c multi	1.50	.15 ☐☐☐☐☐
1379	A801	6c multi	1.50	.15 ☐☐☐☐☐
1379a		Block of 4, #1376-1379	8.00	5.00 ☐☐☐☐☐
1380	A802	6c green	.20	.05 ☐☐☐☐☐
1381	A803	6c yellow, red, black & green	.25	.05 ☐☐☐☐☐
1382	A804	6c red & green	.25	.05 ☐☐☐☐☐
1383	A805	6c blue, black & red	.20	.05 ☐☐☐☐☐
1384	A806	6c dk green & multi	.18	.05 ☐☐☐☐☐
1384a		Precanceled	.60	.06 ☐☐☐☐☐
1385	A807	6c multi	.18	.05 ☐☐☐☐☐
1386	A808	6c multi	.18	.05 ☐☐☐☐☐
1970					
1387	A809	6c multi	.22	.12 ☐☐☐☐☐
1388	A810	6c multi	.22	.12 ☐☐☐☐☐
1389	A811	6c multi	.22	.12 ☐☐☐☐☐
1390	A812	6c multi	.22	.12 ☐☐☐☐☐
1390a		Block of 4, #1387-1390	1.00	1.00 ☐☐☐☐☐
1391	A813	6c black & multi	.18	.05 ☐☐☐☐☐
1392	A814	6c *lt brown*	.18	.05 ☐☐☐☐☐
1970-74		*Perf. 11x10½, 10½x11; 11 (#1394)*		Tagged
1393	A815	6c dk blue gray	.12	.05 ☐☐☐☐☐
1393a		Booklet pane of 8	1.00	.50 ☐☐☐☐☐

A802

A803

A807

A806

A805

A804

A808

A809

A810

A811

A812

A813

A814

A815

A815a

A816

A817

A817a

A818

A818a

A818b

A820

A819

A821

A822

A823

A824

A825

A826

A827

109

A828

A829 A830

A831 A832

A835 A836

A833

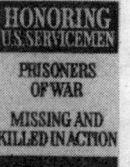
A834

A837

A838

A839

A840

Scott® No.	Illus No.	Description	Unused Price	Used Price	/ / / / / /
1970-74					
1393b		Booklet pane of 5 + label	.85	.35 ☐☐☐☐☐	
1393c		Untagged (Bureau precanceled)		.10 ☐☐☐☐☐	
1393D	A816	7c bright blue ('72)	.14	.05 ☐☐☐☐☐	
1393e		Untagged (Bureau precanceled)		.10 ☐☐☐☐☐	
1394	A815a	8c black, red & blue gray ('71)	.16	.05 ☐☐☐☐☐	
1395	A815	8c dp claret ('71)	.16	.05 ☐☐☐☐☐	
1395a		Booklet pane of 8	1.50	1.25 ☐☐☐☐☐	
1395b		Booklet pane of 6	1.00	.75 ☐☐☐☐☐	
1395c		Booklet pane of 4 + 2 labels ('72)	1.00	.50 ☐☐☐☐☐	
1395d		Booklet pane of 7 + label ('72)	1.25	1.00 ☐☐☐☐☐	
1396	A817	8c multi ('71)	.25	.05 ☐☐☐☐☐	
1397	A817a	14c gray brown ('72)	.32	.05 ☐☐☐☐☐	
1397a		Untagged (Bureau precanceled)		.25 ☐☐☐☐☐	
1398	A818	16c brown ('71)	.35	.05 ☐☐☐☐☐	
1398a		Untagged (Bureau precanceled)		.25 ☐☐☐☐☐	
1399	A818a	18c violet ('74)	.40	.06 ☐☐☐☐☐	
1400	A818b	21c green ('73)	.45	.06 ☐☐☐☐☐	
		Coil Stamps; *Perf. 10 Vert.*			
1401	A815	6c dk blue gray	.20	.05 ☐☐☐☐☐	
1401a		Untagged (Bureau precanceled)		.10 ☐☐☐☐☐	
1402	A815	8c dp claret ('71)	.22	.05 ☐☐☐☐☐	
1402b		Untagged (Bureau precanceled)		.20 ☐☐☐☐☐	
1970					
1405	A819	6c black & olive bister	.18	.05 ☐☐☐☐☐	
1406	A820	6c blue	.18	.05 ☐☐☐☐☐	
1407	A821	6c bister, black & red	.18	.05 ☐☐☐☐☐	
1408	A822	6c gray	.18	.05 ☐☐☐☐☐	
1409	A823	6c yellow & multi	.18	.05 ☐☐☐☐☐	
1410	A824	6c multi	.45	.13 ☐☐☐☐☐	
1411	A825	6c multi	.45	.13 ☐☐☐☐☐	
1412	A826	6c multi	.45	.13 ☐☐☐☐☐	
1413	A827	6c multi	.45	.13 ☐☐☐☐☐	
1413a		Block of 4, #1410-1413	2.50	2.00 ☐☐☐☐☐	
1414	A828	6c multi	.20	.05 ☐☐☐☐☐	
1414a		Precanceled	.35	.08 ☐☐☐☐☐	
1415	A829	6c multi	.85	.10 ☐☐☐☐☐	
1415a		Precanceled	2.00	.15 ☐☐☐☐☐	

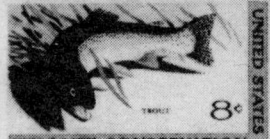
A841

A842

A843

A844

A845

A846

A847

A848

A849

A850

A851

A852

A853

Scott® No.	Illus No.	Description	Unused Price	Used Price	/ / / / / /
1970					
1416	A830	6c multi	.85	.10	☐☐☐☐☐
1416a		Precanceled	2.00	.15	☐☐☐☐☐
1417	A831	6c multi	.85	.10	☐☐☐☐☐
1417a		Precanceled	2.00	.15	☐☐☐☐☐
1418	A832	6c multi	.85	.10	☐☐☐☐☐
1418a		Precanceled	2.00	.15	☐☐☐☐☐
1418b		Block of 4, #1415-1418	4.50	3.50	☐☐☐☐☐
1418c		As "b," precanceled	9.00	6.00	☐☐☐☐☐
1419	A833	6c black, vermilion & ultra	.18	.05	☐☐☐☐☐
1420	A834	6c black, orange, yellow, brown, magenta & blue	.18	.05	☐☐☐☐☐
1421	A835	6c multi	.20	.10	☐☐☐☐☐
1421a		Pair, #1421-1422	.50	.65	☐☐☐☐☐
1422	A836	6c dk blue, black & red	.20	.10	☐☐☐☐☐
1971					
1423	A837	6c multi	.18	.05	☐☐☐☐☐
1424	A838	6c black, red & dk blue	.18	.05	☐☐☐☐☐
1425	A839	6c lt blue, scarlet & indigo	.18	.05	☐☐☐☐☐
1426	A840	8c multi	.20	.05	☐☐☐☐☐
1427	A841	8c multi	.30	.10	☐☐☐☐☐
1428	A842	8c multi	.30	.10	☐☐☐☐☐
1429	A843	8c multi	.30	.10	☐☐☐☐☐
1430	A844	8c multi	.30	.10	☐☐☐☐☐
1430a		Block of 4, #1427-1430	1.30	1.00	☐☐☐☐☐
1431	A845	8c red & dk blue	.25	.05	☐☐☐☐☐
1432	A846	8c red, blue, gray & black	.50	.05	☐☐☐☐☐
1433	A847	8c multi	.20	.05	☐☐☐☐☐
1434	A848	8c black, blue, yellow & red	.20	.10	☐☐☐☐☐
1434a		Pair, #1434-1435	.50	.65	☐☐☐☐☐
1435	A849	8c black, blue, yellow & red	.20	.10	☐☐☐☐☐
1436	A850	8c multi, *greenish*	.18	.05	☐☐☐☐☐
1437	A851	8c multi	.18	.05	☐☐☐☐☐
1438	A852	8c blue, dp blue & black	.18	.05	☐☐☐☐☐
1439	A853	8c multi	.18	.05	☐☐☐☐☐
1440	A854	8c black brown & ocher	.25	.12	☐☐☐☐☐
1441	A855	8c black brown & ocher	.25	.12	☐☐☐☐☐
1442	A856	8c black brown & ocher	.25	.12	☐☐☐☐☐
1443	A857	8c black brown & ocher	.25	.12	☐☐☐☐☐
1443a		Block of 4, #1440-1443	1.20	1.20	☐☐☐☐☐
1444	A858	8c gold & multi	.18	.05	☐☐☐☐☐
1445	A859	8c dk green, red & multi	.18	.05	☐☐☐☐☐
1972					
1446	A860	8c black, brown & lt blue	.18	.05	☐☐☐☐☐
1447	A861	8c dk blue, lt blue & red	.18	.05	☐☐☐☐☐

A854

A855

A856

A857

A862

A863

A864

A865

A858

A860

A859

A867

A861

A866

A868

Scott® No.	Illus No.	Description	Unused Price	Used Price	/ / / / / /
1972					
1448	A862	2c black & multi	.06	.06 ☐☐☐☐☐
1449	A863	2c black & multi	.06	.06 ☐☐☐☐☐
1450	A864	2c black & multi	.06	.06 ☐☐☐☐☐
1451	A865	2c black & multi	.06	.06 ☐☐☐☐☐
1451a		Block of 4, #1448-1451	.25	.30 ☐☐☐☐☐
1452	A866	6c black & multi	.16	.08 ☐☐☐☐☐
1453	A867	8c black, blue, brown & multi	.18	.05 ☐☐☐☐☐
1454	A868	15c black & multi	.35	.22 ☐☐☐☐☐
1455	A869	8c black & multi	.16	.05 ☐☐☐☐☐
1456	A870	8c dp brown	.30	.08 ☐☐☐☐☐
1457	A871	8c dp brown	.30	.08 ☐☐☐☐☐
1458	A872	8c dp brown	.30	.08 ☐☐☐☐☐
1459	A873	8c dp brown	.30	.08 ☐☐☐☐☐
1459a		Block of 4, #1456-1459	1.25	1.25 ☐☐☐☐☐
1460	A874	6c multi	.16	.12 ☐☐☐☐☐
1461	A875	8c multi	.16	.05 ☐☐☐☐☐
1462	A876	15c multi	.35	.18 ☐☐☐☐☐
1463	A877	8c yellow & black	.16	.05 ☐☐☐☐☐
1464	A878	8c multi	.25	.08 ☐☐☐☐☐
1465	A879	8c multi	.25	.08 ☐☐☐☐☐
1466	A880	8c multi	.25	.08 ☐☐☐☐☐
1467	A881	8c multi	.25	.08 ☐☐☐☐☐
1467a		Block of 4, #1464-1467	1.10	.85 ☐☐☐☐☐
1468	A882	8c multi	.16	.05 ☐☐☐☐☐
1469	A883	8c yellow, orange & dk brown	.16	.05 ☐☐☐☐☐
1470	A884	8c black & multi	.16	.05 ☐☐☐☐☐
1471	A885	8c multi	.16	.05 ☐☐☐☐☐
1472	A886	8c multi	.16	.05 ☐☐☐☐☐
1473	A887	8c black & multi	.16	.05 ☐☐☐☐☐
1474	A888	8c dk blue green, black & brown	.16	.05 ☐☐☐☐☐
1973					
1475	A889	8c red, emerald & violet blue	.16	.05 ☐☐☐☐☐
1476	A890	8c ultra, greenish black & red	.20	.05 ■☐☐☐☐
1477	A891	8c black, vermilion & ultra	.20	.05 ☐☐☐☐☐
1478	A892	8c multi	.20	.05 ☐☐☐☐☐
1479	A893	8c multi	.20	.05 ☐☐☐☐☐
1480	A894	8c black & multi	.20	.10 ☐☐☐☐☐
1481	A895	8c black & multi	.20	.10 ☐☐☐☐☐
1482	A896	8c black & multi	.20	.10 ☐☐☐☐☐
1483	A897	8c black & multi	.20	.10 ☐☐☐☐☐
1483a		Block of 4, #1480-1483	.85	.80 ☐☐☐☐☐
1484	A898	8c dp green & multi	.16	.05 ☐☐☐☐☐
1485	A899	8c Prus. blue & multi	.16	.05 ☐☐☐☐☐

A869

A870

A871

A872

A873

A874

A875

A876

A877

A878

A879

A880

A881

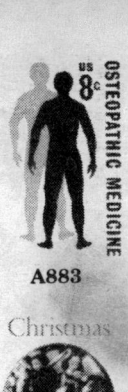
A883

A882

A884

A885

A887

A886

A888

A889

A890

A891

A892

A893

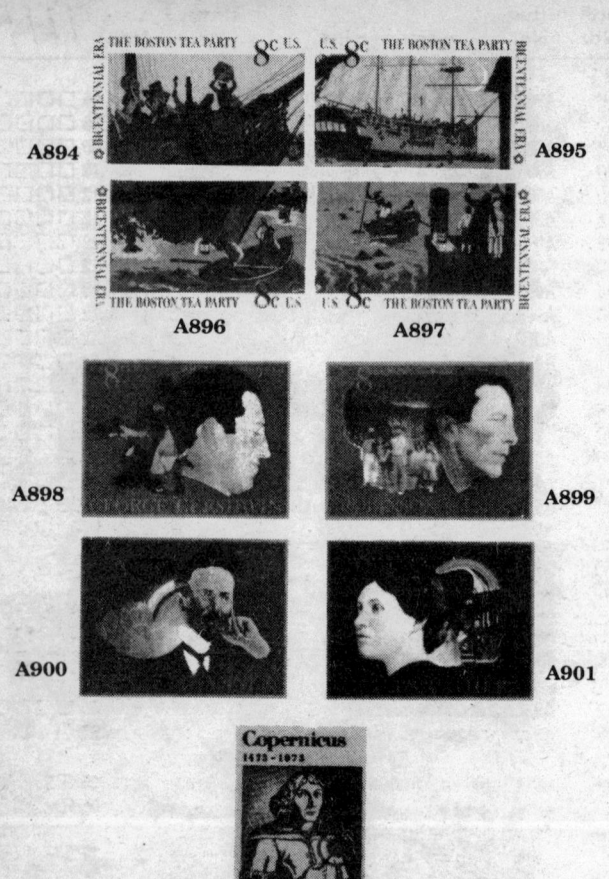

HOW TO USE THIS BOOK

The number in the first column is its Scott number or identifying number. The letter and number that come next (A41) indicate the design and refer to the illustration so designated. Following that is the denomination of the stamp and its color. Finally, the price, unused and used is shown.

Scott® No.	Illus No.	Description	Unused Price	Used Price	/ / / / / /
1973					
1486	A900	8c yellow brown & multi	.16	.05 ☐☐☐☐☐
1487	A901	8c dp brown & multi	.16	.05 ☐☐☐☐☐
1488	A902	8c black & orange	.16	.05 ☐☐☐☐☐
1489	A903	8c multi	.20	.12 ☐☐☐☐☐
1490	A904	8c multi	.20	.12 ☐☐☐☐☐
1491	A905	8c multi	.20	.12 ☐☐☐☐☐
1492	A906	8c multi	.20	.12 ☐☐☐☐☐
1493	A907	8c multi	.20	.12 ☐☐☐☐☐
1494	A908	8c multi	.20	.12 ☐☐☐☐☐
1495	A909	8c multi	.20	.12 ☐☐☐☐☐
1496	A910	8c multi	.20	.12 ☐☐☐☐☐
1497	A911	8c multi	.20	.12 ☐☐☐☐☐
1498	A912	8c multi	.20	.12 ☐☐☐☐☐
1498a		Strip of 10, Nos. 1489-1498	2.25	2.00 ☐☐☐☐☐
1499	A913	8c carmine rose, black & blue	.16	.05 ☐☐☐☐☐
1500	A914	6c lilac & multi	.12	.10 ☐☐☐☐☐
1501	A915	8c tan & multi	.16	.05 ☐☐☐☐☐
1502	A916	15c gray green & multi	.30	.20 ☐☐☐☐☐
1503	A917	8c black & multi	.16	.05 ☐☐☐☐☐
1973-74					
1504	A918	8c multi	.16	.05 ☐☐☐☐☐
1505	A919	10c multi ('74)	.20	.05 ☐☐☐☐☐
1506	A920	10c multi ('74)	.20	.05 ☐☐☐☐☐
1973					
1507	A921	8c tan & multi	.16	.05 ☐☐☐☐☐
1508	A922	8c green & multi	.16	.05 ☐☐☐☐☐
1973-74		Tagged Perf. 11x10½			
1509	A923	10c red & blue	.20	.05 ☐☐☐☐☐
1510	A924	10c blue	.20	.05 ☐☐☐☐☐
1510a		Untagged (Bureau precanceled)		.20 ☐☐☐☐☐
1510b		Bklt. pane of 5 + label	1.00	.30 ☐☐☐☐☐
1510c		Bklt. pane of 8	1.60	.30 ☐☐☐☐☐
1510d		Bklt. pane of 6 ('74)	1.20	.30 ☐☐☐☐☐
1511	A925	10c multi, photo	.20	.05 ☐☐☐☐☐
		Coil Stamps Perf. 10 Vert.			
1518	A926	6.3c brick red	.13	.07 ☐☐☐☐☐
1518a		Untagged (Bureau precanceled)		.13 ☐☐☐☐☐
1519	A923	10c red & blue	.25	.05 ☐☐☐☐☐
1520	A924	10c blue	.20	.05 ☐☐☐☐☐
1520a		Untagged (Bureau precanceled)		.25 ☐☐☐☐☐
1974					
1525	A928	10c red & dk blue	.20	.05 ☐☐☐☐☐

A903

A904

A905

A906

A907

A908

A909

A910

A911   A912

A913

A914

A915

A916

120

A917

A918

A919

A920

A921

A922

A923

A924

A925

A926

A929

A928

A930

A931

A932

Letters
mingle souls
Dumas   Raphael
    10c US

A933

Universal
Postal Union
1874-1974   10c US

A934

Letters
mingle souls
Dumas   10c US

A935

Universal
Postal Union
1874-1974   10c US

A936

Letters
mingle souls
Dumas   10c US

A937

Universal
Postal Union
1874-1974   10c US

A938

Letters
mingle souls
Dumas   Gainsborough
   10c US

A939

Universal
Postal Union
1874-1974   10c US

A940

122

Scott® No.	Illus No.	Description	Unused Price	Used Price	/ / / / / /
1974					
1526	A929	10c black	.20	.05 ☐☐☐☐☐
1527	A930	10c multi	.20	.05 ☐☐☐☐☐
1528	A931	10c yellow & multi	.20	.05 ☐☐☐☐☐
1529	A932	10c multi	.20	.05 ☐☐☐☐☐
1530	A933	10c multi	.20	.18 ☐☐☐☐☐
1531	A934	10c multi	.20	.18 ☐☐☐☐☐
1532	A935	10c multi	.20	.18 ☐☐☐☐☐
1533	A936	10c multi	.20	.18 ☐☐☐☐☐
1534	A937	10c multi	.20	.18 ☐☐☐☐☐
1535	A938	10c multi	.20	.18 ☐☐☐☐☐
1536	A939	10c multi	.20	.18 ☐☐☐☐☐
1537	A940	10c multi	.20	.18 ☐☐☐☐☐
1537a		Block or strip of 8, #1530-1537	1.60	2.00 ☐☐☐☐☐
1538	A941	10c lt blue & multi	.20	.10 ☐☐☐☐☐
1539	A942	10c lt blue & multi	.20	.10 ☐☐☐☐☐
1540	A943	10c lt blue & multi	.20	.10 ☐☐☐☐☐
1541	A944	10c lt blue & multi	.20	.10 ☐☐☐☐☐
1541a		Block of 4, #1538-1541	.80	.80 ☐☐☐☐☐
1542	A945	10c green & multi	.20	.05 ☐☐☐☐☐
1543	A946	10c dk blue & red	.20	.10 ☐☐☐☐☐
1544	A947	10c gray, dk blue & red	.20	.10 ☐☐☐☐☐
1545	A948	10c gray, dk blue & red	.20	.10 ☐☐☐☐☐
1546	A949	10c red & dk blue	.20	.10 ☐☐☐☐☐
1546a		Block of 4, #1543-1546	.80	.80 ☐☐☐☐☐
1547	A950	10c multi	.20	.05 ☐☐☐☐☐
1548	A951	10c dk blue, black, orange & yellow	.20	.05 ☐☐☐☐☐
1549	A952	10c brown red & dk brown	.20	.05 ☐☐☐☐☐
1550	A953	10c multi	.20	.05 ☐☐☐☐☐
1551	A954	10c multi	.20	.05 ☐☐☐☐☐
1552	A955	10c multi	.20	.08 ☐☐☐☐☐

Unused price of No. 1552 is for copy on rouletted paper backing as issued. Used price is for copy on piece, with or without postmark. Die cutting includes crossed slashes through dove, applied to prevent removal and re-use of stamp. The stamp will separate into layers if soaked. No. 1552 is untagged.

Scott® No.	Illus No.	Description	Unused Price	Used Price	
1975					
1553	A956	10c multi	.20	.05 ☐☐☐☐☐
1554	A957	10c multi	.20	.05 ☐☐☐☐☐
1555	A958	10c multi	.20	.05 ☐☐☐☐☐
1556	A959	10c violet blue, yellow & red	.20	.05 ☐☐☐☐☐
1557	A960	10c black, red, ultra & bister	.20	.05 ☐☐☐☐☐
1558	A961	10c multi	.20	.05 ☐☐☐☐☐
1559	A962	8c multi	.16	.13 ☐☐☐☐☐
1560	A963	10c multi	.20	.05 ☐☐☐☐☐
1561	A964	10c multi	.20	.05 ☐☐☐☐☐
1562	A965	18c multi	.36	.20 ☐☐☐☐☐

A941
A942
A943
A944

A946

A947

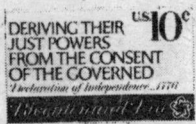

A948

A949

A945

A951

A950

Scott® No.	Illus No.	Description	Unused Price	Used Price	/ / / / /
1975					
1563	A966	10c multi	.20	.05	☐☐☐☐☐
1564	A967	10c multi	.20	.05	☐☐☐☐☐
1565	A968	10c multi	.20	.08	☐☐☐☐☐
1566	A969	10c multi	.20	.08	☐☐☐☐☐
1567	A970	10c multi	.20	.08	☐☐☐☐☐
1568	A971	10c multi	.20	.08	☐☐☐☐☐
1568a		Block of 4, #1565-1568	.80	.70	☐☐☐☐☐
1569	A972	10c multi	.20	.10	☐☐☐☐☐
1569a		Pair, #1569-1570	.40	.25	☐☐☐☐☐
1570	A973	10c multi	.20	.10	☐☐☐☐☐
1571	A974	10c blue, orange & dk blue	.20	.05	☐☐☐☐☐
1572	A975	10c multi	.20	.08	☐☐☐☐☐
1573	A976	10c multi	.20	.08	☐☐☐☐☐
1574	A977	10c multi	.20	.08	☐☐☐☐☐
1575	A978	10c multi	.20	.08	☐☐☐☐☐
1575a		Block of 4, #1572-1575	.80	.80	☐☐☐☐☐
1576	A979	10c green, Prussian blue & rose brown	.20	.05	☐☐☐☐☐
1577	A980	10c multi	.20	.08	☐☐☐☐☐
1577a		Pair, #1577-1578	.40	.20	☐☐☐☐☐
1578	A981	10c multi	.20	.08	☐☐☐☐☐
1579	A982	(10c) multi	.20	.05	☐☐☐☐☐
1580	A983	(10c) multi	.20	.05	☐☐☐☐☐
1580b		Perf. 10½x11	.50	.05	☐☐☐☐☐
1975-81		*Perf. 11x10½*			
1581	A984	1c dk blue, *greenish* ('77)	.05	.05	☐☐☐☐☐
1581a		Untagged (Bureau precanceled)		.05	☐☐☐☐☐
1582	A985	2c red brown, *greenish* ('77)	.05	.05	☐☐☐☐☐
1582a		Untagged (Bureau precanceled)		.06	☐☐☐☐☐
1582b		Cream paper ('81)	.05	.05	☐☐☐☐☐
1584	A987	3c olive, *greenish* ('77)	.06	.05	☐☐☐☐☐
1584a		Untagged (Bureau precanceled)		.06	☐☐☐☐☐
1585	A988	4c rose magenta, *cream* ('77)	.08	.05	☐☐☐☐☐
1585a		Untagged (Bureau precanceled)		.08	☐☐☐☐☐
1590	A994	9c slate green ('77)	.75	.20	☐☐☐☐☐
1590a		Perf. 10	25.00	6.00	☐☐☐☐☐
1591	A994	9c slate green, *gray*	.18	.05	☐☐☐☐☐
1591a		Untagged (Bureau precanceled)		.18	☐☐☐☐☐
1592	A995	10c violet, *gray* ('77)	.20	.05	☐☐☐☐☐
1592a		Untagged (Bureau precanceled)		.25	☐☐☐☐☐
1593	A996	11c orange, *gray*	.22	.05	☐☐☐☐☐
1594	A997	12c brown red, *beige* ('81)	.24	.05	☐☐☐☐☐
1595	A998	13c brown	.26	.05	■☐☐☐☐
1595a		Booklet pane of 6	1.60	.50	☐☐☐☐☐
1595b		Booklet pane of 7 + label	1.80	.50	☐☐☐☐☐
1595c		Booklet pane of 8	2.10	.50	☐☐☐☐☐
1595d		Booklet pane of 5 + label ('76)	1.30	.50	☐☐☐☐☐

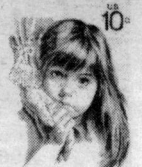
Retarded Children
Can Be Helped

A952

A953

A954

A955

Benjamin West

American artist
10 cents U.S. postage

A956

A958

Paul Laurence Dunbar

American poet
10 cents U.S. postage

A957

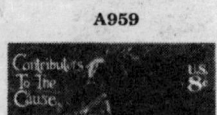

A959

A960

Sybil Ludington — Youthful Heroine

A962

Salem Poor — Gallant Soldier

A963

Haym Salomon — Financial Hero

A964

Peter Francisco — Fighter Extraordinary

A965

A961

A966

A967

A968   A969   A970   A971

A972

A973

A974

A979

A975

A976

A977

A978

A980

A981

A982

A983

 A984
 A985
 A987
 A988

 A994
 A995
 A996
 A997
 A998

 A999
 A1001
 A1002
 A1006

 A1007
 A1008
 A1009
 1011

 A1013
 A1013a
 A1014

 A1014a
 A1015
 A1016
 A1017
 A1018
 A1018a
 A1019
 A1020
 A1021
 A1022

HOW TO USE THIS BOOK

The number in the first column is its Scott number or identifying number. The letter and number that come next (A41) indicate the design and refer to the illustration so designated. Following that is the denomination of the stamp and its color. Finally, the price, unused and used is shown.

Scott® No.	Illus No.	Description	Unused Price	Used Price	/ / / / / /
1975-79					
1596	A999	13c multi	.26	.05 ☐☐☐☐☐
		Perf. 11			
1597	A1001	15c gray, dk blue & red ('78)	.30	.05 ▪☐☐☐☐
		Perf. 11x10½			
1598	A1001	15c gray, dk blue & red ('78)	.30	.05 ☐☐☐☐☐
1598a		Booklet pane of 8	2.40	.60 ☐☐☐☐☐
1599	A1002	16c blue ('78)	.32	.05 ☐☐☐☐☐
1603	A1006	24c red, *blue*	.48	.09 ☐☐☐☐☐
1604	A1007	28c brown, *blue* ('78)	.56	.08 ☐☐☐☐☐
1605	A1008	29c blue, *blue* ('78)	.58	.08 ☐☐☐☐☐
1606	A1009	30c green, *blue* ('79)	.60	.08 ☐☐☐☐☐
1608	A1011	50c black & orange, *tan* ('79)	1.00	.25 ☐☐☐☐☐
1610	A1013	$1 brown, orange & yellow, *tan* ('79)	2.00	.25 ☐☐☐☐☐
1611	A1013a	$2 dk green & orange, *buff* ('78)	4.00	.50 ☐☐☐☐☐
1612	A1014	$5 $5 multi ('79)	10.00	2.00 ☐☐☐☐☐
		Coil Stamps *Perf. 10 Vertically*			
1613	A1014a	3.1c brown, *yellow* ('79)	.11	.05 ☐☐☐☐☐
1613a		Untagged (Bureau precanceled)		.10 ☐☐☐☐☐
1614	A1015	7.7c brown, *bright yellow* ('76)	.20	.08 ☐☐☐☐☐
1614a		Untagged (Bureau precanceled)		.16 ☐☐☐☐☐
1615	A1016	7.9c carmine, *yellow* ('76)	.20	.08 ☐☐☐☐☐
1615a		Untagged (Bureau precanceled)		.16 ☐☐☐☐☐
1615C	A1017	8.4c dk blue, *yellow* ('78)	.20	.08 ☐☐☐☐☐
1615d		Untagged (Bureau precanceled)		.16 ☐☐☐☐☐
1616	A994	9c slate green, *gray*	.18	.05 ☐☐☐☐☐
1616b		Untagged (Bureau precanceled)		.18 ☐☐☐☐☐
1617	A995	10c violet, *gray* ('77)	.20	.05 ☐☐☐☐☐
1617a		Untagged (Bureau precanceled)		.25 ☐☐☐☐☐
1618	A998	13c brown	.26	.05 ☐☐☐☐☐
1618a		Untagged (Bureau precanceled)		.25 ☐☐☐☐☐
1618C	A1001	15c gray, dk blue & red ('78)	.40	.03 ☐☐☐☐☐
1619	A1002	16c blue ('78)	.32	.05 ☐☐☐☐☐
1975-77		*Perf. 11x10½*			
1622	A1018	13c dk blue & red	.26	.05 ☐☐☐☐☐
1622c		13c *perf. 11*	.30	.05 ☐☐☐☐☐
1623	A1018a	13c blue & red ('77)	.26	.05 ☐☐☐☐☐
1623a		Booklet pane of 8 (1 #1590 and 7 #1623)	2.50	.60 ☐☐☐☐☐
1623b		Perf. 10	1.00	.50 ☐☐☐☐☐
1623c		Booklet pane of 8 (1 #1590a + 7 #1623b)	32.50	— ☐☐☐☐☐
		Coil Stamp *Perf. 10 Vertically*			
1625	A1018	13c dk blue & red	.30	.05 ☐☐☐☐☐
1976					
1629	A1019	13c multi	.26	.08 ☐☐☐☐☐
1630	A1020	13c multi	.26	.08 ☐☐☐☐☐
1631	A1021	13c multi	.26	.08 ☐☐☐☐☐
1631a		Strip of 3, #1629-1631	.78	.60 ☐☐☐☐☐

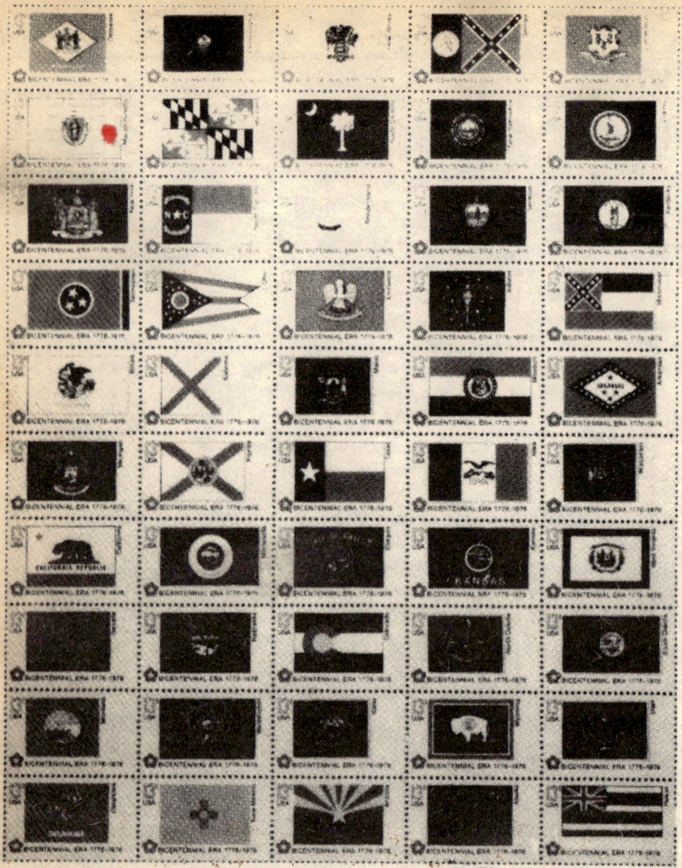

State Flags A1023-A1072

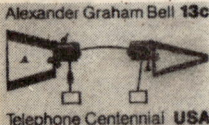

A1073

A1074

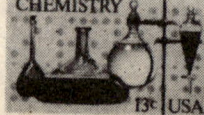

A1075

Scott® No.	Illus No.	Description	Unused Price	Used Price	//////
1976					
1632	A1022	13c dk blue, red & ultra	.26	.05	☐☐☐☐☐
1633	A1023	13c *Delaware*	.45	.30	☐☐☐☐☐
1634	A1024	13c *Pennsylvania*	.45	.30	☐☐☐☐☐
1635	A1025	13c *New Jersey*	.45	.30	☐☐☐☐☐
1636	A1026	13c *Georgia*	.45	.30	☐☐☐☐☐
1637	A1027	13c *Connecticut*	.45	.30	☐☐☐☐☐
1638	A1028	13c *Massachusetts*	.45	.30	☐☐☐☐☐
1639	A1029	13c *Maryland*	.45	.30	☐☐☐☐☐
1640	A1030	13c *South Carolina*	.45	.30	☐☐☐☐☐
1641	A1031	13c *New Hampshire*	.45	.30	☐☐☐☐☐
1642	A1032	13c *Virginia*	.45	.30	☐☐☐☐☐
1643	A1033	13c *New York*	.45	.30	☐☐☐☐☐
1644	A1034	13c *North Carolina*	.45	.30	☐☐☐☐☐
1645	A1035	13c *Rhode Island*	.45	.30	☐☐☐☐☐
1646	A1036	13c *Vermont*	.45	.30	☐☐☐☐☐
1647	A1037	13c *Kentucky*	.45	.30	☐☐☐☐☐
1648	A1038	13c *Tennessee*	.45	.30	☐☐☐☐☐
1649	A1039	13c *Ohio*	.45	.30	☐☐☐☐☐
1650	A1040	13c *Louisiana*	.45	.30	☐☐☐☐☐
1651	A1041	13c *Indiana*	.45	.30	☐☐☐☐☐
1652	A1042	13c *Mississippi*	.45	.30	☐☐☐☐☐
1653	A1043	13c *Illinois*	.45	.30	☐☐☐☐☐
1654	A1044	13c *Alabama*	.45	.30	☐☐☐☐☐
1655	A1045	13c *Maine*	.45	.30	☐☐☐☐☐
1656	A1046	13c *Missouri*	.45	.30	☐☐☐☐☐
1657	A1047	13c *Arkansas*	.45	.30	☐☐☐☐☐
1658	A1048	13c *Michigan*	.45	.30	☐☐☐☐☐
1659	A1049	13c *Florida*	.45	.30	☐☐☐☐☐
1660	A1050	13c *Texas*	.45	.30	☐☐☐☐☐
1661	A1051	13c *Iowa*	.45	.30	☐☐☐☐☐
1662	A1052	13c *Wisconsin*	.45	.30	☐☐☐☐☐
1663	A1053	13c *California*	.45	.30	☐☐☐☐☐
1664	A1054	13c *Minnesota*	.45	.30	☐☐☐☐☐
1665	A1055	13c *Oregon*	.45	.30	☐☐☐☐☐
1666	A1056	13c *Kansas*	.45	.30	☐☐☐☐☐
1667	A1057	13c *West Virginia*	.45	.30	☐☐☐☐☐
1668	A1058	13c *Nevada*	.45	.30	☐☐☐☐☐
1669	A1059	13c *Nebraska*	.45	.30	☐☐☐☐☐
1670	A1060	13c *Colorado*	.45	.30	☐☐☐☐☐
1671	A1061	13c *North Dakota*	.45	.30	☐☐☐☐☐
1672	A1062	13c *South Dakota*	.45	.30	☐☐☐☐☐
1673	A1063	13c *Montana*	.45	.30	☐☐☐☐☐
1674	A1064	13c *Washington*	.45	.30	☐☐☐☐☐
1675	A1065	13c *Idaho*	.45	.30	☐☐☐☐☐
1676	A1066	13c *Wyoming*	.45	.30	☐☐☐☐☐
1677	A1067	13c *Utah*	.45	.30	☐☐☐☐☐
1678	A1068	13c *Oklahoma*	.45	.30	☐☐☐☐☐

Surrender of Cornwallis at Yorktown, by John Trumbull— **A1076**

Declaration of Independence, by John Trumbull— **A1077**

Scott® No.	Illus No.	Description	Unused Price	Used Price	/ / / / / /

1976

1679	A1069	13c *New Mexico*	.45	.30	☐☐☐☐☐
1680	A1070	13c *Arizona*	.45	.30	☐☐☐☐☐
1681	A1071	13c *Alaska*	.45	.30	☐☐☐☐☐
1682	A1072	13c *Hawaii*	.45	.30	☐☐☐☐☐
1682a		Sheet of 50	25.00	—	☐☐☐☐☐

1976

1683	A1073	13c black, purple & red, *tan*	.26	.05	☐☐☐☐☐
1684	A1074	13c blue & multi	.26	.05	☐☐☐☐☐
1685	A1075	13c multi	.26	.05	☐☐☐☐☐
1686	A1076	13c sheet of 5	4.50	—	☐☐☐☐☐
1687	A1077	18c sheet of 5	6.00	—	☐☐☐☐☐
1688	A1078	24c sheet of 5	7.50	—	☐☐☐☐☐
1689	A1079	31c sheet of 5	9.00	—	☐☐☐☐☐
1690	A1080	13c ultra & multi	.26	.05	☐☐☐☐☐
1691	A1081	13c multi	.26	.08	☐☐☐☐☐
1692	A1082	13c multi	.26	.08	☐☐☐☐☐
1693	A1083	13c multi	.26	.08	☐☐☐☐☐
1694	A1084	13c multi	.26	.08	☐☐☐☐☐
1694a		Strip of 4, #1691-1694	1.10	.75	☐☐☐☐☐
1695	A1085	13c multi	.26	.08	☐☐☐☐☐
1696	A1086	13c multi	.26	.08	☐☐☐☐☐
1697	A1087	13c multi	.26	.08	☐☐☐☐☐
1698	A1088	13c multi	.26	.08	☐☐☐☐☐
1698a		Block of 4, #1695-1698	1.10	1.00	☐☐☐☐☐
1699	A1089	13c multi	.26	.06	☐☐☐☐☐
1700	A1090	13c black & gray	.26	.05	☐☐☐☐☐
1701	A1091	13c multi	.26	.05	☐☐☐☐☐
1702	A1092	13c Overall tagging	.26	.05	☐☐☐☐☐
1703	A1092	13c Block tagging	.26	.05	☐☐☐☐☐

No. 1702 has overall tagging. Lettering at base is black and usually ½mm. below design. As a rule, no "snowflaking" in sky or pond. Pane of 50 has margins on 4 sides with slogans.

No. 1703 has block tagging the size of printed area. Lettering at base is gray black and usually ¾mm. below design. "Snowflaking" generally in sky and pond. Pane has margin only at right or left, and no slogans.

1977

1704	A1093	13c multi	.26	.05	☐☐☐☐☐
1705	A1094	13c black & multi	.26	.05	☐☐☐☐☐
1706	A1095	13c multi	.26	.08	☐☐☐☐☐
1707	A1096	13c multi	.26	.08	☐☐☐☐☐
1708	A1097	13c multi	.26	.08	☐☐☐☐☐
1709	A1098	13c multi	.26	.08	☐☐☐☐☐
1709a		Block or strip of 4	1.05	1.00	☐☐☐☐☐
1710	A1099	13c multi	.26	.05	☐☐☐☐☐

Washington Crossing the Delaware
From a Painting by Emanuel Leutze / Eastman Johnson

Washington Crossing the Delaware, by Emanuel Leutze/Eastman Johnson— A1078

Washington Reviewing His Ragged Army at Valley Forge
From a Painting by William T. Trego

Washington Reviewing Army at Valley Forge, by William T. Trego— A1079

A1080

JULY 4,1776: JULY 4,1776: JULY 4,1776: JULY 4,1776
Declaration of Independence, by John Trumbull

A1081   A1082   A1083   A1084

A1085

A1086   A1089

A1087   A1088

A1090

A1091

A1092

A1093

A1094

Zia: Museum of New Mexico
Pueblo Art USA 13c
A1095

San Ildefonso: Denver Art Museum
Pueblo Art USA 13c
A1096

Hopi: Heard Museum Phoenix
Pueblo Art USA 13c
A1097

Acoma: School of American Research
Pueblo Art USA 13c
A1098

A1099

COLORADO

A1100

Lafayette

US Bicentennial 13c
A1105

A1101

A1102

A1103

A1104

138

Scott® No.	Illus No.	Description	Unused Price	Used Price	//////
1977					
1711	A1100	13c multi	.26	.05	☐☐☐☐☐
1712	A1101	13c tan & multi	.26	.08	☐☐☐☐☐
1713	A1102	13c tan & multi	.26	.08	☐☐☐☐☐
1714	A1103	13c tan & multi	.26	.08	☐☐☐☐☐
1715	A1104	13c tan & multi	.26	.08	☐☐☐☐☐
1715a		Block of 4, #1712-1715	1.05	.90	☐☐☐☐☐
1716	A1105	13c blue, black & red	.26	.05	☐☐☐☐☐
1717	A1106	13c multi	.26	.08	☐☐☐☐☐
1718	A1107	13c multi	.26	.08	☐☐☐☐☐
1719	A1108	13c multi	.26	.08	☐☐☐☐☐
1720	A1109	13c multi	.26	.08	☐☐☐☐☐
1720a		Block of 4, #1717-1720	1.05	.90	☐☐☐☐☐
1721	A1110	13c blue	.26	.05	☐☐☐☐☐
1722	A1111	13c multi	.26	.05	☐☐☐☐☐
1723	A1112	13c multi	.26	.08	☐☐☐☐☐
1723a		Pair, #1723-1724	.52	.35	☐☐☐☐☐
1724	A1113	13c multi	.26	.08	☐☐☐☐☐
1725	A1114	13c black & multi	.26	.05	☐☐☐☐☐
1726	A1115	13c red & brown, *cream*	.26	.05	☐☐☐☐☐
1727	A1116	13c multi	.26	.05	☐☐☐☐☐
1728	A1117	13c multi	.26	.05	☐☐☐☐☐
1729	A1118	13c multi	.26	.05	☐☐☐☐☐
1730	A1119	13c multi	.26	.05	☐☐☐☐☐
1978					
1731	A1120	13c black & brown	.26	.05	☐☐☐☐☐
1732	A1121	13c dk blue	.26	.08	☐☐☐☐☐
1732a		Pair, #1732-1733	.55	.30	☐☐☐☐☐
1733	A1122	13c green	.26	.08	☐☐☐☐☐
1734	A1123	13c brown & blue green, *bister*	.26	.10	☐☐☐☐☐
1735	A1124(15c)	orange, Perf. 11	.30	.03	☐☐☐☐☐
1736	A1124(15c)	orange, Perf. 10½ x 11	.30	.05	☐☐☐☐☐
1736a		Booklet pane of 8	2.40	.60	☐☐☐☐☐
1737	A1126	15c multi	.30	.06	☐☐☐☐☐
1737a		Booklet pane of 8	2.40	.60	☐☐☐☐☐
1980					
1738	A1127	15c sepia, *yellow*	.30	.05	☐☐☐☐☐
1739	A1128	15c sepia, *yellow*	.30	.05	☐☐☐☐☐
1740	A1129	15c sepia, *yellow*	.30	.05	■☐☐☐☐
1741	A1130	15c sepia, *yellow*	.30	.05	☐☐☐☐☐
1742	A1131	15c sepia, *yellow*	.30	.05	☐☐☐☐☐
1742a		Booklet pane of 10	3.25	.60	☐☐☐☐☐
1743	A1124(15c)	orange, Perf. 10 vert.	.30	.05	☐☐☐☐☐
1978					
1744	A1133	13c multi	.26	.05	☐☐☐☐☐
1745	A1134	13c multi	.26	.08	☐☐☐☐☐
1746	A1135	13c multi	.26	.08	☐☐☐☐☐

A1106 A1107

A1108 A1109

A1110 A1112 A1111

A1114 A1113 A1115

A1116 A1117

A1118 A1120 A1119

A1121

A1122

A1134

A1135

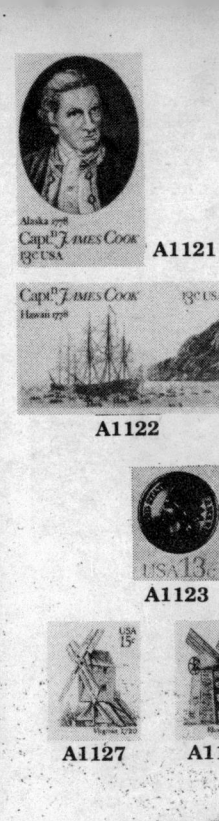

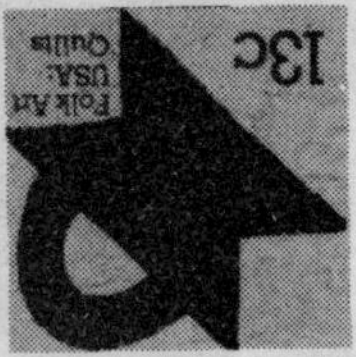

A1136

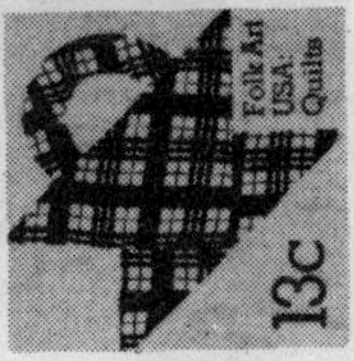

A1137

A1123

A1124

A1126

A1127

A1128

A1129

A1130

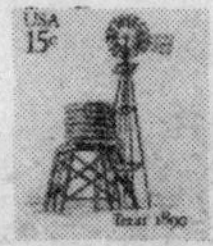

A1131

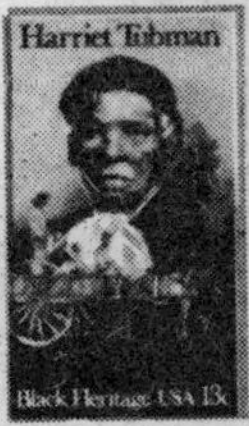

A1133

A1138

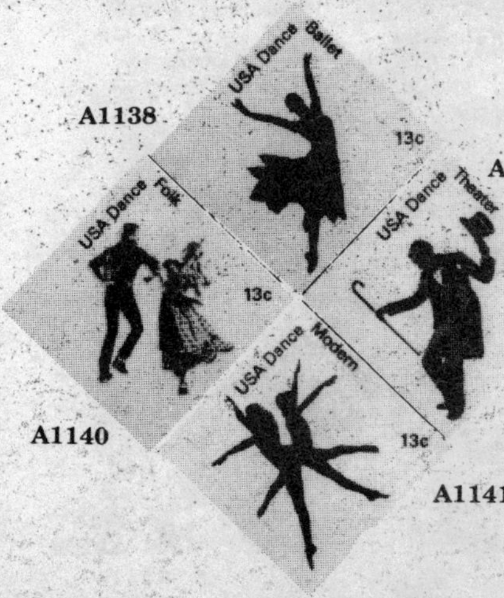

A1139

A1140

A1141

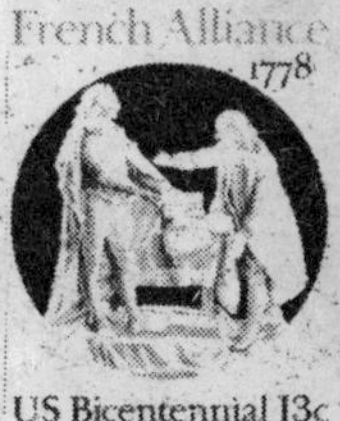

A1142

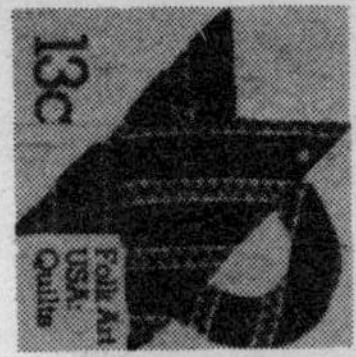

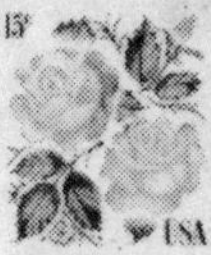

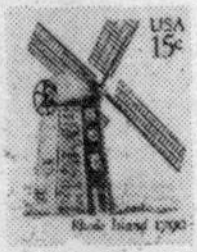

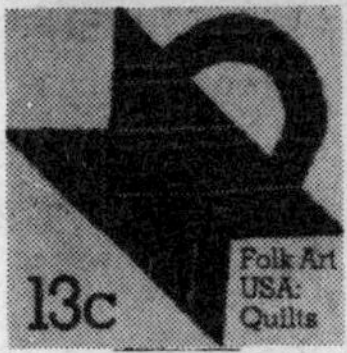

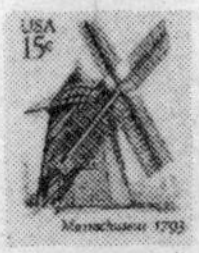

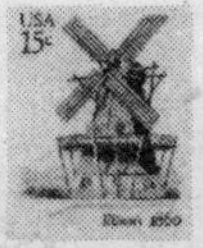

A1143
A1146 
A1144 
A1149 
A1150 
A1145 
A1151 
A1152 
A1147 
A1153
A1154
A1155
A1156

A1148

A1157

A1158

A1159

A1161

A1160

A1162

A1163

A1164

A1165

A1166

A1167

 A1168

 A1169

 A1170

 A1171

 A1172

 A1173

 A1174

 A1175

 A1176

 A1177

 A1178

Scott® No.	Illus No.	Description	Unused Price	Used Price	/ / / / / /
1747	A1136	13c multi	.26	.08	☐☐☐☐☐
1748	A1137	13c multi	.26	.08	☐☐☐☐☐
1748a		Block of 4, #1745-1748	1.05	.75	☐☐☐☐☐
1749	A1138	13c multi	.26	.08	☐☐☐☐☐
1750	A1139	13c multi	.26	.08	☐☐☐☐☐
1751	A1140	13c multi	.26	.08	☐☐☐☐☐
1752	A1141	13c multi	.26	.08	☐☐☐☐☐
1752a		Block of 4, #1749-1752	1.05	.75	☐☐☐☐☐
1753	A1142	13c blue, black & red	.26	.05	☐☐☐☐☐
1754	A1143	13c brown	.26	.05	☐☐☐☐☐
1755	A1144	13c multi	.26	.05	☐☐☐☐☐
1756	A1145	15c multi	.30	.05	☐☐☐☐☐
1757	A1146	13c Block of 8, multi	2.10	2.50	☐☐☐☐☐
1757a		*Cardinal*	.26	.10	☐☐☐☐☐
1757b		*Mallard*	.26	.10	☐☐☐☐☐
1757c		*Canada goose*	.26	.10	☐☐☐☐☐
1757d		*Blue jay*	.26	.10	☐☐☐☐☐
1757e		*Moose*	.26	.10	☐☐☐☐☐
1757f		*Chipmunk*	.26	.10	☐☐☐☐☐
1757g		*Red fox*	.26	.10	☐☐☐☐☐
1757h		*Raccoon*	.26	.10	☐☐☐☐☐
1758	A1147	15c multi	.30	.05	☐☐☐☐☐
1759	A1148	15c multi	.30	.05	☐☐☐☐☐
1760	A1149	15c multi	.30	.08	☐☐☐☐☐
1761	A1150	15c multi	.30	.08	☐☐☐☐☐
1762	A1151	15c multi	.30	.08	☐☐☐☐☐
1763	A1152	15c multi	.30	.08	☐☐☐☐☐
1763a		Block of 4, #1760-1763	1.25	.85	☐☐☐☐☐
1764	A1153	15c multi	.30	.08	☐☐☐☐☐
1765	A1154	15c multi	.30	.08	☐☐☐☐☐
1766	A1155	15c multi	.30	.08	☐☐☐☐☐
1767	A1156	15c multi	.30	.08	☐☐☐☐☐
1767a		Block of 4, #1764-1767	1.25	.85	☐☐☐☐☐
1768	A1157	15c blue & multi	.30	.05	☐☐☐☐☐
1769	A1158	15c red & multi	.30	.05	☐☐☐☐☐

1979-80

Scott® No.	Illus No.	Description	Unused Price	Used Price	/ / / / / /
1770	A1159	15c blue	.30	.05	☐☐☐☐☐
1771	A1160	15c multi	.30	.05	☐☐☐☐☐
1772	A1161	15c orange red	.30	.05	☐☐☐☐☐
1773	A1162	15c dk blue	.30	.05	☐☐☐☐☐
1774	A1163	15c chocolate	.30	.05	☐☐☐☐☐
1775	A1164	15c multi	.30	.08	☐☐☐☐☐
1776	A1165	15c multi	.30	.08	☐☐☐☐☐
1777	A1166	15c multi	.30	.08	☐☐☐☐☐
1778	A1167	15c multi	.30	.08	☐☐☐☐☐
1778a		Block of 4, #1775-1778	1.20	.85	☐☐☐☐☐
1779	A1168	15c black & brick red	.30	.08	☐☐☐☐☐

A1179

A1180

A1181

A1182

A1183

A1184

A1185

A1186

A1187

A1188

A1191

A1189

Scott® No.	Illus No.	Description	Unused Price	Used Price	/ / / / / /
1780	A1169	15c black & brick red	.30	.08 ☐☐☐☐☐
1781	A1170	15c black & brick red	.30	.08 ☐☐☐☐☐
1782	A1171	15c black & brick red	.30	.08 ☐☐☐☐☐
1782a		Block of 4, #1779-1782	1.20	.85 ☐☐☐☐☐
1783	A1172	15c multi	.30	.06 ☐☐☐☐☐
1784	A1173	15c multi	.30	.08 ☐☐☐☐☐
1785	A1174	15c multi	.30	.08 ☐☐☐☐☐
1786	A1175	15c multi	.30	.08 ☐☐☐☐☐
1786a		Block of 4, #1783-1786	1.25	.85 ☐☐☐☐☐
1787	A1176	15c multi	.30	.05 ☐☐☐☐☐
1788	A1177	15c multi	.30	.05 ☐☐☐☐☐
1789	A1178	15c multi	.30	.05 ☐☐☐☐☐
1790	A1179	10c multi	.25	.22 ☐☐☐☐☐
1791	A1180	15c multi	.35	.08 ☐☐☐☐☐
1792	A1181	15c multi	.35	.08 ☐☐☐☐☐
1793	A1182	15c multi	.35	.08 ☐☐☐☐☐
1794	A1183	15c multi	.35	.08 ☐☐☐☐☐
1794a		Block of 4, #1791-1794	1.50	.85 ☐☐☐☐☐
1795	A1184	15c multi	.45	.08 ☐☐☐☐☐
1796	A1185	15c multi	.45	.08 ☐☐☐☐☐
1797	A1186	15c multi	.45	.08 ☐☐☐☐☐
1798	A1187	15c multi	.45	.08 ☐☐☐☐☐
1798b		Block of 4, #1795-1798	1.90	.85 ☐☐☐☐☐
1799	A1188	15c multi	.30	.05 ☐☐☐☐☐
1800	A1189	15c multi	.30	.05 ☐☐☐☐☐
1801	A1190	15c multi	.30	.05 ☐☐☐☐☐
1802	A1191	15c multi	.30	.05 ☐☐☐☐☐

1980

Scott® No.	Illus No.	Description	Unused Price	Used Price
1803	A1192	15c multi	.30	.05 ☐☐☐☐☐
1804	A1193	15c multi	.30	.05 ☐☐☐☐☐
1805	A1194	15c multi	.30	.08 ☐☐☐☐☐
1806	A1195	15c claret & multi	.30	.08 ☐☐☐☐☐
1807	A1196	15c multi	.30	.08 ☐☐☐☐☐
1808	A1195	15c green & multi	.30	.08 ☐☐☐☐☐
1809	A1197	15c multi	.30	.08 ☐☐☐☐☐
1810	A1195	15c red & multi	.30	.08 ☐☐☐☐☐
1810a		Strip of 6 #1805-1810	1.80	1.25 ☐☐☐☐☐

1980-81 *Coil Perf, 10 vert.*

1811	A984	1c dk blue, *greenish*	.05	.05 ☐☐☐☐☐
1813	A1199	3.5c purple, *yellow*	.08	.05 ☐☐☐☐☐
1816	A997	12c brown red, *beige* ('81)	.24	.05 ☐☐☐☐☐

1981

1818	A1207(18c)	violet	.36	.05 ☐☐☐☐☐
1819	A1207(18c)	violet from booklet pane	.36	.05 ☐☐☐☐☐
1819a		Booklet pane of 8	3.00	— ☐☐☐☐☐
1820	A1207(18c)	(18c) violet, coil	.36	.05 ☐☐☐☐☐
1821	A1208	15c Prussian blue	.30	.05 ☐☐☐☐☐
1822	A1209	15c red brown & sepia	.30	.05 ☐☐☐☐☐

A1190

A1192

A1193

A1196

A1194

A1197

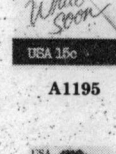

A1195

A1208

A1209

A1210

A1211

A1212

A1213

Scott® No.	Illus No.	Denom	Description	Unused Price	Used Price	/ / / / / /
1980						
1823	A1210	15c	black & red	.30	.05 ☐☐☐☐☐	
1824	A1211	15c	multi	.30	.05 ☐☐☐☐☐	
1825	A1212	15c	carmine & violet blue	.30	.05 ☐☐☐☐☐	
1826	A1213	15c	multi	.30	.05 ☐☐☐☐☐	
1827	A1214	15c	multi	.30	.08 ☐☐☐☐☐	
1828	A1215	15c	multi	.30	.08 ☐☐☐☐☐	
1829	A1216	15c	multi	.30	.08 ☐☐☐☐☐	
1830	A1217	15c	multi	.30	.08 ☐☐☐☐☐	
1831	A1218	15c	multi	.30	.05 ☐☐☐☐☐	
1832	A1219	15c	purple	.30	.05 ☐☐☐☐☐	
1833	A1220	15c	multi	.30	.05 ☐☐☐☐☐	
1834	A1221	15c	multi	.30	.08 ☐☐☐☐☐	
1835	A1222	15c	multi	.30	.08 ☐☐☐☐☐	
1836	A1223	15c	multi	.30	.08 ☐☐☐☐☐	
1837	A1224	15c	multi	.30	.08 ☐☐☐☐☐	
1838	A1225	15c	black & brick red	.30	.08 ☐☐☐☐☐	
1839	A1226	15c	black & brick red	.30	.08 ☐☐☐☐☐	
1840	A1227	15c	black & brick red	.30	.08 ☐☐☐☐☐	
1841	A1228	15c	black & brick red	.30	.08 ☐☐☐☐☐	
1842	A1229	15c	multi	.30	.05 ☐☐☐☐☐	
1843	A1230	15c	multi	.30	.05 ☐☐☐☐☐	
1980-84						
1843A	A1230a	1c	black ('83)	.05	.05 ☐☐☐☐☐	
1844	A1231	2c	brown black ('82)	.05	.05 ☐☐☐☐☐	
1844A	A1231a	3c	olive green ('83)	.06	.05 ☐☐☐☐☐	
1845	A1232	4c	violet ('83)	.08	.05 ☐☐☐☐☐	
1846	A1233	5c	henna brown ('83)	.10	.05 ☐☐☐☐☐	
1846A	A1233a	10c	Prussian blue ('84)	.20	.05 ☐☐☐☐☐	
1847	A1234	13c	lt maroon ('82)	.26	.05 ☐☐☐☐☐	
1849	A1236	17c	green ('81)	.34	.05 ☐☐☐☐☐	
1850	A1237	18c	dk blue ('81)	.36	.05 ☐☐☐☐☐	
1851	A1238	19c	brown	.38	.07 ☐☐☐☐☐	
1852	A1239	20c	rose lake ('80)	.40	.05 ☐☐☐☐☐	
1853	A1240	20c	green ('83)	.40	.05 ☐☐☐☐☐	
1854	A1241	20c	black ('84)	.40	.05 ☐☐☐☐☐	
1858	A1245	30c	olive gray ('84)	.60	.06 ☐☐☐☐☐	
1859	A1246	35c	gray ('81)	.70	.08 ☐☐☐☐☐	
1860	A1247	37c	blue ('82)	.75	.06 ☐☐☐☐☐	
1861	A1248	40c	dk green ('84)	.80	.08 ☐☐☐☐☐	
1981						
1874	A1261	15c	gray	.30	.05 ☐☐☐☐☐	
1875	A1262	15c	multi	.30	.05 ☐☐☐☐☐	
1876	A1263	18c	multi	.36	.08 ☐☐☐☐☐	
1877	A1264	18c	multi	.36	.08 ☐☐☐☐☐	
1878	A1265	18c	multi	.36	.08 ☐☐☐☐☐	
1879	A1266	18c	multi	.36	.08 ☐☐☐☐☐	
1880	A1267	18c	*Bighorn*	.36	.05 ☐☐☐☐☐	

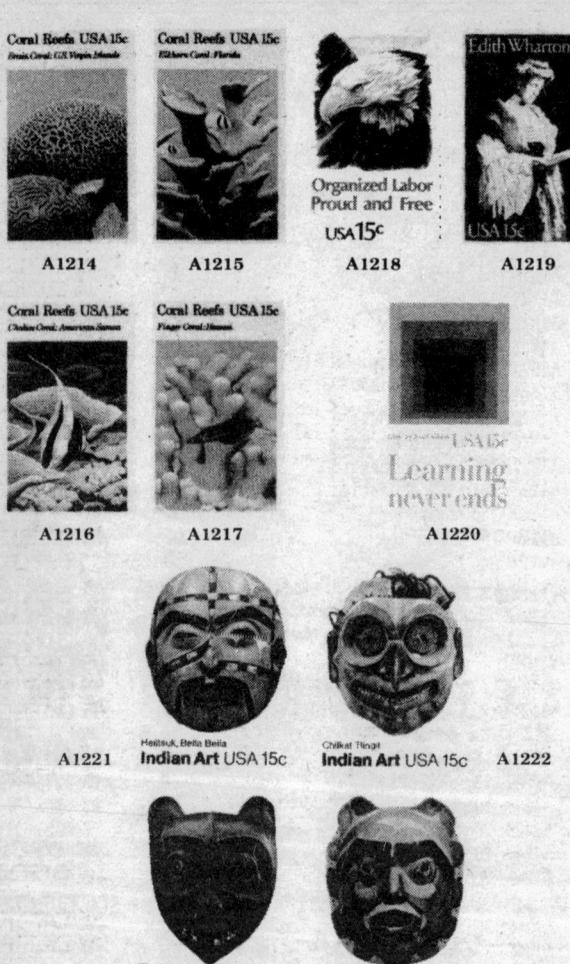

HOW TO USE THIS BOOK

The number in the first column is its Scott number or identifying number. The letter and number that come next (A41) indicate the design and refer to the illustration so designated. Following that is the denomination of the stamp and its color. Finally, the price, unused and used is shown.

Scott® No.	Illus No.	Denom	Description	Unused Price	Used Price	/////
1881	A1268	18c	*Puma*	.36	.05	☐☐☐☐☐
1882	A1269	18c	*Harbor seal*	.36	.05	☐☐☐☐☐
1883	A1270	18c	*Bison*	.36	.05	☐☐☐☐☐
1884	A1271	18c	*Brown bear*	.36	.05	☐☐☐☐☐
1885	A1272	18c	*Polar bear*	.36	.05	☐☐☐☐☐
1886	A1273	18c	*Elk (wapiti)*	.36	.05	☐☐☐☐☐
1887	A1274	18c	*Moose*	.36	.05	☐☐☐☐☐
1888	A1275	18c	*White-tailed deer*	.36	.05	☐☐☐☐☐
1889	A1276	18c	*Pronghorn*	.36	.05	☐☐☐☐☐
1889a			Booklet pane of 10	3.60		☐☐☐☐☐
1890	A1277	18c	multi	.36	.05	☐☐☐☐☐
1891	A1278	18c	multi	.36	.05	☐☐☐☐☐
1892	A1279	6c	multi	.12	.10	☐☐☐☐☐
1893	A1280	18c	multi	.36	.05	☐☐☐☐☐
1893a			Booklet pane of 8 (2 #1892, 6 #1893)	2.40		☐☐☐☐☐
1894	A1281	20c	black, dk blue & red	.40	.05	☐☐☐☐☐
1895	A1281	20c	black, dk blue & red	.40	.05	☐☐☐☐☐
1896	A1281	20c	black, dk blue & red	.40	.05	☐☐☐☐☐
1896a			Booklet pane of 6	2.50	—	☐☐☐☐☐

1981-84   Coil Stamps *Perf. 10 Vert.*

Scott® No.	Illus No.	Denom	Description	Unused Price	Used Price	/////
1897	A1283	1c	violet ('83)	.05	.05	■☐☐☐☐
1897A	A1284	2c	black ('82)	.05	.05	☐☐☐☐☐
1898	A1284a	3c	dark green ('83)	.06	.05	☐☐☐☐☐
1898A	A1285	4c	reddish brown('82)	.08	.05	☐☐☐☐☐
1898b			Untagged (Bureau Prec.)		.08	☐☐☐☐☐
1899	A1286	5c	gray green ('83)	.10	.05	☐☐☐☐☐
1900	A1287	5.2c	carmine ('83)	.12	.05	☐☐☐☐☐
1900a			Untagged (Bureau Prec.)		.12	☐☐☐☐☐
1901	A1288	5.9c	blue ('82)	.12	.05	☐☐☐☐☐
1901a			Untagged (Bureau Precanceled, lines only)		.12	☐☐☐☐☐
1902	A1288a	7.4c	brown ('84)	.15	.08	☐☐☐☐☐
1902a			Untagged (Bureau Prec.)		.15	☐☐☐☐☐
1903	A1289	9.3c	carmine rose ('81)	.20	.08	☐☐☐☐☐
1903a			Untagged (Bureau Prec., lines only)		.20	☐☐☐☐☐
1904	A1290	10.9c	purple ('82)	.22	.05	☐☐☐☐☐
1904a			Untagged (Bureau Precanceled, lines only)		.22	☐☐☐☐☐

A1225 Architecture USA 15c

Architecture USA 15c A1226

A1227 Architecture USA 15c

Architecture USA 15c A1228

Christmas USA 15c
A1229

USA 15c
Season's Greetings
A1230

USA 15c
Everett Dirksen
A1261

Whitney Moore Young
Black Heritage USA 15c
A1262

A1263

Rose USA 18c

Camellia USA 18c
A1264

A1265

Dahlia USA 18c

Lily USA 18c
A1266

 A1230a
 A1231
 A1231a
 A1232

 A1233
 A1233a
 A1234
 A1236

 A1237
 A1238
 A1239
 A1240

 A1241
 A1245
 A1246
 A1247

 A1248

A1283

A1284

A1284a

A1285

A1286

A1287

A1288

A1288a

A1289

A1290

A1290a

A1291

A1292

A1294

A1296

A1207

A1281

A1267   A1268

A1269  A1270

A1271   A1272

A1273  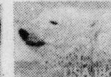 A1274

A1275 A1276

A1277 A1278 A1279 A1280

A1332 A1333 A1334 A1390

155

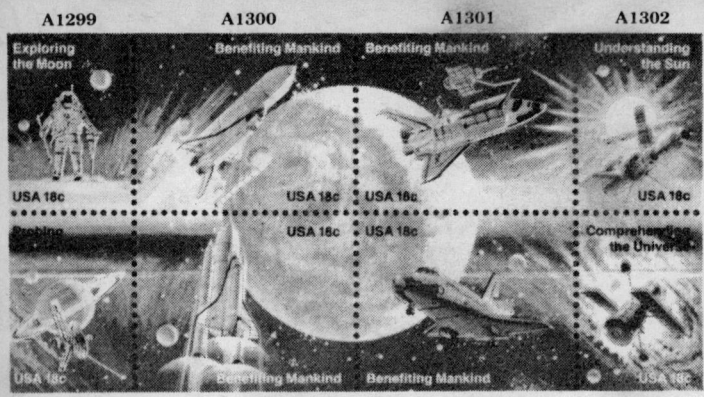

| A1299 | A1300 | A1301 | A1302 |
| A1303 | A1304 | A1305 | A1306 |

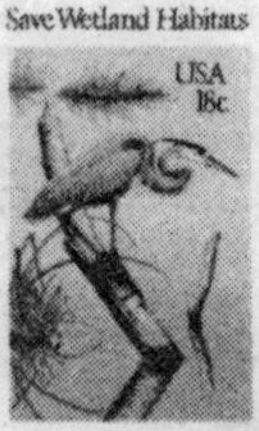

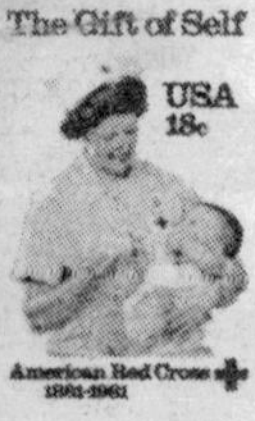

The Gift of Self

USA 18c

American Red Cross
1881-1981

A1297

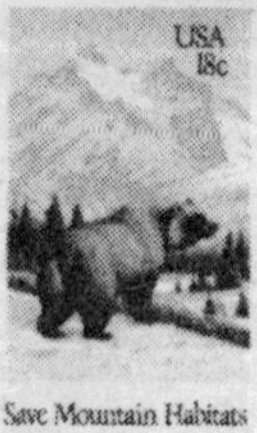

Save Wetland Habitats

USA 18c

A1308

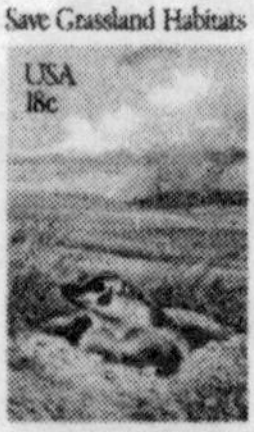

Save Grassland Habitats

USA 18c

A1309

Save Mountain Habitats

USA 18c

A1310

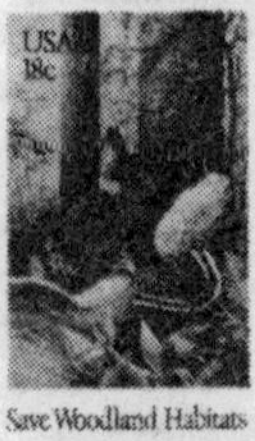

Save Woodland Habitats

USA 18c

A1311

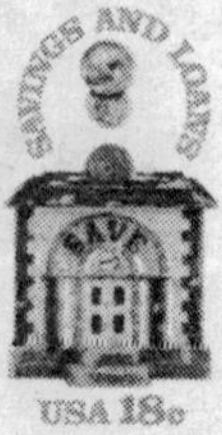

SAVINGS AND LOANS

SAVE

USA 18c

A1298

156

Scott® No.	Illus No.	Denom	Description	Unused Price	Used Price	/////
1905	A1290a	11c	red ('84)	.22	.08	☐☐☐☐☐
1905a			Untagged (Bureau Prec.)		.22	☐☐☐☐☐
1906	A1291	17c	ultramarine ('81)	.34	.05	☐☐☐☐☐
1906a			Untagged (Bureau Precanceled, Presorted First Class)		.34	☐☐☐☐☐
1907	A1292	18c	dark brown ('81)	.36	.05	☐☐☐☐☐
1908	A1294	20c	vermilion ('81)	.40	.05	☐☐☐☐☐
1909	A1296	$9.35	multi, perf. 10 vert.	19.00	—	☐☐☐☐☐
1909a			Booklet pane of 3	60.00	—	☐☐☐☐☐

1981

Scott® No.	Illus No.	Denom	Description	Unused Price	Used Price	/////
1910	A1297	18c	multi	.36	.05	☐☐☐☐☐
1911	A1298	18c	multi	.36	.05	☐☐☐☐☐
1912	A1299	18c	multi	.36	.10	☐☐☐☐☐
1913	A1300	18c	multi	.36	.10	☐☐☐☐☐
1914	A1301	18c	multi	.36	.10	☐☐☐☐☐
1915	A1302	18c	multi	.36	.10	☐☐☐☐☐
1916	A1303	18c	multi	.36	.10	☐☐☐☐☐
1917	A1304	18c	multi	.36	.10	☐☐☐☐☐
1918	A1305	18c	multi	.36	.10	☐☐☐☐☐
1919	A1306	18c	multi	.36	.10	☐☐☐☐☐
1919a			Block of 8, #1912-1919	3.00	2.25	☐☐☐☐☐
1920	A1307	18c	blue & black	.36	.05	☐☐☐☐☐
1921	A1308	18c	multi	.36	.08	☐☐☐☐☐
1922	A1309	18c	multi	.36	.08	☐☐☐☐☐
1923	A1310	18c	multi	.36	.08	☐☐☐☐☐
1924	A1311	18c	multi	.36	.08	☐☐☐☐☐
1924a			Block of 4, #1921-1924	1.50	.85	☐☐☐☐☐
1925	A1312	18c	multi	.36	.05	☐☐☐☐☐
1926	A1313	18c	multi	.36	.05	☐☐☐☐☐
1927	A1314	18c	blue & black	.36	.05	☐☐☐☐☐
1928	A1315	18c	black & red	.36	.08	☐☐☐☐☐
1929	A1316	18c	black & red	.36	.08	☐☐☐☐☐
1930	A1317	18c	black & red	.36	.08	☐☐☐☐☐
1931	A1318	18c	black & red	.36	.08	☐☐☐☐☐
1931a			Block of 4, #1928-1931	1.50	.85	☐☐☐☐☐
1932	A1319	18c	purple	.36	.05	☐☐☐☐☐
1933	A1320	18c	green	.36	.05	☐☐☐☐☐
1934	A1321	18c	gray, green & brown	.36	.05	☐☐☐☐☐
1935	A1322	18c	multi	.50	.25	☐☐☐☐☐
1936	A1322	20c	multi	.40	.05	☐☐☐☐☐
1937	A1323	18c	multi	.36	.06	☐☐☐☐☐
1938	A1324	18c	multi	.36	.06	☐☐☐☐☐
1939	A1325	(20c)	multi	.40	.05	☐☐☐☐☐
1940	A1326	(20c)	multi	.40	.05	☐☐☐☐☐

A1307   A1312

 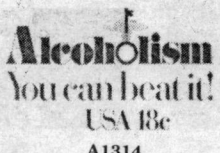

A1313   A1314   A1327

A1315   A1316

A1317   A1318

A1321

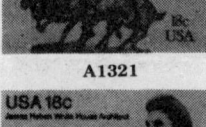 

A1319   A1322   A1320

158

 A1323
 A1324

 A1325
 A1326

 A1328
 A1329
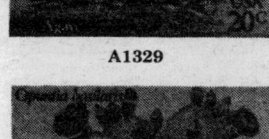 A1330
 A1331

 A1335
 A1336
 A1337

A1338-A1387—State Birds and Flowers

A1388

A1395

A1389

A1391  A1392

A1393  A1394

Scott® No.	Illus No.	Denom	Description	Unused Price	Used Price	/ / / / / /
1941	A1327	20c	multi	.40	.05 ☐☐☐☐☐
1942	A1328	20c	multi	.40	.06 ☐☐☐☐☐
1943	A1329	20c	multi	.40	.06 ☐☐☐☐☐
1944	A1330	20c	multi	.40	.06 ☐☐☐☐☐
1945	A1331	20c	multi	.40	.06 ☐☐☐☐☐
1945a			Block of 4, #1942-1945	1.60	.85 ☐☐☐☐☐
1946	A1332	(20c)	brown	.40	.05 ☐☐☐☐☐
1947	A1332	(20c)	(20c) brown, coil	.40	.05 ☐☐☐☐☐
1948	A1333	(20c)	brown	.40	.05 ☐☐☐☐☐
1948a			Booklet pane of 10	4.25	— ☐☐☐☐☐

1982

Scott® No.	Illus No.	Denom	Description	Unused Price	Used Price	/ / / / / /
1949	A1334	20c	dk blue (from booklet pane)	.40	.05 ☐☐☐☐☐
1949a			Booklet pane of 10	4.00	☐☐☐☐☐
1950	A1335	20c	blue	.40	.05 ☐☐☐☐☐
1951	A1336	20c	multi	.40	.05 ☐☐☐☐☐
1952	A1337	20c	multi	.40	.05 ☐☐☐☐☐
1953	A1338	20c	*Alabama*	.40	.25 ☐☐☐☐☐
1954	A1339	20c	*Alaska*	.40	.25 ☐☐☐☐☐
1955	A1340	20c	*Arizona*	.40	.25 ☐☐☐☐☐
1956	A1341	20c	*Arkansas*	.40	.25 ☐☐☐☐☐
1957	A1342	20c	*California*	.40	.25 ☐☐☐☐☐
1958	A1343	20c	*Colorado*	.40	.25 ☐☐☐☐☐
1959	A1344	20c	*Connecticut*	.40	.25 ☐☐☐☐☐
1960	A1345	20c	*Delaware*	.40	.25 ☐☐☐☐☐
1961	A1346	20c	*Florida*	.40	.25 ☐☐☐☐☐
1962	A1347	20c	*Georgia*	.40	.25 ☐☐☐☐☐
1963	A1348	20c	*Hawaii*	.40	.25 ☐☐☐☐☐
1964	A1349	20c	*Idaho*	.40	.25 ☐☐☐☐☐
1965	A1350	20c	*Illinois*	.40	.25 ☐☐☐☐☐
1966	A1351	20c	*Indiana*	.40	.25 ☐☐☐☐☐
1967	A1352	20c	*Iowa*	.40	.25 ☐☐☐☐☐
1968	A1353	20c	*Kansas*	.40	.25 ☐☐☐☐☐
1969	A1354	20c	*Kentucky*	.40	.25 ☐☐☐☐☐
1970	A1355	20c	*Louisiana*	.40	.25 ☐☐☐☐☐
1971	A1356	20c	*Maine*	.40	.25 ☐☐☐☐☐
1972	A1357	20c	*Maryland*	.40	.25 ☐☐☐☐☐
1973	A1358	20c	*Massachusetts*	.40	.25 ☐☐☐☐☐
1974	A1359	20c	*Michigan*	.40	.25 ☐☐☐☐☐
1975	A1360	20c	*Minnesota*	.40	.25 ☐☐☐☐☐
1976	A1361	20c	*Mississippi*	.40	.25 ☐☐☐☐☐
1977	A1362	20c	*Missouri*	.40	.25 ☐☐☐☐☐
1978	A1363	20c	*Montana*	.40	.25 ☐☐☐☐☐
1979	A1364	20c	*Nebraska*	.40	.25 ☐☐☐☐☐
1980	A1365	20c	*Nevada*	.40	.25 ☐☐☐☐☐
1981	A1366	20c	*New Hampshire*	.40	.25 ☐☐☐☐☐
1982	A1367	20c	*New Jersey*	.40	.25 ☐☐☐☐☐

A1396

A1399

A1397

A1398

A1400

A1401

A1402

A1403

A1404

A1405

A1406

A1407

Scott® No.	Illus No.	Denom	Description	Unused Price	Used Price	/ / / / / /
1983	A1368	20c	*New Mexico*	.40	.25	☐☐☐☐☐
1984	A1369	20c	*New York*	.40	.25	☐☐☐☐☐
1985	A1370	20c	*North Carolina*	.40	.25	☐☐☐☐☐
1986	A1371	20c	*North Dakota*	.40	.25	☐☐☐☐☐
1987	A1372	20c	*Ohio*	.40	.25	☐☐☐☐☐
1988	A1373	20c	*Oklahoma*	.40	.25	☐☐☐☐☐
1989	A1374	20c	*Oregon*	.40	.25	☐☐☐☐☐
1990	A1375	20c	*Pennsylvania*	.40	.25	☐☐☐☐☐
1991	A1376	20c	*Rhode Island*	.40	.25	☐☐☐☐☐
1992	A1377	20c	*South Carolina*	.40	.25	☐☐☐☐☐
1993	A1378	20c	*South Dakota*	.40	.25	☐☐☐☐☐
1994	A1379	20c	*Tennessee*	.40	.25	☐☐☐☐☐
1995	A1380	20c	*Texas*	.40	.25	☐☐☐☐☐
1996	A1381	20c	*Utah*	.40	.25	☐☐☐☐☐
1997	A1382	20c	*Vermont*	.40	.25	☐☐☐☐☐
1998	A1383	20c	*Virginia*	.40	.25	☐☐☐☐☐
1999	A1384	20c	*Washington*	.40	.25	☐☐☐☐☐
2000	A1385	20c	*West Virginia*	.40	.25	☐☐☐☐☐
2001	A1386	20c	*Wisconsin*	.40	.25	☐☐☐☐☐
2002	A1387	20c	*Wyoming*	.40	.25	☐☐☐☐☐
2002a			1953-2002a, single, perf. 11	.40	.25	☐☐☐☐☐
2002b			Sheet of 50, perf. 10½ x 11	21.00	—	☐☐☐☐☐
2002c			**Sheet of 50, perf. 11**	25.00	—	☐☐☐☐☐
2003	A1388	20c	vermilion, bright blue & gray black	.40	.05	☐☐☐☐☐
2004	A1389	20c	red & black	.40	.05	☐☐☐☐☐
2005	A1390	20c	sky blue, coil	.40	.05	☐☐☐☐☐
2006	A1391	20c	multi	.40	.08	☐☐☐☐☐
2007	A1392	20c	multi	.40	.08	☐☐☐☐☐
2008	A1393	20c	multi	.40	.08	☐☐☐☐☐
2009	A1394	20c	multi	.40	.08	☐☐☐☐☐
2009a			Block of 4, #2006-2009	1.60	.85	☐☐☐☐☐
2010	A1395	20c	red & black, *tan*	.40	.05	☐☐☐☐☐
2011	A1396	20c	brown	.40	.05	☐☐☐☐☐
2012	A1397	20c	multi	.40	.05	☐☐☐☐☐
2013	A1398	20c	multi	.40	.05	☐☐☐☐☐
2014	A1399	20c	multi	.40	.05	☐☐☐☐☐
2015	A1400	20c	red & black	.40	.05	☐☐☐☐☐
2016	A1401	20c	multi	.40	.05	☐☐☐☐☐
2017	A1402	20c	multi	.40	.05	☐☐☐☐☐
2018	A1403	20c	multi	.40	.05	☐☐☐☐☐
2019	A1404	20c	black & brown	.40	.08	☐☐☐☐☐
2020	A1405	20c	black & brown	.40	.08	☐☐☐☐☐
2021	A1406	20c	black & brown	.40	.08	☐☐☐☐☐
2022	A1407	20c	black & brown	.40	.08	☐☐☐☐☐
2022a			Block of 4, #2019-2022	1.60	.85	☐☐☐☐☐
2023	A1408	20c	multi	.40	.05	☐☐☐☐☐
2024	A1409	20c	multi	.40	.05	☐☐☐☐☐
2025	A1410	13c	multi	.26	.05	☐☐☐☐☐

A1408

A1409

A1411

A1410

A1416

A1412

A1413

A1414

A1415

A1421

A1422

A1418

A1417

A1419

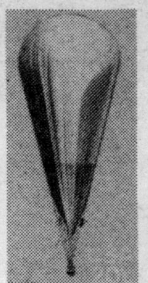
A1420

A1423

A1429

A1431

A1432

A1424

A1425

A1426

A1427

A1428

A1430

A1438

A1437

A1433 A1434

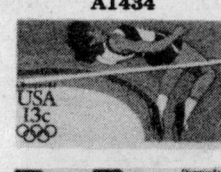

A1435 A1436

A1440 A1441

A1442 A1443

Scott® No.	Illus No.	Denom	Description	Unused Price	Used Price	/ / / / / /
2026	A1411	20c	multi	.40	.05	☐☐☐☐☐
2027	A1412	20c	multi	.40	.05	☐☐☐☐☐
2028	A1413	20c	multi	.40	.05	☐☐☐☐☐
2029	A1414	20c	multi	.40	.05	☐☐☐☐☐
2030	A1415	20c	multi	.40	.05	☐☐☐☐☐
2030a			Block of 4, #2027-2030	1.60	.85	☐☐☐☐☐
1983						
2031	A1416	20c	multi	.40	.05	☐☐☐☐☐
2032	A1417	20c	multi	.40	.08	☐☐☐☐☐
2033	A1418	20c	multi	.40	.08	☐☐☐☐☐
2034	A1419	20c	multi	.40	.08	☐☐☐☐☐
2035	A1420	20c	multi	.40	.08	☐☐☐☐☐
2035a			Block of 4, #2032-2035	1.60	.85	☐☐☐☐☐
2036	A1421	20c	multi	.40	.05	☐☐☐☐☐
2037	A1422	20c	multi	.40	.05	☐☐☐☐☐
2038	A1423	20c	multi	.40	.05	☐☐☐☐☐
2039	A1424	20c	red & black	.40	.05	☐☐☐☐☐
2040	A1425	20c	brown	.40	.05	☐☐☐☐☐
2041	A1426	20c	blue	.40	.05	☐☐☐☐☐
2042	A1427	20c	multi	.40	.05	☐☐☐☐☐
2043	A1428	20c	multi	.40	.05	☐☐☐☐☐
2044	A1429	20c	multi	.40	.05	☐☐☐☐☐
2045	A1430	20c	multi	.40	.05	☐☐☐☐☐
2046	A1431	20c	blue	.40	.05	☐☐☐☐☐
2047	A1432	20c	multi	.40	.05	☐☐☐☐☐
2048	A1433	13c	multi	.26	.05	☐☐☐☐☐
2049	A1434	13c	multi	.26	.05	☐☐☐☐☐
2050	A1435	13c	multi	.26	.05	☐☐☐☐☐
2051	A1436	13c	multi	.26	.05	☐☐☐☐☐
2051a			Block of 4, #2048-2051	1.05	.65	☐☐☐☐☐
2052	A1437	20c	multi	.40	.05	☐☐☐☐☐
2053	A1438	20c	multi	.40	.05	☐☐☐☐☐
2054	A1439	20c	yellow & maroon	.40	.05	☐☐☐☐☐
2055	A1440	20c	orange & black	.40	.08	☐☐☐☐☐
2056	A1441	20c	orange & black	.40	.08	☐☐☐☐☐
2057	A1442	20c	orange & black	.40	.08	☐☐☐☐☐
2058	A1443	20c	orange & black	.40	.08	☐☐☐☐☐
2058a			Block of 4, #2055-2058	1.60	.85	☐☐☐☐☐
2059	A1444	20c	multi	.40	.08	☐☐☐☐☐
2060	A1445	20c	multi	.40	.08	☐☐☐☐☐
2061	A1446	20c	multi	.40	.08	☐☐☐☐☐
2062	A1447	20c	multi	.40	.08	☐☐☐☐☐
2062a			Block of 4, #2059-2062	1.60	.85	☐☐☐☐☐
2063	A1448	20c	multi	.40	.05	☐☐☐☐☐
2064	A1449	20c	multi	.40	.05	☐☐☐☐☐
2065	A1450	20c	multi	.40	.05	☐☐☐☐☐

A1439

A1448

A1449

A1444 A1445

A1446 A1447

A1450

A1452 A1453

A1451

A1456

A1454 A1455

A1457

168

A1458

A1461 A1462

A1463 A1464

A1459

A1460

A1467 A1468

A1469 A1470

A1466

A1473

A1474

A1465

A1471

A1472

169

A1475

A1476

A1477

A1478

A1479

A1480

A1481

A1482

A1483

A1484

A1485 A1486

Scott® No.	Illus No.	Denom	Description	Unused Price	Used Price	/ / / / / /
1984						
2066	A1451	20c multi		.40	.05	☐☐☐☐☐
2067	A1452	20c multi		.40	.08	☐☐☐☐☐
2068	A1453	20c multi		.40	.08	☐☐☐☐☐
2069	A1454	20c multi		.40	.08	☐☐☐☐☐
2070	A1455	20c multi		.40	.08	☐☐☐☐☐
2070a			Block of 4, #2067-2070	1.60	.85	☐☐☐☐☐
2071	A1456	20c multi		.40	.05	■☐☐☐☐
2072	A1457	20c multi		.40	.05	☐☐☐☐☐
2073	A1458	20c multi		.40	.05	☐☐☐☐☐
2074	A1459	20c multi		.40	.05	☐☐☐☐☐
2075	A1460	20c multi		.40	.05	☐☐☐☐☐
2076	A1461	20c multi		.40	.08	☐☐☐☐☐
2077	A1462	20c multi		.40	.08	☐☐☐☐☐
2078	A1463	20c multi		.40	.08	☐☐☐☐☐
2079	A1464	20c multi		.40	.08	☐☐☐☐☐
2079a			Block of 4, #2076-2079	1.60	.85	☐☐☐☐☐
2080	A1465	20c multi		.40	.05	☐☐☐☐☐
2081	A1466	20c multi		.40	.05	☐☐☐☐☐
2082	A1467	20c multi		.40	.08	☐☐☐☐☐
2083	A1468	20c multi		.40	.08	☐☐☐☐☐
2084	A1469	20c multi		.40	.08	☐☐☐☐☐
2085	A1470	20c multi		.40	.08	☐☐☐☐☐
2085a			Block of 4, #2082-2085	1.60	.85	☐☐☐☐☐
2086	A1471	20c multi		.40	.05	☐☐☐☐☐
2087	A1472	20c multi		.40	.05	☐☐☐☐☐
2088	A1473	20c multi		.40	.05	☐☐☐☐☐
2089	A1474	20c brown		.40	.05	☐☐☐☐☐
2090	A1475	20c multi		.40	.05	☐☐☐☐☐
2091	A1476	20c multi		.40	.05	☐☐☐☐☐
2092	A1477	20c blue		.40	.05	☐☐☐☐☐
2093	A1478	20c multi		.40	.05	☐☐☐☐☐
2094	A1479	20c sage green		.40	.05	☐☐☐☐☐
2095	A1480	20c orange & dark brown		.40	.05	☐☐☐☐☐
2096	A1481	20c multi		.40	.05	☐☐☐☐☐
2097	A1482	20c multi		.40	.05	☐☐☐☐☐
2098	A1483	20c multi		.40	.08	☐☐☐☐☐
2099	A1484	20c multi		.40	.08	■☐☐☐☐
2100	A1485	20c multi		.40	.08	☐☐☐☐☐
2101	A1486	20c multi		.40	.08	☐☐☐☐☐
2101a			Block of 4, #2098-2101	1.60	.85	☐☐☐☐☐

Scott® No.	Illus No.	Description	Unused Price	Used Price	//////

Scott® No.	Illus No.	Description	Unused Price	Used Price	/ / / / /

 AP1
 AP2
 AP3
 AP4
 AP5
 AP6
 AP7
 AP8
 AP9
 AP10
 AP11
 AP12
 AP13
 AP14
 AP15

AIR POST STAMPS

For prepayment of postage on all mailable matter sent by airmail.

Scott® No.	Illus No.	Description	Unused Price	Used Price	/ / / / / /
1918					
C1	AP1	6c orange	130.00	45.00	☐☐☐☐☐
C2	AP1	16c green	175.00	52.50	☐☐☐☐☐
C3	AP1	24c carmine rose & blue	175.00	65.00	☐☐☐☐☐
C3a		Center inverted	110000.00		☐☐☐☐☐
1923					
C4	AP2	8c dk green	55.00	20.00	☐☐☐☐☐
C5	AP3	16c dk blue	175.00	50.00	☐☐☐☐☐
C6	AP4	24c carmine	225.00	40.00	☐☐☐☐☐
1926-28		(Perf. 11)			
C7	AP5	10c dk blue	6.00	.50	☐☐☐☐☐
C8	AP5	15c olive brown	7.00	2.75	☐☐☐☐☐
C9	AP5	20c yellow green ('27)	20.00	2.25	☐☐☐☐☐
C10	AP6	10c dk blue	15.00	3.00	☐☐☐☐☐
C10a		Booklet pane of 3	140.00	60.00	☐☐☐☐☐
C11	AP7	5c carmine & blue	7.50	.65	☐☐☐☐☐
C12	AP8	5c violet	18.50	.45	☐☐☐☐☐
1930					
C13	AP9	65c green	450.00	350.00	☐☐☐☐☐
C14	AP10	$1.30 brown	1000.00	650.00	☐☐☐☐☐
C15	AP11	$2.60 blue	1650.00	1000.00	☐☐☐☐☐
1931-32		*Perf. 10½x11*			
C16	AP8	5c violet	10.00	.50	☐☐☐☐☐
C17	AP8	8c olive bister ('32)	4.00	.30	☐☐☐☐☐
1933					
C18	AP12	50c green	150.00	125.00	☐☐☐☐☐
1934					
C19	AP8	6c dl orange	4.50	.12	☐☐☐☐☐
1935					
C20	AP13	25c blue	2.50	1.75	☐☐☐☐☐
1937					
C21	AP14	20c green	20.00	2.25	☐☐☐☐☐
C22	AP14	50c carmine	19.00	6.50	☐☐☐☐☐
1938					
C23	AP15	6c dk blue & carmine	.65	.06	☐☐☐☐☐
1939					
C24	AP16	30c dl blue	19.00	1.50	☐☐☐☐☐
1941-1944					
C25	AP17	6c carmine	.18	.05	☐☐☐☐☐
C25a		Booklet pane of 3 ('43)	6.50	1.00	☐☐☐☐☐
C26	AP17	8c olive green ('44)	.25	.05	☐☐☐☐☐
C27	AP17	10c violet	2.00	.20	☐☐☐☐☐
C28	AP17	15c brown carmine	4.50	.35	☐☐☐☐☐
C29	AP17	20c bright green	3.25	.30	☐☐☐☐☐

AP16

AP17

AP19

AP18

AP20

AP21

AP22

AP24

AP23

AP25

AP26

AP27

AP28

AP29

AP30

Scott® No.	Illus No.	Description	Unused Price	Used Price / / / / / /
C30	AP17	30c blue	4.00	.30 ☐☐☐☐☐
C31	AP17	50c orange	22.50	4.00 ☐☐☐☐☐

1946
Perf. 10½x11.

C32	AP18	5c carmine	.12	.05 ☐☐☐☐☐

1947

C33	AP19	5c carmine	.12	.05 ☐☐☐☐☐
C34	AP20	10c black	.30	.06 ☐☐☐☐☐
C35	AP21	15c bright blue green	.35	.05 ☐☐☐☐☐
C36	AP22	25c blue	1.60	.12 ☐☐☐☐☐

1948
Coil Stamp. *Perf. 10 Horizontally*

C37	AP19	5c carmine	2.00	1.10 ☐☐☐☐☐

1948

C38	AP23	5c bright carmine	.18	.18 ☐☐☐☐☐

1949
Perf. 10½x11.

C39	AP19	6c carmine	.18	.05 ☐☐☐☐☐
C39a		Bklt. pane of 6	13.50	5.00 ☐☐☐☐☐

1949

C40	AP24	6c carmine	.18	.10 ☐☐☐☐☐

Coil Stamp. *Perf. 10 Horizontally.*

C41	AP19	6c carmine	4.50	.05 ☐☐☐☐☐

1949

C42	AP25	10c violet	.35	.35 ☐☐☐☐☐
C43	AP26	15c ultra	.50	.50 ☐☐☐☐☐
C44	AP27	25c rose carmine	.85	.85 ☐☐☐☐☐
C45	AP28	6c magenta	.20	.10 ☐☐☐☐☐

1952-58

C46	AP29	80c bright red violet	12.50	1.50 ☐☐☐☐☐
C47	AP30	6c carmine	.16	.10 ☐☐☐☐☐
C48	AP31	4c bright blue	.12	.08 ☐☐☐☐☐
C49	AP32	6c blue	.20	.10 ☐☐☐☐☐
C50	AP31	5c rose red	.22	.15 ☐☐☐☐☐

Perf. 10½x11

C51	AP33	7c blue	.22	.05 ☐☐☐☐☐
C51a		Bklt. pane of 6	16.50	6.50 ☐☐☐☐☐

Coil Stamp *Perf. 10 Horizontally*

C52	AP33	7c blue	4.50	.20 ☐☐☐☐☐
C53	AP34	7c dk blue	.25	.12 ☐☐☐☐☐
C54	AP35	7c dk blue & red	.25	.12 ☐☐☐☐☐
C55	AP36	7c rose red	.25	.12 ☐☐☐☐☐
C56	AP37	10c violet blue & bright red	.40	.40 ☐☐☐☐☐

1959-66

C57	AP38	10c black & green ('60)	3.00	1.00 ☐☐☐☐☐
C58	AP39	15c black & orange	.75	.06 ☐☐☐☐☐
C59	AP40	25c black & maroon ('60)	.75	.06 ☐☐☐☐☐
C59a		Tagged ('66)	.75	.15 ☐☐☐☐☐

AP31   AP32   AP33

AP34   AP35   AP36

AP38   AP37   AP39

AP40   AP42   AP41-Redrawn

AP43   AP45   AP44

AP46   AP47

178

Scott® No.	Illus No.	Description	Unused Price	Used Price	/////
		Perf. 10½x11			
C60	AP33	7c carmine	.30	.05	☐☐☐☐☐
C60a		Booklet pane of 6	22.50	7.00	☐☐☐☐☐
		Coil Stamp *Perf. 10 Horizontally*			
C61	AP33	7c carmine	8.00	.25	☐☐☐☐☐

1961-67

C62	AP38	13c black & red	.65	.10	☐☐☐☐☐
C62a		Tagged ('67)	.80	.25	☐☐☐☐☐
C63	AP41	15c black & orange	.40	.08	☐☐☐☐☐
C63a		Tagged ('67)	.50	.12	☐☐☐☐☐
		Perf. 10½x11			
C64	AP42	8c carmine	.22	.05	☐☐☐☐☐
C64a		Tagged ('63)	.22	.05	☐☐☐☐☐
C64b		Bklt. pane 5 + label	7.50	1.25	☐☐☐☐☐
C64c		As "b," tagged ('64)	2.25	.50	☐☐☐☐☐
		Coil Stamp *Perf. 10 Horizontally*			
C65	AP42	8c carmine	.50	.08	☐☐☐☐☐
C65a		Tagged ('65)	.60	.10	☐☐☐☐☐
C66	AP43	15c carmine, dp claret & blue	1.40	.75	☐☐☐☐☐
C67	AP44	6c red	.20	.15	☐☐☐☐☐
C67a		Tagged ('67)	3.00	.50	☐☐☐☐☐
C68	AP45	8c carmine & maroon	.40	.15	☐☐☐☐☐
C69	AP46	8c blue, red & bister	1.20	.15	☐☐☐☐☐
C70	AP47	8c brown	.45	.20	☐☐☐☐☐
C71	AP48	20c multi	1.50	.15	☐☐☐☐☐

1968

		Perf. 11x10½			
C72	AP49	10c carmine	.30	.05	☐☐☐☐☐
C72b		Booklet pane of 8	4.00	.75	☐☐☐☐☐
C72c		Booklet pane of 5 + label	2.50	.75	☐☐☐☐☐
		Coil Stamp *Perf. 10 Vertically*			
C73	AP49	10c carmine	.50	.05	☐☐☐☐☐
C74	AP50	10c blue, black & red	.60	.15	☐☐☐☐☐
C75	AP51	20c red, blue & black	1.00	.06	☐☐☐☐☐

1969

C76	AP52	10c multi	.30	.15	☐☐☐☐☐

1971-73

C77	AP53	9c red	.22	.15	☐☐☐☐☐
C78	AP54	11c carmine, Perf. 11 x 10½	.30	.05	☐☐☐☐☐
C78a		Booklet pane of 4 + 2 labels	1.50	.40	☐☐☐☐☐
C78b		Untagged (Bureau precanceled)		.25	☐☐☐☐☐
C79	AP55	13c carmine ('73)	.32	.10	☐☐☐☐☐
C79a		Booklet pane of 5 + label ('73)	1.35	.70	☐☐☐☐☐
C79b		Untagged (Bureau precanceled)		.30	☐☐☐☐☐

AP50

AP48

AP51

AP49

AP52

AP53

AP54

AP55

AP56

AP57

AP58

AP59

AP60

AP61

AP62

AP63

AP70

AP64 **AP66** **AP68**

AP71

AP65 **AP67** **AP69**

AP72 **AP73**

AP74

AP75

AP76

AP77

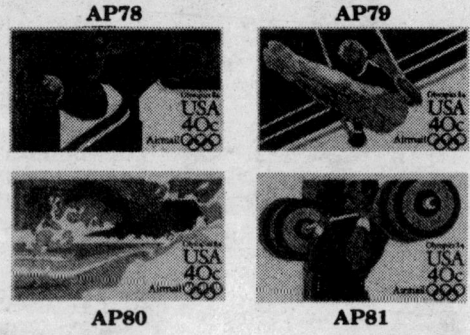

Scott® No.	Illus No.	Description	Unused Price	Used Price	/////
1971-73					
C80	AP56	17c bluish black, red & dk green	.55	.15	☐☐☐☐☐
C81	AP51	21c red, blue & black	.55	.10	☐☐☐☐☐
		Rotary Press Printing	*Perf. 10 Vertically*		
C82	AP54	11c carmine	.40	.06	☐☐☐☐☐
C83	AP55	13c carmine ('73)	.40	.10	☐☐☐☐☐
1972-74					
C84	AP57	11c orange & multi	.30	.15	☐☐☐☐☐
C85	AP58	11c multi	.30	.15	☐☐☐☐☐
C86	AP59	11c rose lilac & multi	.30	.15	☐☐☐☐☐
C87	AP60	18c carmine, black & ultra	.45	.45	☐☐☐☐☐
C88	AP61	26c ultra, black & carmine	.60	.15	☐☐☐☐☐
1976					
C89	AP62	25c ultra, red & black	.60	.18	☐☐☐☐☐
C90	AP63	31c ultra, red & black	.62	.10	☐☐☐☐☐
1978					
C91	AP64	31c ultra & multi	.85	.15	☐☐☐☐☐
C92	AP65	31c ultra & multi	.85	.15	☐☐☐☐☐
C92a		Pair, #C91-C92	1.75	.65	☐☐☐☐☐
1979					
C93	AP66	21c ultra & multi	.85	.32	☐☐☐☐☐
C94	AP67	21c ultra & multi	.85	.32	☐☐☐☐☐
C94a		Pair, #C93-C94	1.75	.75	☐☐☐☐☐
C95	AP68	25c ultra & multi	.85	.35	☐☐☐☐☐
C96	AP69	25c ultra & multi	.85	.35	☐☐☐☐☐
C96a		Pair, #C95-C96	1.75	.85	☐☐☐☐☐
C97	AP70	31c multi	.70	.30	☐☐☐☐☐
1980					
C98	AP71	40c multi	.90	.30	☐☐☐☐☐
C99	AP72	28c multi	.70	.15	☐☐☐☐☐
C100	AP73	35c multi	.70	.15	☐☐☐☐☐
C101	AP74	28c Gymnast	.56	.28	☐☐☐☐☐
C102	AP75	28c Hurdler	.56	.28	☐☐☐☐☐
C103	AP76	28c Basketball	.56	.28	☐☐☐☐☐
C104	AP77	28c Soccer	.56	.28	☐☐☐☐☐
C104a		Block of 4, #C101-C104	2.25	2.00	☐☐☐☐☐
C105	AP78	40c Shot put	.80	.40	☐☐☐☐☐
C106	AP79	40c Gymnast	.80	.40	☐☐☐☐☐
C107	AP80	40c Swimmer	.80	.40	☐☐☐☐☐
C108	AP81	40c Weightlifting	.80	.40	☐☐☐☐☐
C108a		Block of 4, #C105-C108	3.25	2.75	☐☐☐☐☐
C109	AP82	35c multi	.70	.35	☐☐☐☐☐
C110	AP83	35c multi	.70	.35	☐☐☐☐☐
C111	AP84	35c multi	.70	.35	☐☐☐☐☐
C112	AP85	35c multi	.70	.35	☐☐☐☐☐
C112a		Block of 4, #C109-C112	3.00	1.85	☐☐☐☐☐

Scott® No.	Illus No.	Description	Unused Price	Used Price	/ / / / / /

Scott® No.	Illus No.	Description	Unused Price	Used Price	//////
					☐☐☐☐☐

ASPD1

SD1

SD2

SD3

SD4

SD5

SD6

SD7

SD8

SD9

Scott® No.	Illus No.	Description	Unused Price	Used Price	//////

AIR POSTAGE SPECIAL DELIVERY

1934
CE1	APSD1	16c dk blue	1.00	.95	☐☐☐☐☐
CE2	APSD1	16c red & blue	.50	.25	☐☐☐☐☐

SPECIAL DELIVERY STAMPS

1885-93
E1	SD1	10c blue	275.00	30.00	☐☐☐☐☐
E2	SD2	10c blue	275.00	7.50	☐☐☐☐☐
E3	SD2	10c orange	185.00	14.00	☐☐☐☐☐

1894 — Line under "Ten Cents".
E4	SD3	10c blue	775.00	17.50	☐☐☐☐☐

1895 — Wmkd. USPS (191)
E5	SD3	10c blue	150.00	2.50	☐☐☐☐☐

1902
E6	SD4	10c ultra	100.00	2.50	☐☐☐☐☐

1908
E7	SD5	10c green	65.00	27.50	☐☐☐☐☐

1911 — Wmkd. USPS (190) Perf. 12
E8	SD4	10c ultra	100.00	4.00	☐☐☐☐☐

1914 — Perf. 10
E9	SD4	10c ultra	200.00	5.25	☐☐☐☐☐

1916 — Perf. 10. Unwmkd.
E10	SD4	10c pale ultra	350.00	21.00	☐☐☐☐☐

1917-25 — Perf. 11
E11	SD4	10c ultra	17.00	.30	☐☐☐☐☐
E12	SD6	10c gray violet	27.50	.15	☐☐☐☐☐
E13	SD6	15c dp orange	21.00	.65	☐☐☐☐☐
E14	SD7	20c black	3.50	1.75	☐☐☐☐☐

1927-51 — Perf. 11x10½
E15	SD6	10c gray violet	.70	.05	☐☐☐☐☐
E16	SD6	15c orange	.80	.08	☐☐☐☐☐
E17	SD6	13c blue	.65	.06	☐☐☐☐☐
E18	SD6	17c orange yellow	5.00	2.25	☐☐☐☐☐
E19	SD7	20c black	2.00	.12	☐☐☐☐☐

1954-57
E20	SD8	20c dp blue	.60	.08	☐☐☐☐☐
E21	SD8	30c lake ('57)	.90	.05	☐☐☐☐☐

1969-71
E22	SD9	45c carmine & violet blue	2.25	.20	☐☐☐☐☐
E23	SD9	60c violet blue & carmine ('71)	1.20	.12	☐☐☐☐☐

REGISTRATION STAMP
CERTIFIED MAIL STAMP

RS1

CM1

Scott® No.	Illus No.	Description	Unused Price	Used Price	//////
1911	Wmkd.	USPS (190) Engraved.			
F1	RS1	10c ultra	85.00	4.50	☐☐☐☐☐
1955					
FA1	CM1	15c red	.50	.30	☐☐☐☐☐

POSTAGE DUE STAMPS

D1

D2

D3

D4

D5

Scott® No.	Illus No.	Description	Unused Price	Used Price	//////
1879		*Perf. 12.*			
J1	D1	1c brown	22.50	5.00	☐☐☐☐☐
J2	D1	2c brown	150.00	4.00	☐☐☐☐☐
J3	D1	3c brown	17.50	2.50	☐☐☐☐☐
J4	D1	5c brown	225.00	20.00	☐☐☐☐☐
J5	D1	10c brown	300.00	8.00	☐☐☐☐☐
J6	D1	30c brown	125.00	20.00	☐☐☐☐☐
J7	D1	50c brown	190.00	30.00	☐☐☐☐☐

Scott® No.	Illus No.	Description	Unused Price	Used Price	/ / / / / /
1879		Special Printing.			
J8	D1	1c dp brown	5000.00		☐☐☐☐☐
J9	D1	2c dp brown	3250.00		☐☐☐☐☐
J10	D1	3c dp brown	3000.00		☐☐☐☐☐
J11	D1	5c dp brown	2500.00		☐☐☐☐☐
J12	D1	10c dp brown	1450.00		☐☐☐☐☐
J13	D1	30c dp brown	1450.00		☐☐☐☐☐
J14	D1	50c dp brown	1450.00		☐☐☐☐☐
1884-89					
J15	D1	1c red brown	25.00	2.50	☐☐☐☐☐
J16	D1	2c red brown	32.50	2.50	☐☐☐☐☐
J17	D1	3c red brown	400.00	75.00	☐☐☐☐☐
J18	D1	5c red brown	185.00	7.25	☐☐☐☐☐
J19	D1	10c red brown ('87)	140.00	3.50	☐☐☐☐☐
J20	D1	30c red brown	80.00	20.00	☐☐☐☐☐
J21	D1	50c red brown	900.00	110.00	☐☐☐☐☐
1891-93					
J22	D1	1c bright claret	7.50	.50	☐☐☐☐☐
J23	D1	2c bright claret	10.00	.45	☐☐☐☐☐
J24	D1	3c bright claret	22.50	2.75	☐☐☐☐☐
J25	D1	5c bright claret	25.00	2.75	☐☐☐☐☐
J26	D1	10c bright claret	50.00	6.50	☐☐☐☐☐
J27	D1	30c bright claret	200.00	70.00	☐☐☐☐☐
J28	D1	50c bright claret	225.00	75.00	☐☐☐☐☐
1894					
J29	D2	1c vermilion	400.00	65.00	☐☐☐☐☐
J30	D2	2c vermilion	175.00	27.50	☐☐☐☐☐
J31	D2	1c dp claret	15.00	3.00	☐☐☐☐☐
J32	D2	2c dp claret	12.50	1.75	☐☐☐☐☐
J33	D2	3c dp claret	50.00	15.00	☐☐☐☐☐
J34	D2	5c dp claret	55.00	20.00	☐☐☐☐☐
J35	D2	10c dp claret	50.00	10.00	☐☐☐☐☐
J36	D2	30c dp claret	175.00	40.00	☐☐☐☐☐
J36a		30c carmine	160.00	37.50	☐☐☐☐☐
J36b		30c pale rose	150.00	37.50	☐☐☐☐☐
J37	D2	50c dp claret	400.00	85.00	☐☐☐☐☐
J37a		50c pale rose	350.00	80.00	☐☐☐☐☐
1895		Wmkd. USPS (191)			
J38	D2	1c dp claret	4.00	.30	☐☐☐☐☐
J39	D2	2c dp claret	4.00	.20	☐☐☐☐☐
J40	D2	3c dp claret	25.00	1.00	☐☐☐☐☐
J41	D2	5c dp claret	25.00	1.00	☐☐☐☐☐
J42	D2	10c dp claret	27.50	2.00	☐☐☐☐☐
J43	D2	30c dp claret	225.00	15.00	☐☐☐☐☐
J44	D2	50c dp claret	150.00	16.50	☐☐☐☐☐

Scott® No.	Illus No.	Description	Unused Price	Used Price	/ / / / / /
1910-12		Wmkd. USPS (190)			
J45	D2	1c dp claret	17.50	2.00 ☐☐☐☐☐
J45a		1c rose carmine	16.00	1.75 ☐☐☐☐☐
J46	D2	2c dp claret	17.50	.15 ☐☐☐☐☐
J46a		2c rose carmine	16.00	.15 ☐☐☐☐☐
J47	D2	3c dp claret	300.00	10.00 ☐☐☐☐☐
J48	D2	5c dp claret	40.00	2.50 ☐☐☐☐☐
J49	D2	10c dp claret	45.00	6.00 ☐☐☐☐☐
J50	D2	50c dp claret ('12)	550.00	55.00 ☐☐☐☐☐
1914-15		*Perf. 10.*			
J52	D2	1c carmine lake	35.00	6.00 ☐☐☐☐☐
J53	D2	2c carmine lake	20.00	.20 ☐☐☐☐☐
J53a		2c dl rose	20.00	.20 ☐☐☐☐☐
J53b		2c vermilion	20.00	.20 ☐☐☐☐☐
J54	D2	3c carmine lake	325.00	8.50 ☐☐☐☐☐
J55	D2	5c carmine lake	17.50	1.50 ☐☐☐☐☐
J56	D2	10c carmine lake	27.50	.85 ☐☐☐☐☐
J56a		10c dl rose	27.50	.85 ☐☐☐☐☐
J57	D2	30c carmine lake	125.00	12.00 ☐☐☐☐☐
J58	D2	50c carmine lake	4500.00	300.00 ☐☐☐☐☐
1916		*Perf. 10* Unwmkd.			
J59	D2	1c rose	800.00	130.00 ☐☐☐☐☐
J60	D2	2c rose	60.00	3.00 ☐☐☐☐☐
1917		*Perf. 11*			
J61	D2	1c carmine rose	1.50	.08 ☐☐☐☐☐
J62	D2	2c carmine rose	1.25	.05 ☐☐☐☐☐
J63	D2	3c carmine rose	6.50	.08 ☐☐☐☐☐
J63a		3c rose red	6.50	.07 ☐☐☐☐☐
J63b		3c dp claret	7.50	.25 ☐☐☐☐☐
J64	D2	5c carmine	6.50	.08 ☐☐☐☐☐
J64a		5c rose red	6.50	.08 ☐☐☐☐☐
J64b		5c dp claret	6.50	.05 ☐☐☐☐☐
J65	D2	10c carmine rose	9.00	.20 ☐☐☐☐☐
J65a		10c rose red	9.00	.06 ☐☐☐☐☐
J65b		10c dp claret	9.00	.06 ☐☐☐☐☐
J66	D2	30c carmine rose	45.00	.40 ☐☐☐☐☐
J66a		30c dp claret	45.00	.40 ☐☐☐☐☐
J67	D2	50c carmine rose	60.00	.12 ☐☐☐☐☐
J68	D2	½c dl red	.50	.06 ☐☐☐☐☐
1930-31		*Perf. 11*			
J69	D3	½c carmine	3.50	.70 ☐☐☐☐☐
J70	D3	1c carmine	2.50	.15 ☐☐☐☐☐
J71	D3	2c carmine	3.50	.15 ☐☐☐☐☐
J72	D3	3c carmine	20.00	1.00 ☐☐☐☐☐
J73	D3	5c carmine	20.00	1.50 ☐☐☐☐☐
J74	D3	10c carmine	35.00	.50 ☐☐☐☐☐
J75	D3	30c carmine	120.00	1.00 ☐☐☐☐☐

Scott® No.	Illus No.	Description	Unused Price	Used Price	/////
1930-31					
J76	D3	50c carmine	135.00	.30	☐☐☐☐☐
J77	D4	$1 carmine	30.00	.06	☐☐☐☐☐
J77a		$1 scarlet	25.00	.06	☐☐☐☐☐
J78	D4	$5 carmine	45.00	.12	☐☐☐☐☐
J78a		$5 scarlet	40.00	.12	☐☐☐☐☐
1931-56		*Perf. 11x10½.*	*Perf. 10½x11*		
J79	D3	½c dl carmine	1.25	.08	☐☐☐☐☐
J80	D3	1c dl carmine	.15	.05	☐☐☐☐☐
J81	D3	2c dl carmine	.15	.05	☐☐☐☐☐
J82	D3	3c dl carmine	.25	.05	☐☐☐☐☐
J83	D3	5c dl carmine	.35	.05	☐☐☐☐☐
J84	D3	10c dl carmine	1.10	.05	☐☐☐☐☐
J85	D3	30c dl carmine	8.50	.08	☐☐☐☐☐
J86	D3	50c dl carmine	9.50	.06	☐☐☐☐☐
J87	D4	$1 scarlet ('56)	45.00	.20	☐☐☐☐☐
1959					
J88	D5	½c carmine rose	1.25	.85	☐☐☐☐☐
J89	D5	1c carmine rose	.05	.05	☐☐☐☐☐
J90	D5	2c carmine rose	.06	.05	☐☐☐☐☐
J91	D5	3c carmine rose	.07	.05	☐☐☐☐☐
J92	D5	4c carmine rose	.08	.05	☐☐☐☐☐
J93	D5	5c carmine rose	.10	.05	☐☐☐☐☐
J94	D5	6c carmine rose	.12	.05	☐☐☐☐☐
J95	D5	7c carmine rose	.14	.06	☐☐☐☐☐
J96	D5	8c carmine rose	.16	.05	☐☐☐☐☐
J97	D5	10c carmine rose	.20	.05	☐☐☐☐☐
J98	D5	30c carmine rose	.70	.05	☐☐☐☐☐
J99	D5	50c carmine rose	1.10	.05	☐☐☐☐☐
J100	D5	$1 carmine rose	2.00	.05	☐☐☐☐☐
J101	D5	$5 carmine rose	8.00	.15	☐☐☐☐☐
1978					
J102	D5	11c carmine rose	.22	.05	☐☐☐☐☐
J103	D5	13c carmine rose	.26	.05	☐☐☐☐☐

U.S. Offices in China

Scott® No.	Illus No.	Description	Unused Price	Used Price	/ / / / / /
		United States Stamps of 1917-19 Surcharged	**SHANGHAI 2¢ CHINA**		
1919					
K1	A140	2c on 1c green	20.00	22.50	☐☐☐☐☐
K2	A140	4c on 2c rose	20.00	22.50	☐☐☐☐☐
K3	A140	6c on 3c violet	37.50	50.00	☐☐☐☐☐
K4	A140	8c on 4c brown	45.00	50.00	☐☐☐☐☐
K5	A140	10c on 5c blue	50.00	57.50	☐☐☐☐☐
K6	A140	12c on 6c red orange	60.00	72.50	☐☐☐☐☐
K7	A140	14c on 7c black	65.00	80.00	☐☐☐☐☐
K8	A148	16c on 8c olive bister	50.00	55.00	☐☐☐☐☐
K8a		16c on 8c olive green	45.00	47.50	☐☐☐☐☐
K9	A148	18c on 9c salmon red	50.00	60.00	☐☐☐☐☐
K10	A148	20c on 10c orange yellow	45.00	52.50	☐☐☐☐☐
K11	A148	24c on 12c brown carmine	52.50	62.50	☐☐☐☐☐
K12	A148	30c on 15c gray	65.00	80.00	☐☐☐☐☐
K13	A148	40c on 20c dp ultra	100.00	125.00	☐☐☐☐☐
K14	A148	60c on 30c orange red	90.00	110.00	☐☐☐☐☐
K15	A148	$1 on 50c lt violet	650.00	500.00	☐☐☐☐☐
K16	A148	$2 on $1 violet brown	450.00	450.00	☐☐☐☐☐
		Nos. 498 and 528B Surcharged	**SHANGHAI 2 Cts. CHINA**		
1922					
K17	A140	2c on 1c green	90.00	75.00	☐☐☐☐☐
K18	A140	4c on 2c carmine, Type VII	80.00	70.00	☐☐☐☐☐
....	....				☐☐☐☐☐
....	....				☐☐☐☐☐
....	....				☐☐☐☐☐
....	....				☐☐☐☐☐
....	....				☐☐☐☐☐
....	....				☐☐☐☐☐
....	....				☐☐☐☐☐
....	....				☐☐☐☐☐
....	....				☐☐☐☐☐
....	....				☐☐☐☐☐

HOW TO USE THIS BOOK

The number in the first column is its Scott number or identifying number. The letter and number that come next (A41) indicate the design and refer to the illustration so designated. Following that is the denomination of the stamp and its color. Finally, the price, unused and used is shown.

OFFICIAL STAMPS

1873			**Dept. of Agriculture.**		
O1	O1	1c yellow		55.00	30.00 ☐☐☐☐☐
O2	O1	2c yellow		37.50	13.50 ☐☐☐☐☐
O3	O1	3c yellow		30.00	3.50 ☐☐☐☐☐
O4	O1	6c yellow		40.00	12.50 ☐☐☐☐☐
O5	O1	10c yellow		95.00	47.50 ☐☐☐☐☐
O6	O1	12c yellow		130.00	70.00 ☐☐☐☐☐
O7	O1	15c yellow		130.00	70.00 ☐☐☐☐☐
O8	O1	24c yellow		90.00	47.50 ☐☐☐☐☐
O9	O1	30c yellow		150.00	85.00 ☐☐☐☐☐
			Executive Dept.		
O10	O1	1c carmine		225.00	85.00 ☐☐☐☐☐
O11	O1	2c carmine		150.00	70.00 ☐☐☐☐☐
O12	O1	3c carmine		175.00	60.00 ☐☐☐☐☐
O12a	O1	3c violet rose		150.00	60.00 ☐☐☐☐☐
O13	O1	6c carmine		275.00	140.00 ☐☐☐☐☐
O14	O1	10c carmine		235.00	140.00 ☐☐☐☐☐
			Dept. of the Interior.		
O15	O1	1c vermilion		15.00	2.25 ☐☐☐☐☐
O16	O1	2c vermilion		12.00	1.50 ☐☐☐☐☐
O17	O1	3c vermilion		20.00	1.50 ☐☐☐☐☐

Scott® No.	Illus No.	Description	Unused Price	Used Price	/ / / / / /
1873					
O18	O1	6c vermilion	15.00	1.50	☐☐☐☐☐
O19	O1	10c vermilion	12.50	3.50	☐☐☐☐☐
O20	O1	12c vermilion	18.50	2.50	☐☐☐☐☐
O21	O1	15c vermilion	37.50	7.25	☐☐☐☐☐
O22	O1	24c vermilion	27.50	5.50	☐☐☐☐☐
O23	O1	30c vermilion	37.50	5.75	☐☐☐☐☐
O24	O1	90c vermilion	85.00	12.50	☐☐☐☐☐
		Dept. of Justice.			
O25	O1	1c purple	32.50	17.50	☐☐☐☐☐
O26	O1	2c purple	57.50	20.00	☐☐☐☐☐
O27	O1	3c purple	60.00	7.00	☐☐☐☐☐
O28	O1	6c purple	52.50	10.00	☐☐☐☐☐
O29	O1	10c purple	60.00	25.00	☐☐☐☐☐
O30	O1	12c purple	35.00	12.00	☐☐☐☐☐
O31	O1	15c purple	95.00	47.50	☐☐☐☐☐
O32	O1	24c purple	275.00	120.00	☐☐☐☐☐
O33	O1	30c purple	250.00	85.00	☐☐☐☐☐
O34	O1	90c purple	375.00	175.00	☐☐☐☐☐
		Navy Dept.			
O35	O1	1c ultra	30.00	10.00	☐☐☐☐☐
O36	O1	2c ultra	20.00	8.00	☐☐☐☐☐
O37	O1	3c ultra	24.00	3.00	☐☐☐☐☐
O38	O1	6c ultra	20.00	4.50	☐☐☐☐☐
O39	O1	7c ultra	150.00	60.00	☐☐☐☐☐
O40	O1	10c ultra	26.00	10.00	☐☐☐☐☐
O41	O1	12c ultra	37.50	8.25	☐☐☐☐☐
O42	O1	15c ultra	65.00	22.50	☐☐☐☐☐
O43	O1	24c ultra	65.00	30.00	☐☐☐☐☐
O44	O1	30c ultra	55.00	12.50	☐☐☐☐☐
O45	O1	90c ultra	275.00	80.00	☐☐☐☐☐
		Post Office Dept.			
O47	O6	1c black	7.25	3.00	☐☐☐☐☐
O48	O6	2c black	7.00	2.50	☐☐☐☐☐
O49	O6	3c black	2.50	.75	☐☐☐☐☐
O50	O6	6c black	7.00	1.65	☐☐☐☐☐
O51	O6	10c black	32.50	16.50	☐☐☐☐☐
O52	O6	12c black	17.50	3.75	☐☐☐☐☐
O53	O6	15c black	20.00	6.50	☐☐☐☐☐
O54	O6	24c black	25.00	8.25	☐☐☐☐☐
O55	O6	30c black	25.00	7.00	☐☐☐☐☐
O56	O6	90c black	40.00	11.00	☐☐☐☐☐
		Dept. of State.			
O57	O1	1c dk green	35.00	10.00	☐☐☐☐☐
O58	O1	2c dk green	80.00	25.00	☐☐☐☐☐
O59	O1	3c bright green	30.00	7.50	☐☐☐☐☐

Scott® No.	Illus No.	Description	Unused Price	Used Price	/ / / / / /
1873					
O60	O1	6c bright green	25.00	7.50	☐☐☐☐☐
O61	O1	7c dk green	55.00	15.00	☐☐☐☐☐
O62	O1	10c dk green	35.00	12.50	☐☐☐☐☐
O63	O1	12c dk green	70.00	27.50	☐☐☐☐☐
O64	O1	15c dk green	55.00	15.00	☐☐☐☐☐
O65	O1	24c dk green	150.00	75.00	☐☐☐☐☐
O66	O1	30c dk green	135.00	60.00	☐☐☐☐☐
O67	O1	90c dk green	300.00	120.00	☐☐☐☐☐
O68	O8	$2 green & black	500.00	225.00	☐☐☐☐☐
O69	O8	$5 green & black	4000.00	2000.00	☐☐☐☐☐
O70	O8	$10 green & black	2500.00	1300.00	☐☐☐☐☐
O71	O8	$20 green & black	2150.00	1100.00	☐☐☐☐☐
		Treasury Dept.			
O72	O1	1c brown	12.00	1.75	☐☐☐☐☐
O73	O1	2c brown	18.00	1.75	☐☐☐☐☐
O74	O1	3c brown	10.00	1.00	☐☐☐☐☐
O75	O1	6c brown	17.50	1.00	☐☐☐☐☐
O76	O1	7c brown	35.00	11.00	☐☐☐☐☐
O77	O1	10c brown	35.00	3.50	☐☐☐☐☐
O78	O1	12c brown	35.00	1.50	☐☐☐☐☐
O79	O1	15c brown	35.00	3.25	☐☐☐☐☐
O80	O1	24c brown	165.00	55.00	☐☐☐☐☐
O81	O1	30c brown	50.00	3.25	☐☐☐☐☐
O82	O1	90c brown	55.00	3.00	☐☐☐☐☐
		War Dept.			
O83	O1	1c rose	50.00	3.25	☐☐☐☐☐
O84	O1	2c rose	45.00	5.00	☐☐☐☐☐
O85	O1	3c rose	42.50	1.00	☐☐☐☐☐
O86	O1	6c rose	200.00	4.00	☐☐☐☐☐
O87	O1	7c rose	45.00	25.00	☐☐☐☐☐
O88	O1	10c rose	14.00	3.00	☐☐☐☐☐
O89	O1	12c rose	40.00	2.00	☐☐☐☐☐
O90	O1	15c rose	12.00	1.20	☐☐☐☐☐
O91	O1	24c rose	12.50	1.75	☐☐☐☐☐
O92	O1	30c rose	13.00	1.50	☐☐☐☐☐
O93	O1	90c rose	35.00	10.00	☐☐☐☐☐
1879		**Dept. of Agriculture.**			
O94	O1	1c yellow	1350.00		☐☐☐☐☐
O95	O1	3c yellow	160.00	25.00	☐☐☐☐☐
		Dept. of the Interior.			
O96	O1	1c vermilion	110.00	60.00	☐☐☐☐☐
O97	O1	2c vermilion	2.50	.75	☐☐☐☐☐
O98	O1	3c vermilion	2.00	.60	☐☐☐☐☐
O99	O1	6c vermilion	3.00	1.00	☐☐☐☐☐
O100	O1	10c vermilion	27.50	17.50	☐☐☐☐☐

Scott® No.	Illus No.	Description	Unused Price	Used Price	//////
1879					
O101	O1	12c vermilion	50.00	30.00	☐☐☐☐☐
O102	O1	15c vermilion	115.00	60.00	☐☐☐☐☐
O103	O1	24c vermilion	1000.00		☐☐☐☐☐
		Dept. of Justice.			
O106	O1	3c bluish purple	40.00	17.50	☐☐☐☐☐
O107	O1	6c bluish purple	100.00	60.00	☐☐☐☐☐
		Post Office Dept.			
O108	O6	3c black	6.50	1.40	☐☐☐☐☐
		Treasury Dept.			
O109	O1	3c brown	21.00	2.50	☐☐☐☐☐
O110	O1	6c brown	42.50	17.50	☐☐☐☐☐
O111	O1	10c brown	60.00	15.00	☐☐☐☐☐
O112	O1	30c brown	675.00	135.00	☐☐☐☐☐
O113	O1	90c brown	700.00	135.00	☐☐☐☐☐
		War Dept.			
O114	O1	1c rose red	1.75	.75	☐☐☐☐☐
O115	O1	2c rose red	2.75	1.00	☐☐☐☐☐
O116	O1	3c rose red	2.75	.65	☐☐☐☐☐
O117	O1	6c rose red	2.50	.70	☐☐☐☐☐
O118	O1	10c rose red	13.50	6.00	☐☐☐☐☐
O119	O1	12c rose red	10.00	1.75	☐☐☐☐☐
O120	O1	30c rose red	35.00	25.00	☐☐☐☐☐

Official Postal Savings Mail.

1911 Wmkd. USPS (191)

O121	O11	2c black	9.00	1.10	☐☐☐☐☐
O122	O11	50c dk green	100.00	32.50	☐☐☐☐☐
O123	O11	$1 ultra	95.00	9.50	☐☐☐☐☐

Wmkd. USPS (190)

O124	O11	1c dk violet	4.00	1.00	☐☐☐☐☐
O125	O11	2c black	30.00	3.50	☐☐☐☐☐
O126	O11	10c carmine	8.50	1.00	☐☐☐☐☐
1983					
O127	O12	1c red, blue & black	.05	—	☐☐☐☐☐
O128	O12	4c red, blue & black	.08	—	☐☐☐☐☐
O129	O12	13c red, blue & black	.26	—	☐☐☐☐☐
O130	O12	17c red, blue & black	.34	—	☐☐☐☐☐
O132	O12	$1 red, blue & black	2.00	—	☐☐☐☐☐
O133	O12	$5 red, blue & black	10.00	—	☐☐☐☐☐
		Coil Stamps Perf. 10 Vert.			
O135	O12	20c red, blue & black	.40	—	☐☐☐☐☐
......	......				☐☐☐☐☐
......	......				☐☐☐☐☐
......	......				☐☐☐☐☐

NEWSPAPER STAMPS

Scott® No.	Illus No.	Description	Unused Price	Used Price	/ / / / / /
1865		*Thin Hard Paper, No Gum.*			
PR1	N1	5c dk blue	135.00	—	☐☐☐☐☐
PR2	N2	10c blue green	75.00	—	☐☐☐☐☐
PR3	N3	25c orange red	75.00	—	☐☐☐☐☐
		White Border. *Yellowish Paper.*			
PR4	N1	5c lt blue	30.00	25.00	☐☐☐☐☐
1875		*Hard White Paper, No Gum.*			
PR5	N1	5c dl blue	55.00		☐☐☐☐☐
PR6	N2	10c dk bluish green	32.50		☐☐☐☐☐
PR7	N3	25c dk carmine	65.00		☐☐☐☐☐
1880		*Soft Porous Paper.* *White Border.*			
PR8	N1	5c dk blue	110.00		☐☐☐☐☐
1875		*Thin Hard Paper*			
PR9	N4	2c black	8.00	8.00	☐☐☐☐☐
PR10	N4	3c black	11.00	11.00	☐☐☐☐☐
PR11	N4	4c black	9.00	9.00	☐☐☐☐☐
PR12	N4	6c black	12.50	12.50	☐☐☐☐☐
PR13	N4	8c black	17.50	17.50	☐☐☐☐☐
PR14	N4	9c black	40.00	40.00	☐☐☐☐☐
PR15	N4	10c black	17.50	15.00	☐☐☐☐☐
PR16	N5	12c rose	40.00	30.00	☐☐☐☐☐
PR17	N5	24c rose	50.00	35.00	☐☐☐☐☐
PR18	N5	36c rose	55.00	40.00	☐☐☐☐☐
PR19	N5	48c rose	95.00	55.00	☐☐☐☐☐
PR20	N5	60c rose	50.00	40.00	☐☐☐☐☐
PR21	N5	72c rose	125.00	90.00	☐☐☐☐☐
PR22	N5	84c rose	150.00	95.00	☐☐☐☐☐
PR23	N5	96c rose	110.00	85.00	☐☐☐☐☐
PR24	N6	$1.92 dk brown	130.00	90.00	☐☐☐☐☐
PR25	N7	$3 vermilion	175.00	110.00	☐☐☐☐☐
PR26	N8	$6 ultra	325.00	150.00	☐☐☐☐☐
PR27	N9	$9 yellow	425.00	185.00	☐☐☐☐☐
PR28	N10	$12 blue green	500.00	250.00	☐☐☐☐☐
PR29	N11	$24 dk gray violet	500.00	275.00	☐☐☐☐☐
PR30	N12	$36 brown rose	550.00	325.00	☐☐☐☐☐
PR31	N13	$48 red brown	700.00	425.00	☐☐☐☐☐
PR32	N14	$60 violet	700.00	375.00	☐☐☐☐☐
		Special Printing. *Hard White Paper.* *Without Gum.*			
PR33	N4	2c gray black	60.00		☐☐☐☐☐
PR34	N4	3c gray black	65.00		☐☐☐☐☐
PR35	N4	4c gray black	80.00		☐☐☐☐☐
PR36	N4	6c gray black	110.00		☐☐☐☐☐
PR37	N4	8c gray black	130.00		☐☐☐☐☐
PR38	N4	9c gray black	150.00		☐☐☐☐☐
PR39	N4	10c gray black	185.00		☐☐☐☐☐

N1

N2

N3

N4

N5

N6

N7

N8

N9

N10

N11

N12

N13

N14

Scott® No.	Illus No.	Description	Unused Price	Used Price	/////
1875					
PR40	N5	12c pale rose	210.00		☐☐☐☐☐
PR41	N5	24c pale rose	275.00		☐☐☐☐☐
PR42	N5	36c pale rose	375.00		☐☐☐☐☐
PR43	N5	48c pale rose	425.00		☐☐☐☐☐
PR44	N5	60c pale rose	500.00		☐☐☐☐☐
PR45	N5	72c pale rose	650.00		☐☐☐☐☐
PR46	N5	84c pale rose	675.00		☐☐☐☐☐
PR47	N5	96c pale rose	800.00		☐☐☐☐☐
PR48	N6	$1.92 dk brown	2400.00		☐☐☐☐☐
PR49	N7	$3 vermilion	5000.00		☐☐☐☐☐
PR50	N8	$6 ultra	6000.00		☐☐☐☐☐
PR51	N9	$9 yellow	11000.00		☐☐☐☐☐
PR52	N10	$12 blue green	10000.00		☐☐☐☐☐
PR53	N11	$24 dk gray violet	—		☐☐☐☐☐
PR54	N12	$36 brown rose	—		☐☐☐☐☐
PR55	N13	$48 red brown	—		☐☐☐☐☐
PR56	N14	$60 violet	—		☐☐☐☐☐
1879		*Soft Porous Paper*			
PR57	N4	2c black	4.00	3.50	☐☐☐☐☐
PR58	N4	3c black	5.00	4.50	☐☐☐☐☐
PR59	N4	4c black	5.00	4.50	☐☐☐☐☐
PR60	N4	6c black	10.50	9.00	☐☐☐☐☐
PR61	N4	8c black	10.50	9.00	☐☐☐☐☐
PR62	N4	10c black	10.50	9.00	☐☐☐☐☐
PR63	N5	12c red	30.00	20.00	☐☐☐☐☐
PR64	N5	24c red	30.00	18.50	☐☐☐☐☐
PR65	N5	36c red	110.00	85.00	☐☐☐☐☐
PR66	N5	48c red	80.00	50.00	☐☐☐☐☐
PR67	N5	60c red	60.00	50.00	☐☐☐☐☐
PR68	N5	72c red	145.00	90.00	☐☐☐☐☐
PR69	N5	84c red	110.00	75.00	☐☐☐☐☐
PR70	N5	96c red	80.00	55.00	☐☐☐☐☐
PR71	N6	$1.92 pale brown	65.00	50.00	☐☐☐☐☐
PR72	N7	$3 red vermilion	65.00	50.00	☐☐☐☐☐
PR73	N8	$6 blue	110.00	75.00	☐☐☐☐☐
PR74	N9	$9 orange	70.00	50.00	☐☐☐☐☐
PR75	N10	$12 yellow green	110.00	75.00	☐☐☐☐☐
PR76	N11	$24 dk violet	145.00	100.00	☐☐☐☐☐
PR77	N12	$36 indian red	185.00	120.00	☐☐☐☐☐
PR78	N13	$48 yellow brown	250.00	150.00	☐☐☐☐☐
PR79	N14	$60 purple	275.00	150.00	☐☐☐☐☐
1883		*Special Printing.*			
PR80	N4	2c intense black	130.00		☐☐☐☐☐
1885					
PR81	N4	1c black	5.50	3.50	☐☐☐☐☐
PR82	N5	12c carmine	17.50	8.50	☐☐☐☐☐

N15  N16

N17

N18

N19

N20 N21 N22

HOW TO USE THIS BOOK
The number in the first column is its Scott number or identifying number. The letter and number that come next (A41) indicate the design and refer to the illustration so designated. Following that is the denomination of the stamp and its color. Finally, the price, unused and used is shown.

Scott® No.	Illus No.	Description	Unused Price	Used Price
1885				
PR83	N5	24c carmine	20.00	12.50 □□□□□
PR84	N5	36c carmine	30.00	15.00 □□□□□
PR85	N5	48c carmine	40.00	25.00 □□□□□
PR86	N5	60c carmine	60.00	35.00 □□□□□
PR87	N5	72c carmine	70.00	40.00 □□□□□
PR88	N5	84c carmine	140.00	85.00 □□□□□
PR89	N5	96c carmine	100.00	70.00 □□□□□
1894				
PR90	N4	1c intense black	25.00	□□□□□
PR91	N4	2c intense black	25.00	□□□□□
PR92	N4	4c intense black	35.00	□□□□□
PR93	N4	6c intense black	750.00	□□□□□
PR94	N4	10c intense black	65.00	□□□□□
PR95	N5	12c pink	300.00	— □□□□□
PR96	N5	24c pink	275.00	□□□□□
PR97	N5	36c pink	1750.00	□□□□□
PR98	N5	60c pink	1750.00	— □□□□□
PR99	N5	96c pink	2750.00	□□□□□
PR100	N7	$3 scarlet	4000.00	□□□□□
PR101	N8	$6 pale blue	4750.00	3000.00 □□□□□
1895				
PR102	N15	1c black	17.50	5.00 □□□□□
PR103	N15	2c black	18.50	5.00 □□□□□
PR104	N15	5c black	25.00	8.50 □□□□□
PR105	N15	10c black	55.00	25.00 □□□□□
PR106	N16	25c carmine	75.00	25.00 □□□□□
PR107	N16	50c carmine	175.00	75.00 □□□□□
PR108	N17	$2 scarlet	200.00	45.00 □□□□□
PR109	N18	$5 ultra	325.00	135.00 □□□□□
PR110	N19	$10 green	300.00	150.00 □□□□□
PR111	N20	$20 slate	575.00	275.00 □□□□□
PR112	N21	$50 dl rose	600.00	275.00 □□□□□
PR113	N22	$100 purple	675.00	325.00 □□□□□
1895-97		Wmkd. USPS (191)		
PR114	N15	1c black ('96)	2.50	2.00 □□□□□
PR115	N15	2c black	2.50	1.50 □□□□□
PR116	N15	5c black ('96)	4.00	3.00 □□□□□
PR117	N15	10c black	2.50	2.00 □□□□□
PR118	N16	25c carmine	4.00	3.75 □□□□□
PR119	N16	50c carmine	5.00	3.50 □□□□□
PR120	N17	$2 scarlet ('97)	7.50	8.50 □□□□□
PR121	N18	$5 dk blue ('96)	17.50	20.00 □□□□□
PR121a		$5 lt blue	85.00	40.00 □□□□□
PR122	N19	$10 green ('96)	15.00	25.00 □□□□□
PR123	N20	$20 slate ('96)	16.00	27.50 □□□□□
PR124	N21	$50 dl rose ('97)	17.50	27.50 □□□□□
PR125	N22	$100 purple ('96)	20.00	35.00 □□□□□

PP1

PP2

PP3

PP4

PP5

PP6

PP7

PP8

PP9

PP10

PP11

PP12

PP13

Scott® No.	Illus No.	Description	Unused Price	Used Price	/ / / / /

PPD1

OC1

OC2

1912-13 PARCEL POST STAMPS

Q1	PP1	1c carmine rose	4.00	.90	☐☐☐☐☐
Q2	PP2	2c carmine rose	4.50	.70	☐☐☐☐☐
Q3	PP3	3c carmine rose ('13)	11.00	5.00	☐☐☐☐☐
Q4	PP4	4c carmine rose	30.00	2.00	☐☐☐☐☐
Q5	PP5	5c carmine rose	30.00	1.25	☐☐☐☐☐
Q6	PP6	10c carmine rose	45.00	1.75	☐☐☐☐☐
Q7	PP7	15c carmine rose	75.00	9.00	☐☐☐☐☐
Q8	PP8	20c carmine rose	150.00	17.50	☐☐☐☐☐
Q9	PP9	25c carmine rose	85.00	4.50	☐☐☐☐☐
Q10	PP10	50c carmine rose ('13)	250.00	35.00	☐☐☐☐☐
Q11	PP11	75c carmine rose	80.00	25.00	☐☐☐☐☐
Q12	PP12	$1 carmine rose ('13)	450.00	20.00	☐☐☐☐☐

SPECIAL HANDLING STAMPS

1925-29

QE1	PP13	10c yellow green ('28)	1.60	.90	☐☐☐☐☐
QE2	PP13	15c yellow green ('28)	1.75	.90	☐☐☐☐☐
QE3	PP13	20c yellow green ('28)	2.25	1.75	☐☐☐☐☐
QE4	PP13	25c yellow green ('29)	22.50	7.50	☐☐☐☐☐
QE4a		25c dp green ('25)	27.50	4.50	☐☐☐☐☐

PARCEL POSTAGE DUE STAMPS

1912

JQ1	PPD1	1c dk green	10.00	3.00	☐☐☐☐☐
JQ2	PPD1	2c dk green	85.00	15.00	☐☐☐☐☐
JQ3	PPD1	5c dk green	12.50	3.50	☐☐☐☐☐
JQ4	PPD1	10c dk green	165.00	35.00	☐☐☐☐☐
JQ5	PPD1	25c dk green	80.00	3.50	☐☐☐☐☐

1851 CARRIER'S STAMPS

LO1	OC1	(1c) dl blue, *rose*	1850.00	2500.00	☐☐☐☐☐
LO2	OC2	1c blue	20.00	20.00	☐☐☐☐☐

GOVERNMENT REPRINTS

1875

LO3	OC1	BL *rose* imperf.	40.00		☐☐☐☐☐
LO4	OC1	BL perf. 12	1750.00		☐☐☐☐☐
LO5	OC2	1c blue imperf.	20.00		☐☐☐☐☐
LO6	OC2	1c blue perf. 12	90.00		☐☐☐☐☐

PLATE NUMBER BLOCK, SHEET AND FIRST DAY COVER PRICES

The Plate Block and First Day Cover prices have been derived from the 1984 edition of Scott's Specialized Catalogue of United States Stamps. The sheet prices were developed by the Editorial Staff of Scott Publishing Co. exclusively for this edition. Sheet prices start with the 1957 Flag Issue (Scott 1094), the beginning of contemporary multicolor and multiple plate number printing.

All plate blocks are blocks of four, unless otherwise indicated in parenthesis.

Scott No.		Pl. Blk.	Sheet	FDC	Scott No.		Pl. Blk.	Sheet	FDC
1893					281	(6)	800.00		
230	(6)	500.00		2,600.00	282	(6)	1,200.00		
231	(6)	450.00		2,000.00	282C	(6)	3,250.00		
232	(6)	850.00		6,000.00	283	(6)	1,800.00		
233	(6)	1,100.00		6,000.00	284	(6)	2,750.00		
234	(6)	1,600.00		6,250.00	**1898**				
235	(6)	1,300.00		6,750.00	285		265.00		5,250.00
236	(6)	850,000			286		250.00		4,500.00
237	(6)	3,500.00		7,500.00	287		1,500.00		
238	(6)	5,750.00			288		1,400.00		5,500.00
239	(6)	8,500.00			289		2,400.00		8,000.00
240	(6)	12,000.00			290		3,000.00		
241	(6)	23,500.00			291		18,500.00		9,250.00
242	(6)	25,000.00		14,000.00	292		45,000.00		
243	(6)	55,000.00			293		90,000.00		
244	(6)	110,000.00			**1901**				
245	(6)	120,000.00			294		100.00		3,500.00
1894					295		100.00		3,000.00
With Triangles					296		500.00		4,250.00
Unwatermarked					297		525.00		4,500.00
246	(6)	325.00			298		675.00		
247	(6)	650.00			299		1,025.00		
248	(6)	225.00			**1902-03**				
249	(6)	1,250.00			300	(6)	185.00		
250	(6)	325.00			301	(6)	200.00		2,750.00
251	(6)	2,500.00			302	(6)	1,100.00		
252	(6)	1,200.00			303	(6)	1,100.00		
253	(6)	1,000.00			304	(6)	1,250.00		
254	(6)	1,250.00			305	(6)	1,250.00		
255	(6)	875.00			306	(6)	875.00		
256	(6)	1,600.00			307	(6)	1,500.00		
257	(6)	1,000.00			308	(6)	700.00		
258	(6)	2,750.00			309	(6)	4,500.00		
259	(6)	4,250.00			310	(6)	9,500.00		
260	(6)	7,000.00			311	(6)	18,500.00		
261	(6)	16,500.00			312	(6)	27,500.00		
261A	(6)	27,500.00			313	(6)	70,000.00		
262	(6)	40,000.00			**1906-08**				
263	(6)	—			**Imperforate**				
1895					314	(6)	300.00		
With Triangles					315	(6)	5,750.00		
Watermarked					**1903**				
264	(6)	185.00			319	(6)	125.00		
265	(6)	375.00			**1906**				
266	(6)	425.00			**Imperforate**				
267	(6)	135.00			320	(6)	350.00		
268	(6)	650.00			**1904**				
269	(6)	650.00			323		225.00		3,500.00
270	(6)	650.00			324		225.00		3,250.00
271	(6)	1,250.00			325		750.00		3,750.00
272	(6)	700.00			326		900.00		4,750.00
273	(6)	1,300.00			327		2,400.00		7,000.00
274	(6)	3,500.00			**1907**				
275	(6)	6,750.00			328	(6)	325.00		2,500.00
276	(6)	11,500.00			329	(6)	475.00		2,750.00
276A	(6)	23,500.00			330	(6)	3,500.00		
277	(6)	21,000.00			**1908-09**				
278	(6)	60,000.00			331	(6)	80.00		
1898					332	(6)	75.00		
279	(6)	185.00			333	(6)	350.00		
279B	(6)	175.00			334	(6)	400.00		
280	(6)	700.00							

Scott No.	Pl. Blk.	Sheet	FDC	Scott No.	Pl. Blk.	Sheet	FDC
335	(6) 650.00				**1912-14**		
336	(6) 1,000.00				**Perforated 12**		
337	(6) 550.00			414	(6) 575.00		
338	(6) 1,150.00			415	(6) 850.00		
339	(6) 550.00			416	(6) 650.00		
340	(6) 750.00			417	(6) 550.00		
341	(6) 8,000.00			418	(6) 825.00		
342	(6) 12,000.00			419	(6) 2,350.00		
	1908-09			420	(6) 2,150.00		
	Imperforate			421	(6) 10,000.00		
343	(6) 90.00				**1914**		
344	(6) 160.00				**Watermarked**		
345	(6) 300.00				**Double-Line USPS**		
346	(6) 450.00			422	(6) 6,750.00		
347	(6) 750.00			423	(6) 12,500.00		
	1909				**1914-15**		
	Bluish Paper				**Perforated 10**		
357	(6) 1,250.00			424	(6) 60.00		
358	(6) 1,250.00			425	(6) 40.00		
359	(6) 16,500.00			426	(6) 150.00		
361	(6) 35,000.00			427	(6) 450.00		
362	(6) 11,000.00			428	(6) 350.00		
364	(6) 12,000.00			429	(6) 325.00		
365	(6) 18,500.00			430	(6) 1,050.00		
366	(6) 10,000.00			431	(6) 400.00		
				432	(6) 575.00		
				433	(6) 625.00		
	1909			434	(6) 200.00		
367	(6) 200.00		350.00	435	(6) 250.00		
368	(6) 375.00		1,900.00	437	(6) 900.00		
369	(6) 4,750.00			438	(6) 3,200.00		
370	(6) 325.00		1,800.00	439	(6) 4,850.00		
371	(6) 450.00			440	(6) 11,500.00		
372	(6) 375.00		950.00		**1915**		
373	(6) 600.00		2,350.00	460	(6) 13,500.00		
	1910-11				**1915**		
	Watermarked				**Perforated 11**		
	Single-Line USPS			461	(6) 1,000.00		
374	(6) 95.00				**1916-17**		
375	(6) 85.00				**Perforated 10**		
376	(6) 185.00				**Unwatermarked**		
377	(6) 250.00			462	(6) 160.00		
378	(6) 285.00			463	(6) 110.00		
379	(6) 525.00			464	(6) 1,600.00		
380	(6) 1,500.00			465	(6) 850.00		
381	(6) 1,450.00			466	(6) 1,100.00		
382	(6) 3,000.00			468	(6) 1,150.00		
	1911			469	(6) 1,500.00		
	Imperforate			470	(6) 600.00		
383	(6) 85.00			471	(6) 700.00		
384	(6) 250.00			472	(6) 1,600.00		
	1913			473	(6) 325.00		
397	(6) 190.00		3,500.00	474	(6) 600.00		
398	(6) 375.00			475	(6) 2,500.00		
399	(6) 2,900.00		4,500.00	476	(6) 3,750.00		
400	(6) 4,000.00			476A	(6) —		
400A	(6) 11,500.00			477	(6) 25,000.00		
	1914-15			478	(6) 13,500.00		
	Perforated 10			479	(6) 6,500.00		
401	(6) 450.00			480	(6) 5,250.00		
402	(6) 2,500.00				**1916-17**		
403	(6) 5,750.00				**Imperforate**		
404	(6) 19,000.00			481	(6) 16.50		
	1912-14			482	(6) 32.50		
	Perforated 12			483	(6) 200.00		
405	(6) 115.00			484	(6) 150.00		
406	(6) 140.00				**1917-19**		
407	(6) 1,500.00				**Perforated 11**		
	1914			498	(6) 18.00		
	Imperforate			499	(6) 14.00		
408	(6) 30.00			500	(6) 2,500.00		
409	(6) 60.00			501	(6) 190.00		

Scott No.	Pl. Blk.	Sheet	FDC
502	(6) 250.00		
503	(6) 200.00		
504	(6) 165.00		
506	(6) 250.00		
507	(6) 375.00		
508	(6) 250.00		
509	(6) 250.00		
510	(6) 300.00		
511	(6) 150.00		
512	(6) 150.00		
513	(6) 150.00		
514	(6) 800.00		
515	(6) 875.00		
516	(6) 750.00		
517	(6) 1,750.00		
518	(6) 1,300.00		

1917
Type of 1908-09
Perforated 11

Scott No.	Pl. Blk.	Sheet	FDC
519	(6) 2,500.00		

1918

523	(8) 22,500.00		
524	(8) 8,500.00		

1918-20
Offset Printing

525	(6) 35.00		
526	(6) 250.00		825.00
527	(6) 160.00		
528	(6) 65.00		
528A	(6) 375.00		
528B	(6) 170.00		
529	(6) 60.00		
530	(6) 15.00		

1918-20
Offset, Imperforate

531	(6) 100.00		
532	(6) 350.00		
533	(6) 2,500.00		
534	(6) 130.00		
534A	(6) 400.00		
534B	(6) 14,500.00		
535	(6) 90.00		

1919
Offset, Perf. 12½

536	(6) 200.00		

1919

537	(6) 175.00		700.00

1919
Perforated 11X10

538	100.00		
539	15,000.00		
540	110.00		
541	450.00		

1920
Perforated 10X11

542	(6) 135.00		525.00

1921
Rotary

543	20.00		
545	1,100.00		
546	900.00		

1920

547	(8) 9,500.00		
548	(6) 80.00		700.00
549	(6) 110.00		625.00
550	(6) 900.00		

1922-25
Perforated 11

551	(6) 8.50		25.00
552	(6) 35.00		37.50
553	(6) 55.00		40.00

Scott No.	Pl. Blk.	Sheet	FDC
554	(6) 35.00		50.00
555	(6) 300.00		42.50
556	(6) 300.00		55.00
557	(6) 325.00		110.00
558	(6) 600.00		200.00
559	(6) 95.00		110.00
560	(6) 1,100.00		110.00
561	(6) 250.00		110.00
562	(6) 425.00		110.00
563	(6) 60.00		550.00
564	(6) 100.00		150.00
565	(6) 85.00		350.00
566	(6) 325.00		350.00
567	(6) 325.00		400.00
568	(6) 325.00		600.00
569	(6) 500.00		700.00
570	(6) 1,450.00		900.00
571	(6) 600.00		4,250.00
572	(6) 2,000.00		8,500.00
573	(8) 6,500.00		11,000.00

1923-25
Imperforate

575	(6) 145.00		
576	(6) 45.00		50.00
577	(6) 40.00		

1923-26
Perforated 11X10

578	850.00		
579	450.00		

Perforated 10

581	120.00		2,000.00
582	45.00		52.50
583	30.00		
584	325.00		62.50
585	200.00		
586	200.00		62.50
587	65.00		77.50
588	120.00		75.00
589	325.00		80.00
590	45.00		85.00
591	750.00		110.00

Perforated 11
Rotary

595	1,750.00		

1923

610	(6) 40.00		22.50
611	(6) 185.00		100.00
612	425.00		110.00

1924

614	(6) 65.00		40.00
615	(6) 115.00		55.00
616	(6) 575.00		100.00

1925

617	(6) 60.00		40.00
618	(6) 125.00		50.00
619	(6) 450.00		90.00
620	(8) 325.00		32.50
621	(8) 1,000.00		55.00

1925-26

622	(6) 250.00		35.00
623	(6) 275.00		35.00

1926

627	(6) 70.00		17.50
628	(6) 120.00		30.00
629	(6) 70.00		7.00
631	80.00		40.00

1926-34
Perforated 11X10½

632	3.00		60.00
633	110.00		60.00
634	1.20		62.50

Scott No.		Pl. Blk.	Sheet	FDC	Scott No.		Pl. Blk.	Sheet	FDC
634A		2,500.00					**1931**		
635		9.00		52.50	702		2.50		4.00
636		140.00		60.00	703		4.00		5.00
637		25.00		60.00			**1932**		
638		25.00		72.50	704		4.50		5.00
639		25.00		75.00	705		5.50		5.5
640		25.00		77.50	706		25.00		5.5
641		25.00		95.00	707		1.75		5.5
642		42.50		100.00	708		18.00		5.7
		1927			709		7.00		5.7
643		60.00		5.00	710		24.00		6.00
644	(6)	85.00		20.00	711		85.00		6.7
		1928			712		7.50		6.7
645	(6)	65.00		5.00	713		100.00		6.7
646		70.00		22.50	714		65.00		7.7
647		200.00		22.50	715		160.00		10.00
648		400.00		40.00			**1932**		
649	(6)	22.50		12.00	716	(6)	17.50		5.00
650	(6)	110.00		18.00	717		12.50		3.2
		1929			718		25.00		5.7
651	(6)	20.00		7.00	719		40.00		7.5
653		1.00		30.00	720		1.50		10.0
654	(6)	50.00		11.00	724	(6)	20.00		3.0
655		75.00		77.50	725	(6)	32.50		3.0
657	(6)	45.00		4.50			**1933**		
		"Kansas"			726	(6)	22.50		3.00
658		35.00		27.50	727		7.00		3.50
659		55.00		27.50	728		3.00		2.75
660		55.00		27.50	729		4.00		2.75
661		200.00		30.00	732		2.00		3.00
662		185.00		32.50	733	(6)	30.00		7.00
663		200.00		35.00	734	(6)	65.00		6.25
664		550.00		42.50			**1934**		
665		450.00		42.50	736	(6)	15.00		2.00
666		850.00		80.00	737		1.75		2.00
667		225.00		72.50	738	(6)	7.25		2.00
668		425.00		85.00	739	(6)	7.00		2.00
		"Nebraska"			740	(6)	1.50		2.25
669		35.00		27.50	741	(6)	2.00		2.25
670		50.00		25.00	742	(6)	3.50		2.50
671		35.00		25.00	743	(6)	12.00		3.25
672		200.00		32.50	744	(6)	14.50		3.25
673		225.00		37.50	745	(6)	30.00		4.00
674		275.00		37.50	746	(6)	20.00		4.00
675		600.00		55.00	747	(6)	35.00		4.25
676		275.00		57.50	748	(6)	32.50		4.50
677		375.00		60.00	749	(6)	57.50		7.50
678		425.00		62.50			**1935**		
679		1,000.00		70.00	752		16.00		13.00
		1929			753		25.00		15.00
680	(6)	50.00		4.75	754	(6)	40.00		15.00
681	(6)	32.50		4.00	755	(6)	40.00		15.00
		1930			756	(6)	6.50		15.00
682	(6)	55.00		3.75	757	(6)	7.50		15.00
683	(6)	85.00		4.00	758	(6)	22.50		16.00
684	(6)	1.25		4.75	759	(6)	27.50		16.00
685	(6)	8.50		10.00	760	(6)	37.50		16.00
688	(6)	60.00		5.25	761	(6)	47.50		16.50
689	(6)	35.00		5.00	762	(6)	45.00		16.50
		1931			763	(6)	60.00		17.00
690	(6)	25.00		4.00	764	(6)	60.00		18.00
		Regular Issue			765	(6)	80.00		20.00
692		19.00		80.00	771	(6)	100.00		25.00
693		35.00		80.00	772		2.00		9.50
694		17.50		85.00	773		2.00		9.50
695		25.00		85.00	774	(6)	2.75		13.00
696		60.00		95.00	775		2.00		9.00
697		30.00		1,750.00			**1936**		
698		70.00		160.00	776		2.00		9.00
699		60.00		1,750.00	777		2.00		9.00
700		110.00		275.00	782		2.00		9.00
701		325.00		400.00	783		2.00		9.00
					784		.75		17.50

Scott No.	Pl. Blk.	Sheet	FDC	Scott No.	Pl. Blk.	Sheet	FDC
	1936-37			865	1.50		2.00
85	1.00		6.00	866	3.50		2.00
86	1.10		6.00	867	12.00		4.50
87	1.50		6.00	868	55.00		8.25
88	13.00		6.75	869	1.50		2.00
89	15.00		8.00	870	1.40		2.00
90	1.00		6.00	871	3.25		2.00
91	1.10		6.00	872	13.00		4.75
92	1.50		6.00	873	35.00		8.25
93	13.00		6.75	874	1.00		2.00
94	15.00		8.00	875	1.20		2.00
	1937			876	2.00		2.00
95	2.00		8.50	877	10.50		4.50
96	11.50	(6)	9.50	878	35.00		8.25
98	1.65		8.50	879	1.25		2.00
99	2.00		9.50	880	1.25		2.00
00	2.00		9.50	881	1.75		2.00
01	1.75		9.50	882	13.00		4.50
02	2.00		9.50	883	50.00		7.75
	1938			884	1.10		2.00
03	.40		1.25	885	1.10		2.00
04	.25		1.35	886	1.25		2.00
05	.30		1.35	887	12.50		4.00
06	.35		1.65	888	45.00		7.75
07	.50		1.65	889	2.50		2.00
08	1.80		1.65	890	1.50		2.00
09	1.60		2.25	891	2.50		2.00
10	1.80		2.25	892	22.50		5.00
11	2.00		2.25	893	135.00		13.50
12	2.00		2.50		**1940**		
13	2.25		2.50	894	7.50		6.75
14	2.75		2.65	895	7.00		5.25
15	2.00		2.75	896	3.75		5.25
16	4.50		2.75	897	3.25		5.25
17	6.00		3.00	898	3.25		5.25
18	5.50		3.00	899	.60		5.00
19	5.50		3.25	900	.70		5.00
20	3.60		3.25	901	1.40		5.00
21	7.00		3.50	902	8.25		6.00
22	7.00		3.75		**1941-43**		
23	13.00		4.25	903	2.75		5.50
24	8.00		4.25	904	2.25		5.00
25	5.50		4.50	905	.60		4.75
26	8.25		5.00	906	25.00		7.00
27	8.25		5.25	907	.50		4.25
28	26.50		5.25	908	1.00		4.25
29	7.25		6.50	909	15.00		5.75
30	38.50		10.00	910	6.00		5.50
31	52.50		20.00	911	3.50		5.00
32	60.00		55.00	912	3.50		5.00
33	200.00		100.00	913	3.50		5.00
34	575.00		175.00	914	3.50		5.00
	1938			915	3.50		5.00
35	6.00		8.50	916	27.50		5.00
36	6.00	(6)	8.50	917	14.00		5.00
37	16.50		8.50	918	8.50		5.00
38	9.50		8.50	919	8.50		5.00
	1939			920	11.50		5.00
52	1.65		7.50	921	12.50		6.50
53	2.00		8.50		**1944**		
54	4.75	(6)	7.50	922	2.50		6.75
55	3.50		17.50	923	2.50		4.50
56	6.00	(6)	7.50	924	1.60		4.00
57	1.65		7.50	925	3.00		4.00
58	1.65		7.00	926	2.00		4.00
	1940				**1945**		
59	1.10		2.00	927	1.00		4.00
60	1.25		2.00	928	.70		4.00
61	2.00		2.00	929	.60		5.00
62	12.00		5.00		**1945-46**		
63	55.00		8.25	930	.20		3.00
64	1.50		2.00	931	.50		3.00

Scott No.	Pl. Blk.	Sheet	FDC	Scott No.	Pl. Blk.	Sheet	FDC
932	.55		3.00		**1951**		
933	.75		3.00	998	.50		1.5
				999	.50		1.5
	1945			1000	.50		1.5
934	.50		3.00	1001	.50		1.5
935	.50		3.00	1002	.50		1.5
936	.50		3.00	1003	.50		1.5
937	.50		3.00		**1952**		
938	.50		3.00	1004	.50		1.5
	1946			1005	.50		1.5
939	.50		3.00	1006	.50		2.0
940	.55		3.00	1007	.60		.8
941	.50		3.00	1008	.55		.8
942	.50		3.00	1009	.50		.8
943	.50		3.00	1010	.60		.8
944	.50		3.00	1011	.50		.8
	1947			1012	.60		.8
945	.50		3.00	1013	.50		.8
946	.50		3.00	1014	.60		.8
947	.50		3.00	1015	.50		.8
949	.50		2.00	1016	.50		.8
950	.50		2.00		**1953-54**		
951	.50		2.00	1017	.50		.8
952	.50		2.00	1018	.80		.8
				1019	.50		.8
	1948			1020	.50		.8
953	.50		2.00	1021	2.00		.8
954	.50		2.00	1022	.50		.8
955	.50		2.00	1023	.50		1.00
956	.50		2.00	1024	.50		.8
957	.50		2.00	1025	.50		.8
958	1.00		2.00	1026	.50		.8
959	.50		2.00	1027	.50		.8
960	.60		2.00	1028	.50		.8
961	.50		2.00	1029	.50		.8
962	.50		2.00		**1954-68**		
963	.50		2.00	1030	.30		
964	.90		2.00	1031	.25		.8
965	1.70		2.00	1031A	1.75		.8
966	2.50		2.00	1032	7.50		.6
967	.60		1.50	1033	.25		.6
968	.80		1.50	1034	2.00		.6
969	.65		2.00	1035	.40		.6
970	.65		2.00	1036	.50		.6
971	.75		2.00	1037	1.75		.6
972	.75		1.50	1038	.75		.6
973	1.20		1.50	1039	2.00		.6
974	.65		1.50	1040	1.50		.7
975	1.00		1.50	1041	5.00		.8
976	2.00		1.50	1042	1.75		.6
977	.65		1.50	1042A	1.50		.6
978	.70		1.50	1043	1.50		.9
979	.65		1.50	1044	1.65		.9
980	.75		1.50	1044A	1.50		.9
	1949			1045	2.75		.9
981	.50		1.50	1046	3.35		1.00
982	.50		1.50	1047	4.50		1.20
983	.50		1.50	1048	14.00		1.30
984	.50		1.50	1049	10.00		1.50
985	.50		1.50	1050	18.00		1.75
986	.60		1.50	1051	18.00		6.00
	1950			1052	65.00		11.00
987	.50		1.50	1053	475.00		65.00
988	.55		1.50		**1954**		
989	.50		1.50	1060	.50		.75
990	.50		1.50	1061	.50		.75
991	.50		1.50	1062	.60		.75
992	.50		1.50	1063	.50		.75
993	.50		1.50		**1955**		
994	.50		1.50	1064	.50		FD
995	.55		1.50	1065	.50		.75
996	.50		1.50	1066	1.75		.90
997	.50		1.50	1067	.50		.75

Scott No.	Pl. Blk.	Sheet	FDC	Scott No.	Pl. Blk.	Sheet	FDC
68	.50		.75		**1960-61**		
69	.50		.75	1138	.50	7.00	.80
70	.80		.75	1139	1.00	9.25	.80
71	.50		.75	1140	1.00	9.25	.80
72	.60		.75	1141	1.00	9.25	.80
	1956			1142	1.00	9.25	.80
73	.50		.75	1143	1.00	9.25	.80
74	.50		.75	1144	1.00	9.25	.80
76	.50		.75		**1960**		
77	.65		1.00	1145	.50	5.00	.80
78	.65		1.00	1146	.50	5.00	.80
79	.65		1.00	1147	.60	7.25	.80
80	.50		.80	1148	2.50	15.50	.80
81	.50		.80	1149	.50	5.00	.80
82	.50		.80	1150	.65	5.25	.80
83	.50		.80	1151	.50	7.00	.80
84	.50		.80	1152	.50	5.00	.80
85	.50		.80	1153	.50	5.00	.80
	1957			1154	.50	5.00	.80
86	.50		.80	1155	.50	5.00	.80
87	.50		.80	1156	.50	5.00	.80
88	.50		.80	1157	.50	5.00	.80
89	.50		.80	1158	.50	5.00	.80
90	.50		.80	1159	.55	7.25	.80
91	.50		.80	1160	2.00	15.25	.80
92	.60		.80	1161	.50	7.00	.80
93	.50		.80	1162	.50	5.00	.80
94	.60	5.50	.80	1163	.50	5.00	.80
95	.70	7.25	.80	1164	.50	5.00	.80
96	1.90	11.50	.80	1165	.55	7.25	.80
97	.50	5.00	.80	1166	2.25	15.25	.80
98	.65	5.25	1.00	1167	.50	5.00	.80
99	.50	5.00	.80	1168	.55	7.25	.80
	1958			1169	2.25	15.25	.80
100	.50	5.00	.80	1170	.50	7.00	.80
104	.50	5.00	.80	1171	.50	7.00	.80
105	.60	7.25	.80	1172	.55	7.25	.80
106	.50	5.00	.80	1173	2.25	24.00	1.40
107	.75	6.50	.80		**1961**		
108	.50	5.00	.80	1174	.55	7.25	.80
109	.50	5.00	.80	1175	2.25	16.00	.80
110	.60	7.25	.80	1176	.65	5.25	.75
111	6.00	23.00	.80	1177	.55	7.25	.75
112	.50	5.00	.80		**1961-65**		
	1958-59			1178	1.10	9.50	1.25
113	.40	2.75	.80	1179	1.00	8.00	1.25
114	.60	5.25	.80	1180	1.00	8.00	1.25
115	.55	5.25	.80	1181	1.00	8.00	1.25
116	.65	5.25	.80	1182	1.10	9.50	1.25
	1958				**1961**		
117	.60	7.25	.80	1183	.55	5.25	.75
118	4.25	18.50	.80	1184	.55	5.25	.75
119	.50	5.00	.80	1185	.55	5.25	.90
120	.50	5.00	.80	1186	.55	5.25	.75
121	.50	7.00	.80	1187	1.00	8.00	.75
122	.60	5.25	.80	1188	.55	5.25	.75
123	.50	5.00	.80	1189	.55	5.25	.90
	1959			1190	.70	5.25	.75
124	.50	5.00	.80		**1962**		
125	.55	7.25	.80	1191	.55	5.25	.75
126	2.25	15.00	.80	1192	.75	8.25	.75
127	.50	7.00	.80	1193	.75	9.00	1.50
128	.85	6.75	.80	1194	.55	5.25	.75
129	1.50	10.75	.80	1195	.55	5.25	.75
130	.50	5.00	.80	1196	.70	5.25	.75
131	.50	5.00	.80	1197	.55	5.25	.75
132	.50	5.00	.80	1198	.55	5.25	.75
133	.65	5.25	.80	1199	.55	5.25	.75
134	.50	5.00	.80	1200	.75	8.00	.75
135	.50	5.00	.80	1201	.55	5.25	.75
136	.60	7.25	.80	1202	.55	5.25	.75
137	2.25	15.00	.80	1203	.70	6.25	.75

Scott No.	Pl. Blk.	Sheet	FDC	Scott No.		Pl. Blk.	Sheet	FDC
1204	5.00	13.00	6.00	1291		3.00	60.00	1.2
1205	.50	10.00	.75	1292		4.00	80.00	1.6
1206	.55	5.25	.75	1293		5.00	100.00	3.2
1207	1.50	8.50	.75	1294		10.00	200.00	7.5
1962-63				1295		50.00	1,000.00	60.0
1208	.55	12.00	.75	**1966**				
1209	.25	5.00	.75	1306		1.00	8.00	.7
1213	.65	12.00	.75	1307		.90	7.75	.7
1963				1308		.75	6.50	.7
1230	.60	6.00	.75	1309		.90	6.50	.7
1231	.60	6.00	.75	1310		.90	6.50	.7
1232	.60	6.00	.75	1312		.75	6.50	.7
1233	.60	6.00	.75	1313		.90	8.00	.7
1234	.60	6.00	.75	1314		.75	6.50	.7
1235	.60	6.00	.75	1315		1.00	6.75	.7
1236	.60	6.00	.75	1316		1.00	6.75	.7
1237	1.35	10.50	.75	1317		1.00	6.75	.7
1238	.60	6.00	.75	1318		1.25	8.25	.7
1239	.60	6.00	.75	1319		1.00	6.75	.7
1240	.60	12.00	.75	1320		1.00	6.75	.7
1241	1.25	8.50	.75	1321		.75	12.50	.7
1964				1322		2.75	12.50	.7
1242	.60	6.00	.75	**1967**				
1243	1.20	8.25	.75	1323		.90	6.50	
1244	1.00	6.50	.75	1324		.90	6.50	
1245	.60	6.00	.75	1325		.90	6.50	
1246	.60	6.00	.75	1326		.90	6.50	
1247	.60	6.00	.75	1327		.90	6.50	
1248	.60	6.00	.75	1328		.90	6.50	
1249	.60	6.00	.75	1329		1.00	6.75	
1250	.60	6.00	.75	1330		1.00	6.75	
1251	.60	6.00	.75	1331-1332		11.00	95.00	10.0
1252	.60	6.00	.75	1333		2.00	9.50	.7
1253	.60	6.00	.75	1334		2.00	10.00	.7
1254-1257	5.50	120.00	.75ea.	1335		2.50	11.00	.7
1258	.60	6.00	.75	1336		.60	6.25	.7
1259	.75	6.25	.75	1337		2.00	9.50	.7
1260	.75	6.25	.75	**1968-71**				
1965				1338		.60	13.00	.7
1261	.75	6.25	.75	1338D	(20)	3.25	13.00	.7
1262	.75	6.25	.75	1338F	(20)	3.50	16.50	.7
1263	.75	6.25	.75	**1968**				
1264	.75	6.25	.75	1339		1.00	9.50	.7
1265	.75	6.25	.75	1340		1.00	9.50	.7
1266	.75	6.25	.75	1341		32.50	205.00	6.5
1267	.75	6.25	.75	1342		1.00	9.50	.7
1268	.75	6.25	.75	1343		1.00	9.50	.7
1269	.75	6.25	.75	1344		1.00	9.50	.7
1270	.75	6.25	.75	1345-1354	(20)	18.00	45.00	4.00 ea
1271	1.00	6.50	.75	1355		1.75	11.50	1.00
1272	1.00	6.50	.75	1356		1.10	10.50	.7
1273	1.25	9.50	.75	1357		1.10	10.50	.7
1274	15.00	37.50	.75	1358		1.10	10.50	.7
1275	.75	6.25	.75	1359		1.20	10.50	.7
1276	.60	12.00	.75	1360		1.65	11.00	.7
1965-73				1361		2.25	13.50	.7
1278	.20	3.00	.35	1362		3.00	17.00	.7
1279	22.50	40.00	.35	1363	(10)	2.75	10.75	.7
1280	.30	4.25	.35	1364		3.00	18.00	.7
1281	.70	6.75	.35	**1969**				
1282	.40	8.00	.35	1365-1368		10.00	85.00	2.00 ea
1283	.50	10.00	.45	1369		1.10	10.50	.7
1283B	1.00	12.00	.45	1370		1.35	13.00	.7
1284	.65	12.50	.45	1371		3.00	16.50	2.0
1285	1.25	17.00	.50	1372		1.00	10.50	.7
1286	1.30	20.00	.60	1373		1.00	10.50	.7
1286A	1.75	26.00	.50	1374		1.00	10.50	.7
1287	1.65	26.50	.65	1375		1.00	10.50	.7
1288	1.50	31.00	.60	1376-1379		12.00	120.00	2.00 ea
1289	2.00	40.00	.80	1380		1.35	10.50	.7
1290	2.50	50.00	1.00	1381		1.75	13.25	.7

Scott No.		Pl. Blk.	Sheet	FDC
1382		1.85	13.25	.75
1383		1.00	6.75	.75
1384	(10)	2.25	9.50	.75
1385		1.00	9.50	.75
1386		1.20	6.25	.75
1970				
1387-1390		2.75	10.50	2.00 ea.
1391		1.10	9.50	.75
1392		1.10	9.50	.75
1970-74				
1393		.60	12.00	.75
1393D		1.35	15.00	.75
1394		1.00	16.50	.75
1396	(12)	7.50	30.00	.75
1397		2.35	30.00	.85
1398		2.35	33.50	.75
1399		1.80	36.50	1.25
1400		2.10	42.50	1.00
1970				
1405		1.00	9.50	.75
1406		1.00	9.50	.75
1407		1.00	9.50	.75
1408		1.00	9.50	.75
1409		1.00	9.50	.75
1410-1413	(10)	7.00	30.00	1.40 ea.
1414	(8)	3.00	12.00	1.40
1415-1418	(8)	10.00	57.50	1.40 ea.
1419		1.25	9.75	.75
1420		1.25	9.75	.75
1421-1422		7.00	25.00	.75 ea.
1971				
1423		1.00	9.50	.75
1424		1.00	9.50	.75
1425		1.00	9.50	.75
1426	(12)	3.50	11.50	.75
1427-1430		2.25	11.00	1.75 ca.
1431		1.65	13.25	.75
1432		4.00	30.00	.75
1433		1.65	12.00	.75
1434-1435		1.75	13.50	1.75
1436		1.25	9.75	.75
1437		1.25	9.75	.75
1438	(6)	1.85	10.00	.75
1439	(8)	2.10	10.00	.75
1440-1443		1.85	10.50	1.20 ea.
1444	(12)	2.50	9.50	.75
1445	(12)	2.50	9.50	.75
1972				
1446		1.00	9.50	.75
1447		1.50	9.75	.75
1448-1451		1.60	8.50	1.25
1452		1.25	8.75	.75
1453		1.00	6.25	.75
1454		2.50	19.00	.75
1455		1.00	8.50	.75
1456-1459		2.25	16.00	1.00 ea.
1460	(10)	2.00	7.00	.75
1461	(10)	2.25	8.75	.85
1462	(10)	4.00	16.00	1.00
1463		1.00	9.25	.75
1464-1467		1.40	9.00	2.00 ea.
1468	(12)	2.75	9.25	.75
1469	(6)	1.35	9.25	.75
1470		1.00	8.50	.75
1471	(12)	2.75	9.00	.75
1472	(12)	2.75	9.00	.75
1473		1.00	8.50	.75
1474		1.00	6.75	.75
1973				
1475		1.35	8.50	.75
1476		1.35	10.75	.75

Scott No.		Pl. Blk.	Sheet	FDC
1477		1.35	10.75	.75
1478		1.35	10.75	.75
1479		1.35	10.75	.75
1480-1483		1.35	11.50	1.75 ea.
1484	(12)	2.75	6.25	.75
1485	(12)	2.75	6.25	.75
1486	(12)	2.75	6.25	.75
1487	(12)	2.75	6.25	.75
1488		.80	8.25	.75
1489-1498	(20)	4.50	12.00	1.10 ea.
1499		1.00	5.50	.75
1500		1.25	6.75	.75
1501		1.00	8.50	.75
1502		2.25	16.00	.80
1503	(12)	2.50	5.75	.75
1973-74				
1504		1.00	8.50	.75
1505		1.00	10.50	.75
1506		1.00	10.50	.75
1507	(12)	2.10	8.25	.75
1508	(12)	2.10	8.25	.75
1509	(20)	4.50	20.00	.75
1510		1.00	20.00	.75
1511	(8)	1.80	20.00	.75
1974				
1525		1.25	10.50	.75
1526		1.00	10.50	.75
1527	(12)	2.60	8.25	.75
1528	(12)	2.60	10.50	.75
1529		1.00	10.50	1.25
1530-1537	(10)	2.60	6.75	1.10 ea.
1538-1541		1.25	9.75	1.50 ea.
1542		1.00	10.50	.75
1543-1546		1.20	10.75	1.10 ea.
1547		1.00	10.50	.75
1548		1.00	12.00	.75
1549		1.00	10.50	.75
1550	(10)	2.20	10.50	.75
1551	(12)	2.60	10.50	.75
1552	(20)	5.50	12.50	.75
1975				
1553	(10)	2.20	10.50	.75
1554	(10)	2.20	10.50	.75
1555		1.00	10.50	.75
1556		1.00	10.50	1.10
1557		1.00	10.50	1.10
1558	(8)	1.80	10.50	.75
1559	(10)	1.75	8.25	.75
1560	(10)	2.20	10.50	.75
1561	(10)	2.20	10.50	.75
1562	(10)	4.00	19.00	.75
1563	(12)	2.60	8.25	.75
1564	(12)	2.60	8.25	.75
1565-1568	(12)	2.60	10.50	.90 ea.
1569-1570	(12)	2.60	5.00	1.00 ea.
1571	(6)	1.40	10.75	.75
1572-1575	(12)	2.60	10.50	.75 ea.
1576		1.00	10.50	.75
1577-1578		1.00	8.50	.75 ea.
1579	(12)	2.60	10.50	.75
1580	(12)	2.60	10.50	.75
1975-81				
1581		.15	3.00	.40
1582		.20	4.00	.40
1584		.30	6.00	.40
1585		.40	8.00	.40
1591		.90	18.50	.60
1592		1.00	20.50	.60
1593		1.10	19.50	.60
1594		1.15	24.00	.60
1596	(12)	3.50	26.50	.60
1597	(6)	2.10	30.50	.65

212

Scott No.		Pl. Blk.	Sheet	FDC
1599		1.60	32.50	.65
1603		2.40	50.00	.75
1604		2.80	56.50	1.20
1605		2.90	59.00	1.10
1606		3.00	61.00	1.10
1608		5.00	101.00	1.25
1610		10.00	202.50	3.00
1611		20.00	405.00	4.75
1612		50.00	1,010.00	10.00
1622	(20)	5.50	26.50	.65
1976				
1629-1631	(12)	3.40	13.50	.65ea.
1632		1.30	13.50	.65
1633-1682	(50)	25.00	25.00	1.75ea.
1683		1.30	13.50	.65
1684	(10)	2.90	13.50	.65
1685	(12)	3.40	13.50	.65
1690		1.30	13.50	.65
1691-1694	(20)	5.50	14.00	.65ea.
1695-1698	(12)	3.40	14.00	.70ea.
1699	(12)	3.40	11.00	.65
1700		1.30	9.00	.65
1701	(12)	3.40	13.50	.65
1702	(10)	3.00	13.50	.65
1703	(20)	5.70	13.50	.65
1977				
1704	(10)	2.90	10.75	.65
1705		1.30	13.50	.65
1706-1709	(10)	3.00	11.00	.65ea.
1710	(12)	3.65	13.50	.65
1711	(12)	3.65	13.50	.65
1712-1715	(12)	3.65	13.50	.65ea.
1716		1.30	11.00	.65
1717-1720	(12)	3.65	13.50	.65ea.
1721		1.30	13.50	.65
1722	(10)	3.10	11.00	.65ea.
1723-1724	(12)	3.65	11.00	.65ea.
1725		1.30	13.50	.65
1726		1.30	13.50	.65
1727		1.30	13.50	.65
1728	(10)	3.10	11.00	.65
1729	(20)	5.70	26.50	.65
1730	(10)	3.10	26.50	.65
1978				
1731		1.30	13.50	.65
1732		1.30		.70
1733		1.30		.70
1732-1733	(20)	5.75	13.50	
1734		1.30	39.00	.90
1735		1.50	30.00	.65
1744	(12)	3.65	13.50	.65
1745-1748	(12)	3.65	13.00	.65ea.
1749-1752	(12)	3.65	13.00	.65ea.
1753		1.30	13.50	.65
1754		1.30	13.50	.65
1755	(12)	3.65	13.00	.65
1756	(12)	4.20	15.50	.65
1758	(12)	4.20	12.50	.65
1759		1.50	15.50	.80
1760-1763		1.50	15.50	.65ea.
1764-1767	(12)	4.20	12.50	.65ea.
1768	(12)	4.20	30.50	.65
1769	(12)	4.20	30.50	.65ea.
1979				
1770		1.50	15.00	.65
1771	(12)	4.20	15.50	.65
1772		1.50	15.50	.65
1773		1.50	15.50	.65
1774		1.50	15.50	.65
1775-1778	(10)	3.50	12.50	.65ea.
1779-1782		1.50	15.00	.65ea.
1783-1786	(12)	4.20	15.50	.65ea.
1787	(20)	6.50	15.25	.65

Scott No.		Pl. Blk.	Sheet	FDC
1788	(10)	3.50	15.50	.65
1789	(10)	3.50	15.50	.65
1790	(12)	3.75	10.50	.60
1791-1794	(12)	5.25	22.00	.65ea.
1795-1798	(12)	4.25	15.50	.65ea.
1799	(12)	4.25	30.50	.65
1800	(12)	4.25	30.50	.65
1801	(12)	4.25	15.50	.65
1802	(10)	3.50	15.50	.65
1980				
1803	(12)	4.25	15.50	.65
1804	(12)	4.25	15.50	.65
1805-1810	(36)	11.00	18.20	.65
1818		1.80	37.50	.75
1821		1.50	15.50	.65
1822		1.50	23.00	.65
1823		1.50	15.50	.65
1824		1.50	15.50	.65
1825		1.50	15.50	.65
1826		1.50	15.50	.65
1827-1830	(12)	4.50	15.50	.65ea.
1831	(12)	4.50	15.50	.65
1832		1.50	15.50	.65
1833	(6)	2.25	15.50	.65
1834-1837	(10)	3.50	12.50	.65ea.
1838-1841		1.50	12.50	.65
1842	(12)	4.25	15.50	.65
1843	(20)	6.50	15.50	.65
1980-84				
1843A	(20)	1.10	2.25	.60
1844		.20	4.50	.60
1844A		.30	6.50	.60
1845		.40	8.50	.60
1846		.50	10.50	.60
1846A	(20)	4.75	20.40	.65
1847		1.30	26.25	.65
1849		1.75	34.40	.75
1850		1.75	37.00	.75
1851		2.00	39.50	.80
1852		2.00	40.40	.75
1853		2.00	40.40	.75
1854	(20)	8.50	40.40	.75
1858	(20)	13.25	60.50	.90
1859		3.50	70.50	1.00
1860		3.75	75.75	1.00
1861	(20)	18.00	80.50	1.00
1981				
1874		1.50	15.30	.65
1875		1.50	15.50	.65
1876-1879		1.75	17.50	.75ea.
1890	(20)	7.50	36.50	.75
1894	(20)	8.50	40.50	.75
1910		1.75	48.10	.75
1911		1.75	48.10	.75
1912-1919	(8)	3.50	17.90	.75ea.
1920		1.75	18.30	.75
1921-1924		1.75	18.30	.75ea.
1925		1.75	18.30	.75
1926		1.75	18.30	.75
1927	(20)	8.00	18.80	.75
1928-1931		1.75	14.45	.75ea.
1932		1.75	18.30	.75
1933		1.75	18.30	.75
1934		1.75	18.30	.75
1935		1.75	18.30	.75
1936		2.00	20.40	.75
1937-1938		1.75	18.30	.75ea.
1939		2.00	40.40	.75
1940		2.00	20.40	.75
1941		2.00	20.40	.75

Scott No.		Pl. Blk.	Sheet	FDC
1981				
1942-1945		2.00	16.50	.75ea.
1946		2.00	40.40	.75
1982				
1950		2.00	19.60	.75
1951		2.00	20.40	.75
1952		2.00	20.40	.75
1953-2002	(50)	20.00	20.00	.75ea.
2003	(20)	8.50	20.40	.75
2004		2.00	20.40	.75
2006-2009		2.00	20.40	.75ea.
2010		2.00	20.40	.75
2011		2.00	20.40	.75
2012		2.00	20.40	.75
2013		2.00	20.40	.75
2014		2.00	20.40	.75
2015		2.00	20.40	.75
2016		2.00	20.40	.75
2017	(20)	8.50	20.40	.75
2018		2.00	20.40	.75
2019-2022		2.00	16.40	.75ea.
2023		2.00	20.40	.75
2024	(20)	8.50	20.40	.75
2025		1.30	13.25	.75
2026	(20)	8.50	20.40	.75
2027-2030		2.00	20.40	.75ea.
1983				
2031		2.00	20.40	.75
2032-2035		2.00	16.40	.75ea.
2036		2.00	20.40	.75
2037		2.00	20.40	.75
2038		2.00	20.40	.75
2039	(20)	8.50	20.40	.75
2040		2.00	20.40	.75
2041		2.00	20.40	.75
2042	(20)	8.50	20.40	.75
2043	(20)	8.50	20.40	.75
2044		2.00	20.40	.75
2045		2.00	16.40	.75
2046		2.00	20.40	.75
2047		2.00	20.40	.75
2048-2051		1.30	13.30	.75 ea.
2052		2.00	16.40	.75
2053	(20)	8.50	20.40	.75
2054		2.00	20.40	.75
2055-2058		2.00	20.40	.75 ea.
2059-2062		2.00	20.40	.75 ea.
2063		2.00	20.40	.75
2064	(20)	8.50	20.40	.75
2065		2.00	20.40	.75
1984				
2066		2.00	20.40	.75
2067-2070		2.00	20.40	.75 ea.
2071		2.00	20.40	.75
2072	(20)	8.50	20.40	.75
2073		2.00	20.40	.75
2074		2.00	20.40	.75
2075		2.00	20.40	.75
2076-2079		2.00	16.40	.75 ea.
2080		2.00	20.40	.75
2081		2.00	20.40	.75
2082-2085		2.00	20.40	.75 ea.
2086		2.00	16.40	.75
2087		2.00	20.40	.75
2088	(20)	8.50	20.40	.75
2089		2.00	20.40	.75
2090		2.00	20.40	.75
2091		2.00	20.40	.75
2092		2.00	20.40	.75
2093		2.00	20.40	.75
2094		2.00	20.40	.75
2095	(20)	8.50	20.40	.75
2096		2.00	20.40	.75
2097		2.00	20.40	.75
2098-2101		2.00	16.40	.75 ea.

Scott No.	Pl. Blk.	Sheet	FDC	Scott No.	Pl. Blk.	Sheet	FDC
	Air Post			C63		2.25	20.50	1.00
	1918			C64		1.10	18.50	.60
C1	(6)	1,700.00		16,000.00		**1963-64**		
C2	(6)	3,500.00		16,000.00	C66		11.00	90.00	1.35
C3	(6)	950.00		19,000.00	C67		4.00	19.00	.50
	1923			C68		4.50	23.00	2.50
C4	(6)	825.00		500.00	C69		7.50	54.00	2.75
C5	(6)	5,000.00		850.00				
C6	(6)	6,000.00		1,000.00		**1967-69**		
	1926-28			C70		7.00	46.00	.70
C7	(6)	85.00		75.00	C71		10.00	75.00	2.00
C8	(6)	100.00		85.00	C72		2.25	29.00	.60
C9	(6)	250.00		140.00	C74		8.00	52.50	1.50
C10	(6)	275.00		30.00	C75		6.50	51.00	1.10
C11	(6)	90.00		50.00	C76		3.50	13.00	3.50
C12	(6)	350.00		20.00		**1971-73**		
C13	(6)	5,500.00		2,750.00	C77		3.00	22.75	.50
C14	(6)	13,500.00		2,000.00	C78		1.35	22.50	.50
C15	(6)	20,000.00		3,000.00	C79		1.65	30.00	.50
	1931-34			C80		2.75	25.50	.60
C16		210.00		300.00	C81		2.75	25.50	.70
C17		75.00		20.00	C84		2.75	17.00	.60
C18	(6)	1,500.00		300.00	C85	(10)	3.50	13.75	.50
C19		35.00		200.00	C86		1.75	16.00	.50
	1935-39			C87		2.50	23.50	.60
C20	(6)	40.00		35.00	C88		2.85	45.00	.80
C21	(6)	225.00		40.00	C89		2.50	26.00	.80
C22	(6)	210.00		40.00	C90		3.10	32.00	1.10
C23		11.00		20.00				
C24	(6)	325.00		45.00		**1978-79**		
	1941-44			C91-C92		3.10	62.50	1.15ea
C25		1.00		2.25	C93-C94		2.10	42.50	1.00ea
C26		1.50		3.75	C95-C96		2.50	50.50	1.00ea
C27		16.00		7.00	C97	(12)	8.75	31.50	1.1
C28		22.00		10.00		**1980**		
C29		20.00		10.00	C98	(12)	11.00	40.50	1.3
C30		21.00		16.00	C99	(12)	7.75	28.50	1.10
C31		150.00		40.00	C100	(12)	10.00	35.50	1.2
	1946-47				**1983**		
C32		.75		2.00	C101-C104		2.75	28.50	1.10 ea.
C33		.75		2.00	C105-C108		4.00	40.50	1.35 ea.
C34		2.50		2.00	C109-C112		3.50	35.50	1.25 ea.
C35		2.85		2.75		**Air Post**		
C36		7.50		3.50		**Special Delivery**		
	1948-49				**1934-36**		
C38		20.00		1.75	CE1	(6)	30.00		25.00
C39		.85		1.50	CE2		12.00		17.50
C40		.95		1.25		**Special Delivery**		
C42		3.50		1.75		**1885-95**		
C43		3.00		2.25	E1	(8)	15,000.00		8,000.00
C44		11.00		2.75	E2	(8)	15,000.00		
C45		1.00		3.75	E3	(8)	9,000.00		
	1952-54			E4	(6)	16,500.00		
C46		80.00		17.50	E5	(6)	5,500.00		
C47		.85		1.50		**1902-17**		
C48		5.00		.75	E6	(6)	3,250.00		
	1957-59			E7	(6)	1,200.00		
C49		1.50	10.75	1.75	E8	(6)	3,000.00		
C50		5.00	24.00	.80	E9	(6)	5,750.00		
C51		1.30	22.50	.75	E10	(6)	7,500.00		
C53		1.50	13.25	.65	E11	(6)	300.00		
C54		1.50	13.25	1.10		**1922-25**		
C55		1.50	13.25	1.00	E12	(6)	525.00		550.00
C56		5.00	26.50	.90	E13	(6)	325.00		275.00
	1959-62			E14	(6)	50.00		150.00
C57		15.00	152.50	1.50		**1927-51**		
C58		4.00	43.50	1.10	E15		6.50		100.00
C59		4.00	37.50	1.50	E16		6.50		1,000.00
C60		1.50	28.00	.70	E17		5.00		12.00
C62		7.00	31.50	.80	E18		30.00		12.00
				E19		12.00		5.00

Scott No.		Pl. Blk.	Sheet	FDC	Scott No.		Pl. Blk.	Sheet	FDC
	1954-57				J97		1.25		
20		4.50		3.00	J98		5.50		
21		5.25		2.25	J99		6.50		
	1969-71				J100		10.00		
22		14.50		3.50	J101		40.00		
23		6.00		3.50		**1978**			
	Registration				J102		1.10		
	(6)	2,100.00		9,000.00	J103		1.30		
	Certified Mail					**Offices in China**			
A1		6.25		3.25		**1919-22**			
	Postage Due				K1	(6)	350.00		
	1910-12				K2	(6)	350.00		
5	(6)	400.00			K3	(6)	575.00		
6	(6)	350.00			K4	(6)	650.00		
7	(6)	3,850.00			K5	(6)	600.00		
8	(6)	600.00			K6	(6)	800.00		
9	(6)	1,150.00			K7	(6)	900.00		
0	(6)	6,500.00			K8	(6)	700.00		
	1914-15				K9	(6)	750.00		
52	(6)	550.00			K10	(6)	725.00		
53	(6)	350.00			K11	(6)	900.00		
54	(6)	4,500.00			K12	(6)	1,250.00		
55	(6)	285.00			K13	(6)	1,650.00		
56	(6)	675.00			K14	(6)	1,200.00		
57	(6)	2,350.00			K15	(6)	12,500.00		
58	(6)	30,000.00			K16	(6)	8,500.00		
	1916				K17	(6)	775.00		
59	(6)	7,250.00			K18	(6)	675.00		
50	(6)	800.00				**Official Stamps**			
	1917-25					**1910-11**			
61	(6)	40.00			O121	(6)	225.00		
62	(6)	35.00			O122	(6)	2,100.00		
63	(6)	85.00			O123	(6)	1,850.00		
64	(6)	85.00			O124	(6)	120.00		
65	(6)	125.00			O125	(6)	550.00		
66	(6)	575.00			O126	(6)	250.00		
67	(6)	750.00				**1983**			
68	(6)	11.00			O127		.15		.75
	1930-31				O128		.40		.75
	Perforated 11				O129		1.30		.60
69	(6)	35.00			O130		1.70		.75
70	(6)	27.50			O132		10.00		2.25
71	(6)	40.00			O133		50.00		12.50
72	(6)	240.00							
73	(6)	225.00							
74	(6)	400.00							
75	(6)	1,000.00							
76	(6)	1,150.00							
77	(6)	275.00							
78	(6)	375.00							
	1931-56								
	Perforated 11X10½								
J79		22.50							
J80		2.00							
J81		2.00							
J82		3.00							
J83		4.00							
J84		8.50							
J85		45.00							
J86		57.50							
J87		325.00							
	1959								
J88		125.00							
J89		.50							
J90		.60							
J91		.70							
J92		1.25							
J93		.75							
J94		1.40							
J95		1.60							
J96		1.75							

Scott® No.	Illus No.	Description	Unused Price	Used Price	/ / / / / /

Scott® No.	Illus No.	Description	Unused Price	Used Price	/ / / / / /
......	......	....	......	......	☐☐☐☐☐
......	......	....	......	......	☐☐☐☐☐
......	......	....	......	......	☐☐☐☐☐
......	......	....	......	......	☐☐☐☐☐
......	......	....	......	......	☐☐☐☐☐
......	......	....	......	......	☐☐☐☐☐
......	......	....	......	......	☐☐☐☐☐
......	......	....	......	......	☐☐☐☐☐
......	......	....	......	......	☐☐☐☐☐
......	......	....	......	......	☐☐☐☐☐
......	......	....	......	......	☐☐☐☐☐
......	......	....	......	......	☐☐☐☐☐
......	......	....	......	......	☐☐☐☐☐
......	......	....	......	......	☐☐☐☐☐
......	......	....	......	......	☐☐☐☐☐
......	......	....	......	......	☐☐☐☐☐
......	......	....	......	......	☐☐☐☐☐
......	......	....	......	......	☐☐☐☐☐
......	......	....	......	......	☐☐☐☐☐
......	......	....	......	......	☐☐☐☐☐
......	......	....	......	......	☐☐☐☐☐
......	......	....	......	......	☐☐☐☐☐
......	......	....	......	......	☐☐☐☐☐
......	......	....	......	......	☐☐☐☐☐
......	......	....	......	......	☐☐☐☐☐
......	......	....	......	......	☐☐☐☐☐
......	......	....	......	......	☐☐☐☐☐
......	......	....	......	......	☐☐☐☐☐
......	......	....	......	......	☐☐☐☐☐
......	......	....	......	......	☐☐☐☐☐
......	......	....	......	......	☐☐☐☐☐
......	......	....	......	......	☐☐☐☐☐
......	......	....	......	......	☐☐☐☐☐
......	......	....	......	......	☐☐☐☐☐
......	......	....	......	......	☐☐☐☐☐
......	......	....	......	......	☐☐☐☐☐
......	......	....	......	......	☐☐☐☐☐
......	......	....	......	......	☐☐☐☐☐
......	......	....	......	......	☐☐☐☐☐
......	......	....	......	......	☐☐☐☐☐
......	......	....	......	......	☐☐☐☐☐
......	......	....	......	......	☐☐☐☐☐
......	......	....	......	......	☐☐☐☐☐
......	......	....	......	......	☐☐☐☐☐

Scott® No.	Illus No.	Description	Unused Price	Used Price	/ / / / / /
					☐☐☐☐☐
					☐☐☐☐☐
					☐☐☐☐☐
					☐☐☐☐☐
					☐☐☐☐☐
					☐☐☐☐☐
					☐☐☐☐☐
					☐☐☐☐☐
					☐☐☐☐☐
					☐☐☐☐☐
					☐☐☐☐☐
					☐☐☐☐☐
					☐☐☐☐☐
					☐☐☐☐☐
					☐☐☐☐☐
					☐☐☐☐☐
					☐☐☐☐☐
					☐☐☐☐☐
					☐☐☐☐☐
					☐☐☐☐☐
					☐☐☐☐☐
					☐☐☐☐☐
					☐☐☐☐☐
					☐☐☐☐☐
					☐☐☐☐☐
					☐☐☐☐☐
					☐☐☐☐☐
					☐☐☐☐☐
					☐☐☐☐☐
					☐☐☐☐☐
					☐☐☐☐☐
					☐☐☐☐☐
					☐☐☐☐☐
					☐☐☐☐☐
					☐☐☐☐☐
					☐☐☐☐☐
					☐☐☐☐☐
					☐☐☐☐☐
					☐☐☐☐☐
					☐☐☐☐☐
					☐☐☐☐☐
					☐☐☐☐☐
					☐☐☐☐☐
					☐☐☐☐☐
					☐☐☐☐☐
					☐☐☐☐☐
					☐☐☐☐☐
					☐☐☐☐☐
					☐☐☐☐☐

Scott® No.	Illus No.	Description	Unused Price	Used Price	/ / / / / /

Scott® No.	Illus No.	Description	Unused Price	Used Price	/ / / / /

Scott® No.	Illus No.	Description	Unused Price	Used Price	//////

Scott° No.	Illus No.	Description	Unused Price	Used Price	/ / / / /
					☐☐☐☐☐
					☐☐☐☐☐
					☐☐☐☐☐
					☐☐☐☐☐
					☐☐☐☐☐
					☐☐☐☐☐
					☐☐☐☐☐
					☐☐☐☐☐
					☐☐☐☐☐
					☐☐☐☐☐
					☐☐☐☐☐
					☐☐☐☐☐
					☐☐☐☐☐
					☐☐☐☐☐
					☐☐☐☐☐
					☐☐☐☐☐
					☐☐☐☐☐
					☐☐☐☐☐
					☐☐☐☐☐
					☐☐☐☐☐
					☐☐☐☐☐
					☐☐☐☐☐
					☐☐☐☐☐
					☐☐☐☐☐
Scott° No.	Illus No.	Description	Unused Price	Used Price	
					☐☐☐☐☐
					☐☐☐☐☐
					☐☐☐☐☐
					☐☐☐☐☐
					☐☐☐☐☐
					☐☐☐☐☐
					☐☐☐☐☐
					☐☐☐☐☐
					☐☐☐☐☐
					☐☐☐☐☐
					☐☐☐☐☐
					☐☐☐☐☐
					☐☐☐☐☐
					☐☐☐☐☐
					☐☐☐☐☐
					☐☐☐☐☐
					☐☐☐☐☐
					☐☐☐☐☐
					☐☐☐☐☐
					☐☐☐☐☐
					☐☐☐☐☐

Scott® No.	Illus No.	Description	Unused Price	Used Price	//////